QUEER AIRWAVES

MEDIA, COMMUNICATION, AND CULTURE IN AMERICA

Michael C. Keith and Donald Fishman, Series Editors

WAVES OF RANCOR
Tuning in the Radical Right
Robert L. Hilliard and Michael C. Keith

SCREENED OUT
How the Media Control Us and What We Can Do About It
Carla Brooks Johnston

DISCONNECTED AMERICA
The Consequences of Mass Media in a Narcissistic World
Ed Shane

QUEER AIRWAVES
The Story of Gay and Lesbian Broadcasting
Phylis Johnson and Michael C. Keith

INVISIBLE STARS
A Social History of Women in American Broadcasting
Donna L. Halper

QUEER AIRWAVES

The Story of
Gay and Lesbian
Broadcasting

Phylis A. Johnson
and Michael C. Keith

M.E. Sharpe
Armonk, New York
London, England

Library of Congress Cataloging-in-Publication Data

Queer airwaves : the story of gay and lesbian broadcasting / Phylis Johnson,
Michael Keith.
    p. cm.—(Media, communication, and culture in America)
  Includes bibliographical references and index.
  ISBN 0-7656-0400-0 (alk. paper)
    1. Gay broadcasters—United States—Interviews. 2. Radio programs for gays—
United States. 3. Television programs for gays—United States. 4. Homosexuality on
radio. 5. Homosexuality on television. I. Keith, Michael C., 1945– II. Title. III. Series.

PN1990.9.H64 J64 2001
791.44′028′08664—dc21   00-049652

Printed in the United States of America

Lupus est homo homini, non homo, quam qualis sit non novit.
—Plautus

(Translated: "A man is a wolf rather than a man to another man, when he hasn't yet found out what he's like.")

Contents

Foreword

One of the most neglected areas in the history of broadcasting has been the role played by gay and lesbian activists in radio and television. Part of this neglect arose, until recently, from the relative invisibility of gays and lesbians on radio and television. Part of the neglect occurred because network executives, broadcast station owners, and social bigotry operated to limit the opportunities of gays and lesbians to enter broadcasting.

However, the past thirty years have witnessed the coming of age of gay and lesbian programming. At the network level, more television programs began to feature gay and lesbian characters in nonstereotypical roles. On the local level, radio began to program hundreds of shows with special relevance to the gay and lesbian communities. There is even a gay and lesbian presence on the Internet providing online radio services.

The title of this book deserves a special word of commentary because the terminology employed to describe the gay and lesbian community has undergone an important change. The term "queer," once a pejorative word indicating "different from the usual" or "deviant," has now been transformed by the gay and lesbian community into a positive and honorific concept. It has become a benchmark of pride to speak about someone having a "queer sensibility" or providing a "queer perspective." In fact, academic departments now search for professors to teach "queer theory" in literature and cultural studies.

This is a pioneering work in the field of broadcasting. Johnson and Keith have gathered interviews from leading gay and lesbian theorists, activists, and broadcasters. The text not only surveys the explosion of gay and lesbian broadcast stations in the United States, it also provides a glimpse of such broadcasting activities abroad, especially in England and Australia. Most of the material in this book comes from first-hand interviews with producers, performers, and program directors who have changed the landscape of broadcasting.

This is an important book in explaining the voice of a previously underrepresented minority. Of course, the growing market power of the gay and lesbian community has helped accelerate the growth of queer broadcasting. But Johnson and Keith provide us with a discerning glimpse of the human dimensions of the struggle of a minority group to gain recognition and acceptance in what may at best be described as a "straight-jacketed" society. This book will yield more than its quota of insights and useful observations about the evolution of a "queer" perspective in broadcasting.

Donald Fishman
Boston College

Acknowledgments

When Michael Keith initially invited me to coauthor *Queer Airwaves* with him, I never imagined how many hours of my life would be given to this project. I would like to personally thank all the people who gave freely of their time to talk with me during the process of writing this book. Indeed, I would prefer to think that we all wrote this book together. From the beginning, my concept was to allow the contributors an opportunity to share their voice through interview and narrative. It was a technique that had worked well for Michael, my coauthor, in some of his previous works.

I would also like to thank Studs Terkel, one of the leading oral historians of our time, for being an inspiration to writers like myself. I had the honor of meeting him at a dinner presentation at Southern Illinois University, and for that I am grateful. He underscored the importance of working with a good transcriber as part of the interview and writing process.

In my case, without the help of Deborah Morrow and Aisha Cool, I would have never completed this book. I would like to thank Deborah for transcribing the bulk of the interviews in *Queer Airwaves*, and for her words of encouragement in the writing of this book. I would also like to thank Aisha for her assistance in transcribing some of the interviews in this book, and thank her for her willingness to learn about this new area of media study.

In addition, I would like to thank my family for all its support through this two-year process of interviewing and writing. I would also like to thank the faculty and staff in the Department of Radio-Television at Southern Illinois University, Carbondale, for their encouragement along the way.

Last but not least, I would like to thank the M.E. Sharpe editorial staff, in particular Esther Clark, Henrietta Toth, and Suzanne Lobel, for all their hard work during the preparation of this manuscript for publication. I would like to thank Peter Coveney, former executive editor at M.E. Sharpe, for providing Michael Keith and me with the opportunity to share the stories behind *Queer Airwaves*—an account of the personal struggles by many broadcasters who wish to be represented across the American and international airwaves.

List of Appendixes

QUEER AIRWAVES

I listen to other radio talk shows all the time. Rush, I admire, only because he is so arrogant. I consider arrogance to be a quality worth emulating, until you start getting nasty. Self-appreciation as a direction is not such a bad thing, and this is what I appreciate about Rush. I have called his show and have done some very funny things with him. One time, I called Rush Limbaugh, and said our organization wants to give you an award on the air so they put me right on the air. At the time, he was making fun of Ann Richards, the governor of Texas, because she had received an award as an "Honorary Lesbian." And he said, so if it's such an honor to be an honorary lesbian, it must be more important than to be a governor. So instead of calling her governor, he's going to call her "Honorary Lesbian Ann Richards." I got the humor of it, but he was doing it over and over. So I called up and said, "Our organization wants to give you an award." I don't think that he was aware of the juxtaposition, and this had been going on for about two weeks—"Honorary Lesbian Ann Richards" said this and that. So I said, "We had a meeting of Gay Fathers last night, and we decided that we would declare you an 'Honorary Gay Man.'" He said, "That's low." I said, "Low? Actually it is a high honor because our organization is one of the few organizations that you can join overnight . . . even in the twinkling of an eye, and your eyes don't even have to twinkle, and I'm sure in your case they don't." So that was the end of his gay-baiting Ann Richards. I thought it was pretty cool. It was fun.

Alan Ross, *Gaydreams* host (1985–1990)

Chapter One

Coming Out on Air

Personal Histories and Perspectives

I remember the shots of the fence post that Matthew was tied up on. That's pretty grisly when a person sees that. I don't think on television you can get into some of the more detailed and specific aspects of some of these events. With Shepard, they showed shots of the campus. They were pictures of that fence where he was essentially crucified, that's my sense on that one. The specifics—some court testimony or that sort of thing—can be vividly played out in print I think more easily than television, I think the gay press was on the murder sooner and faster than the mainstream, although when you have a national paper, like the New York Times, *stating that they are going to cover gay things thoroughly, exhaustively, completely, and accurately that changes the dynamics.*

—Chuck Colbert, freelance syndicated columnist

Is There a Gay Perspective?

Organizations like the Gay and Lesbian Alliance Against Defamation (GLAAD) and the National Lesbian and Gay Journalists' Association (NLGJA) have played a significant role in the advancement of lesbian, gay, bisexual, and transgender (LGBT) issues and concerns within the media in recent years—in print and electronic media. Although some might argue that there is no such thing as objectivity—that we all bring our own biases to a story as constructors and as individual audience members, others in the gay media feel that there is a definite professional distinction between being a queer journalist or producer and being an advocate for queer rights and justice. Beyond that, many of the storytellers in this book see a unique role for queer broadcasting that cannot be completely fulfilled by the mainstream, even though presenting positive images to straight America is an equally important goal. It's all part of the process of coming out ... in the media.

3

Karen Boothe: As we head into the next millennium, I wish I could say that NLGJA's decade of hard work has paid off so completely that our job is one that's well done. But it's not. We can draw lessons from the other minority journalists' organizations and predict a long future for NLGJA. To be gay or lesbian means nothing to one's professional integrity as a journalist. We still have work to do. Many of our members still lack the same health benefits as their heterosexual peers in the newsroom. Untold members have been surpassed by promotions and key assignments. Others tell stories of being pulled from top assignments, being reduced in air time, and ghettoized in beats and late night shifts. It's not easy to substantiate hurt feelings just because all of the openly gay and lesbian reporters are given desks in a corner of the newsroom—away from the concentration of power—in a newly devised seating chart. It's a new day in the newsroom when, after nine years of promotions and top assignments, a senior political reporter is told by a managing editor that her new leadership role in NLGJA might mean a compromised ethic for some political assignments. Later, the news director approaches the political editor to ask that same reporter if she is "pushing her gay agenda." The editor defends the reporter's story—which is later picked up by the rest of the city's newsrooms.

Joshua Gamson: When I look at TV as a whole rather than just what is going on at the four major networks, I'm more impressed with the level of diversity than when I'm just looking at the sort of old-fashioned four-network way, or three-network way of broadcasting. And I have been thinking about whether I think network TV is the most important battle. When things are so segmented at this point, there are a lot of other ways to get diversity into cultural imagery. Well, for example, if you look at television as a whole, you've actually got a fair amount of diversity because of market segmentation and cable television, even if you look at how staid and puritanical American TV tends to be or how sensitive and asexual cable is about gay characters. I'm not referring to premium cable. On MTV, for instance, I noticed the other night a show clearly geared toward teenagers and those in their early 20s, basically set in a dorm. It is about a bunch of kids' sex lives, more or less; that is the theme. And there's a very incidental gay character, gay Latino character I think, who is just talking with his straight roommate about dating and, you know, they're giving each other advice. And there's some sexual tension between them and, it is just, nothing. There's nothing attractive about the program really. It is nothing terribly smart, but the visibility of those kinds of images and the incidental way the gay character is represented happened because MTV is targeting a particular, narrow demographic. They're narrowcasting, and that is mostly what is going on in TV at this point.

Nicholas Cimorelli: Mainstream service or disservice I think is an important and healthy question. I would say there is really a need for both. There are definitely issues around mainstreaming that have the risk of diluting the focus of issues pertaining to the community of special interests and minorities—in this case we're talking about sexual minorities and certainly the visibility is not with the same pitch and hype. At the same time, there is something to be said about giving the opportunity for sexual minorities to bring their special perspective to a wider audience to educate. I don't believe that it should be one or the other. My sense is there is a need for specialized programs. *OutFM* is still on the air and I think it very much needs to be there because there are issues that we need to talk about, and we're also talking about community radio—community identified and community supported, but that's a whole other issue itself. In respect to broadcasting, to what extent is community radio going to remain community identified or become syndicated, and how will it continue to serve as an information tool to broader audiences around the country? To what extent will the local community involvement be lessened? That's what is so important about having a gay and lesbian program in particular in a city such as New York. We can actually air our views, provide a forum, to be able to dialogue on issues that are really challenging to us, and we're sort of in the process of coming together to really examine radio. It is all about raising healthy questions and really trying to move through ideas perhaps that are binding and going into a more expanded state of consciousness.

Chuck Colbert: I think you should make a distinction between those who do advocacy media for gays and lesbians and those who are professional journalists; there is a difference there. GLAAD has a very powerful role in all this but NLGJA is a professional association of journalists, which is slightly different. We are often accused of being advocates. Anytime I breathe, I am suddenly a "militant" homosexual advocate. That's a tricky thing for the media—labeling everybody who is gay as an activist. Would you say a Catholic is an activist because he's espousing something from the church? I get called a gay activist every time I pick up a pen. People enjoy putting labels on people so they can organize them into little boxes and it isn't always that simple.

Karen Boothe: Another story, which has crossed my desk as NLGJA president, involves a human resources director telling a reporter that the news director likes to keep a "firewall" between his staff and advocacy issues. The reporter reminds the HR director that NLGJA is a professional journalists' organization. It is stories like these that motivate me as NLGJA president. I am convinced that the landscape for gay and lesbian journalists has improved and continues to improve. This is due, in no small part, to NLGJA. I am also convinced that so much work remains to be done until stories like those that have crossed my desk as president are no longer told. I am convinced that coverage has improved too—but even in 1999 members report that newsrooms still lend "balance" to stories pertaining to gays and lesbians with comment from leaders of the religious right. Imagine—one reporter told of a gathering of gay and lesbian travel agents and then "balanced" the piece with a comment from a religious right spokesman saying the gathering jeopardized the state's family-friendly reputation. Excuse me, but could it be that since the reporter wasn't thinking, the segment producer and editor weren't either?

Joe Liberatore: One of our shows on the *Gay News Network* (GNN) from beginning to end was dedicated to Matthew Shepard and the candlelight vigil that was held here at the U.S. capitol. We actually won a documentary award, which was amazing. Most local news stations will never contact us for footage because when we go to shoot something, they're already there. When folks have contacted us, they have been mostly interested in the background of our organization and how we got started—a profile of the organization as opposed to a news article where they quote somebody from GLAAD. You know if Ellen DeGeneres is in town, they may want to call and get our footage, but in terms of relying on us for opinions or a quote, rather it is GLAAD's job to be an advocate and to take a position—take a stand, denounce something—bad practices—or when something's good, put a spotlight on it. That probably will never happen to us. They won't ask us for our opinion or quote us.

Marle Becker: Our community is so diverse. It is so eclectic so I'm not sure that our community won't need gay broadcasting one day in the future. Judith Light said it best at the opening of the Gay Games many years ago. And it was certainly the thing that turned me on to her. She put it very simply and succinctly, and said, "Human rights are not special rights." I thought, wow, you can't get it any simpler than that. So I think that there are certain issues within the gay and lesbian community. Let's face it, there are issues that are very important to me that are not gay issues. Education is important. I think it is important that children are educated because they are the future of our country. And I think the environment is important. The economy is important. I am a human being so all the issues that impact straight people generally affect me too. But then there are those other issues that are very important to me. Relationships. Same-sex marriages. Certainly the AIDS epidemic. So those issues, I think, will always be there for us. So I don't ever see there not being a need for gay broadcasting. Can it be combined comfortably that it would be a nice marriage with straight and gay issues on the same news-cast—maybe one day it will, but I don't think I'll see that day.

Nicholas Cimorelli: It's really that in the end all of us are trying to be more awake and more conscious so I think that exclusively mainstream program-ming probably wouldn't be sufficient to really address the issues that are impacting on the community. On the other hand, if we weren't mainstream, there is a terrific opportunity that is lost in terms of people seeing those positive images in which we're viable and that we're really contributing. One thing that impressed me with GLAAD—the Gay and Lesbian Alliance Against Defamation—which is now a household term for most people is that they are very concerned with positive images of gays and lesbians in the media. The only way those images can really be seen is to have them out there where people who are not gay or lesbian can hear them and experience what they're really about and not necessarily in the context of them talking about their sexual identity or life as a sexual minority but who are from a more integrated place, inclusive of their sexual identity. I think often in our culture we want to simplify things and that's often not the answer. It is im-portant to recognize who we are as multidimensional human beings having lived through a period of great multiple loss and as a result of AIDS in the late '80s and early '90s. It has profoundly impacted all of us and made me see how it put us all—in a sense—on an excellent path in terms of really needing to look at what we're about and what we want to do with our lives.

So the Story Begins. . . .

> *So many images we see in the media are often based on perceptions and prejudices of their creators. This is true for an array of media outlets and minority groups. Even in today's atmosphere of equality, diversity, and political correctness, civil rights groups protest the lack of minority images on television as well as how these images are presented. One of the last minority groups included in television programs are gays and lesbians.*

> —Chuck Hoy, university professor and researcher

The story of gay and lesbian broadcasting is only beginning to be told, and much of its history can be traced back to the people who fought for free expression and civil rights. In 1965, Franklin Kameny, Washington leader of the Mattachine Soci-ety, organized one of the first protests for gay rights, in which participants peace-fully held signs that asked for citizenship.[1] The Mattachine Society, America's first gay rights organization, was founded in 1951 by Harry Hay in Los Angeles.[2] By late 1958, the society had 117 members. It was during this time that San Francisco's KPFA aired what is believed to be the first comprehensive gay rights radio documentary in the United States. The two-hour documentary brought together a small entourage of physicians, lawyers, and criminologists with the mother of a homosexual man and Harold L. Call, an editor for the *Mattachine Review*, to discuss the "condition and rights" of the gay man.[3]

In 1962, WBAI aired "The Homosexual in America," a sixty-minute program focused around the opinions of a panel of psychiatrists, after which vocal protests by Mattachine New York organizer Randolfe Wicker demanded equal time from WBAI management.[4] On July 16, 1962, WBAI aired another show, but this one was centered on a discussion by Wicker and six other gay men. A group of listeners challenged the station's license, filing a complaint with the Federal Communications Commission (FCC). The rejected complaint provided the impetus for future discussion of homosexuality in the electronic media. In 1967, Mike Wallace hosted "CBS Reports: The Homosexuals," a one-hour special documentary on gay men, and in doing so he debunked a number of negative stereotypes. Yet, when all was said and done, Wallace concluded: "The average homosexual, if there be such, is promiscuous. He's not interested in, nor capable of, a lasting relationship like that of a heterosexual marriage."[5]

The '60s and '70s gave way to several queer radio shows, mainly on community radio stations, that continued the dialogue within the gay community. However, for the most part, these programs were almost always volunteer produced and as such were limited financially and regionally. Further, the longevity of these shows was often dependent on the whim of the station manager and program director, and gay and lesbian producers on occasion would be forced to compete among themselves for time slots. These shows, although increasing in number and influence over the years, represented the efforts of only a handful of radio collectives.

But with the onset of Reaganism in the 1980s, right-wing conservatism swept through the nation, and to some gay activists, the United States entered the Dark Ages. The previous victories in civil liberties and free expression were challenged once again by the FCC and the religious right. AIDS provided the justification and rationale for what would become the widespread abuse of human rights and rise in hate propaganda in the years to follow.

ACT UP (AIDS Coalition to Unleash Power) media formed in New York City during the latter half of the Reagan administration, and the government was condemned by activists for minimizing the threat of AIDS within the United States— especially among heterosexual Americans. Nevertheless, ACT UP engaged in well-crafted and well-executed media campaigns designed to attract mainstream media attention to AIDS issues. Among these professionals of the ACT UP generation, according to Larry Gross in *Contested Closets*, were a number of young queer journalists, such as Michelangelo Signorile, who were tired of the press code that provided privacy and privilege to the personal lives of gay and lesbian celebrities, politicians, and elite, in particular those who failed to acknowledge the issues and struggles confronting their community.[6]

It was in this environment that queer broadcasting would push forward and feverishly combat the stereotypical attitudes and hate propaganda targeted toward gays and lesbians into the present. Howard Stern and then later Rush Limbaugh ridiculed gays and lesbians and just about everybody else on the air; subsequently their ratings skyrocketed in many cities across the United States. To some shock jocks and their fans, good taste was a matter of opinion, and the FCC was behind the times. In this climate, gay bashing and epithets by a host of Stern and Rush wannabees became routine across the airwaves. Indeed, it was during the midst of this debate that the FCC warned Pacifica radio station KPFA 94.1 FM no longer to broadcast Allen Ginsberg's controversial poem *Howl* on its airwaves for what some critics describe as its "obscene" and "homosexual overtones."[7] Ginsberg commented,

> I participated in a roundtable discussion at an FCC lawyers' convention with James Quello, the oldest member on the FCC, and Quello pulled out a copy of *Howl*, and said, "This is a perfectly good poem you could broadcast on the air— all you have to do is eliminate a couple paragraphs." That was his idea of art! ... I'm a poet who specializes in oral recitation and performance. I am pleased that my work is good on the page—it should be solid on the page—but there is a dimension of sound, which Ezra Pound emphasized. I'm a specialist in that, I'm very good at vocalization, I'm famous for that around the world, and yet I'm banned from the "main marketplace of ideas" in my own country—radio, television, and God knows what they can do when the FCC gets hold of the information highway. [See Appendix 1A.][8]

As Americans became absorbed by images on the evening news and as hate fueled conservative and shock talk radio, the only way to ensure accurate messages about gays and lesbians and to create any sense of discussion was for the queer community to participate in the media and to seek to control it. Indeed, the LGBT community experienced significant progress during the 1990s, from which new alliances between a number of gay and lesbian media outlets and producers have already set the stage for a new era in queer broadcasting on radio, television, cable, and the Internet.

The Revolution That America Missed

> *I have friends who are so anti-straight. I say wait a minute. I don't want to live in a gay world any more than I want to live in an all straight world. I love the differences. I think we should celebrate our differences. That's the problem. Instead of looking at people because they are different and looking at that as something bad, these differences should be celebrated. We all have something to bring to the table, and that is what is really important. I said to Judith Light, "Boy if we could have given ourselves gay rights we would have done it twenty-five years ago. So we need those straight voices out there supporting us."*

—Marle Becker, host of *OutFM*

The modern gay and lesbian movement began with the Stonewall Rebellion, although its significance is largely unknown to the heterosexual American and often ignored when discussing the civil rights movement. It is a history that parents and educators debate whether to include or exclude from public school textbooks. The gay and lesbian movement has been minimized to a few snapshots here and there, some video clips, and sound bites on the evening news in what is perceived by many as a lifestyle contrary to the American way, with little or no consideration of human rights issues.

The religious right has sought to exorcise what it perceives as increasingly rampant homosexuality within the very fiber (optics) of the American electronic media. What may be perceived as the end of morality for some is in reality the product of an ongoing human rights struggle for freedom that began in 1969. The decision on what needed to be done to achieve equality, tolerance, and ultimately acceptance was made in an instant one fateful Friday night. The modern-day struggle for civil rights among gays, lesbians, bisexuals, and transgendered began officially that night—June 27, 1969—during what became known as the Stonewall Rebellion. For some on the streets of New York City, that night symbolized a new hope, an awareness of one's ability to influence one's life, but most straight Americans paid little attention to what they perceived to be an isolated incident of rebellion. The June 1999 Pride edition of the national Public Broadcast Service's (PBS) *In the Life* newsmagazine series investigates "the cause-and-effect links between the insurrection at Stonewall Inn and the funeral earlier that day for Judy Garland":

> Many of the people who would later become charter members of the Stonewall Veterans Organization were among the more than 20,000 who had crowded the streets outside Garland's funeral earlier in the day, and report that when the police came into the bar that night they felt like they had nothing more to lose. So they fought back, a resistance that rapidly spilled out into the Greenwich Village streets and grew into three nights of riotous rebellion.[9]

It was this event that affirmed the queer community's quest for civil rights— six years after the 1963 March on Washington—if only among themselves that evening. The Ward and June Cleavers of America, although possibly disconcerted by the news reports, were nestled in their homes, snug and secure in their heterosexuality, oblivious to the shock waves emanating from Greenwich Village.

Marle Becker: I was in Stonewall when it was raided, but I don't consider myself a Stonewall veteran. I think Stonewall happened because it was a bar that reflected the diversity of our community. There were women, blacks, Hispanics, whites, drag queens—every part our community was represented in the Stonewall. And that was the only bar in New York at the time that really had that kind of representation of clientele. And if they had raided a bar that catered to a black and gay community, or raided the women's bar, or even the white-collar gay male bar, the patrons wouldn't have fought back. They just happened to hit the wrong bar that night. When they hit the Stonewall, everyone in that bar realized they were not raiding the bar because I'm black, or I'm a drag queen, or I'm Hispanic, or I'm a woman. The thing that everyone had in common that night was they were gay. I think that's why everyone said, "Hey, wait a minute. It is time to fight back."

The social ramifications of how one event would impact American broadcasting would be underestimated that night by straight America. The world was changing too rapidly for most Americans. In 1969, a routine police raid on a Greenwich Village bar that served transvestites turned violent after patrons decided not to run away from the police, but instead to stand their ground on the street in front of Stonewall Inn. Because the bar ignored a state law against selling alcohol to homosexuals, Stonewall Inn had become the social center for drag queens, gays, and lesbians in New York City, as well a popular site for police raids. As several people were arrested, someone in the crowd pushed an officer. The crowd began to throw bricks at the police, and the rest is history. The riots continued in New York City for three days, and the Gay Liberation Front was formed within weeks. The Stonewall Rebellion propelled the gay and lesbian movement with a new synergy and openness: the demand for respect and visibility in the media and in society in general.

To many gay media activists, the failure to move into the mainstream, beyond their own community, is a form of "gay ghettoization." Regardless of their limitations, the gay and lesbian media have been "out" there and everywhere, mainly since Stonewall, in helping to provide in-depth coverage of events and issues impacting the gay and lesbian community—sometimes by merely reporting on these events and at other times by inspiring the gay and lesbian community through music and social commentary to become involved in these issues and in the media themselves. It is through the eyes of these producers, writers, and hosts that this book is written, in an effort to tell not only the story of gay and lesbian broadcasting, but to call attention to its role in providing voice and opportunity to a community closeted by the policies and traditions of some in the mainstream media and in society in general.

Yet it would not be accurate to say that discrimination in broadcast policies and practices is exclusive to American broadcasting. Legal and social roadblocks vary by country and region. For example, the Gay Solidarity Group (GSG) formed in 1978 in Sydney, Australia, and a product of its struggles is *Gay Waves*, a weekly gay and lesbian radio program on 2SER-FM. The group changed its name to Lesbian and Gay Solidarity in 1992, and it continues to fight for civil rights:

> As GSG, we were the organisers of the first Lesbian and Gay Mardi Gras which was preceded by a gay rights street march through Sydney on the morning of Saturday, 24 June 1978, followed by an open lesbian and gay Forum in the afternoon and that night at 10 p.m. the Mardi Gras parade. These Sydney events were to serve a double purpose—to highlight the Stonewall gay rights events in the United States and to draw attention to our own discriminatory laws, violence against us and demands for equality and an end to police harass-

ment. What happened at the night parade—the brutal arrests of 53 lesbians and gays—shocked not only Sydney but the world via television and newspaper pictures of the police violence. It proved to be the catalyst for change. That change has been slow and hard fought and still has a long way to go despite the appearance the present Gay and Lesbian Mardi Gras gives which incidentally was originally a mid-winter parade and only later changed to mid-summer.[10]

Struggles confronting the international gay and lesbian media, especially in Canada, New Zealand, and Australia, are documented in this book. *The Third Pink Book* is an excellent source for a global view of lesbian and gay liberation and oppression.[11] In many countries and within America, the LGBT community must compete for resources, in terms of airtime and equipment, with other disenfranchised or minority groups. Aside from these major inconveniences, a number of quality shows are produced on television, radio, and the Internet internationally.

Gay and lesbian media are very much a part of the American popular culture, a part that is often embraced internationally (and overlooked nationally) and viewed as an extension of American life in general. The Canadian radio show *Out and About* debuted in 1993, and its Web site features a time line of significant gay and lesbian events. Several accomplishments listed are Canadian, but many also occurred in the United States. (See Appendix 1B). That is not to say that America is leading the way in queer broadcasting, but only an observation that many countries are monitoring closely the gay and lesbian struggle toward visibility and audibility on U.S. airwaves.

Sometimes It's Just Personal. . . .

> *We're all minorities. There's the people with blue eyes. Would you say I'm a gay male Protestant. What am I first? Am I Protestant? Am I male first? Am I a gay first? I think that you would be amazed at the different words that would come up from different people when asked to describe themselves. Who would think of it that way. . . . This is the sum of my parts.*

—Marle Becker, host of *OutFM*

Little is written about the producers and reporters within queer broadcasting, who not only report news and events from a queer perspective, but whose very involvement often reflects their personal struggle to be viewed and heard as equals in the mainstream media and in life itself. For a number of people, the ability to participate in gay and lesbian media has eased the transition from the closet to the public arena. Personal expression through queer media released and empowered gays, lesbians, bisexuals, and transgender communities to seek new ways to work collectively toward providing information, resources, and fellowship to others. The electronic LGBT media were, and still are, an extension of the quest for basic human rights for all people, regardless of ethnicity, race, or gender.

What is then relevant, in this discussion, is the personal motivations of the producers and entrepreneurs who have become part of the queer airwaves—their history and their future. The reason for these people's involvement is often very similar, indeed among many gay and lesbian broadcasters across the world: the need to tell their stories—not for personal gratification, but rather to make life a little easier for the next generation.

A number of broadcasters, academicians, entrepreneurs, and industry observers were interviewed in the making of this book. More than a hundred people responded to our call for personal stories and perspectives related to the rise of queer broadcasting. A number of people declined to be interviewed, but were happy to pass along the names of friends and colleagues and leaders within the queer media—those individuals who were among the first to air gay and lesbian programming in the United States or beyond.

Throughout this book, we have woven personal interviews, personal narratives, and personal perspectives from an eclectic mix of producers, entrepreneurs, and media analysts—most of whom have worked specifically within queer broadcasting. So it seems only natural for us to start this book with a collection of personal thoughts on the coming-out process within a media culture that narrowly defines gender identity. This chapter represents the ongoing dialogue among queer broadcasters—often one of self-discovery and personal activism—and also represents their need to pass along a sense of community to queer youth whose self-image is often defined by what they hear and see in the mainstream media.

Karen Boothe: I was not the most popular kid on my block. While the other kids in the neighborhood spent their summer playing kickball, I consumed bowls of ice cream while glued to the televised proceedings of Watergate. I was captured by the story, the process, and the drama. I also read the newspaper every afternoon as soon as the afternoon edition landed on the front porch. I was thirteen years old. I like to say my first news job was when I was eleven years old. My family was living in the southern Minnesota town of Mankato. I began my first neighborhood newsletter when I pounded out a story on a turquoise typewriter my parents bought for my use at J.C. Penney. I told the story of how our boxer dog Lady Jane attacked Bobby Probach only after he stopped each day after school to taunt and throw rocks at her. The eight stitches in his head meant Lady Jane had to go live on a farm with another family. It was a story, I felt, that needed to be told to the neighborhood so that Lady Jane would be understood. Little did I, or anyone else for that matter, figure that my compulsion to tell the story more fully would lead to a career in journalism nineteen years later.

Paul Graham: At one time I thought of myself as lucky for being able to be myself and not hide my sexuality. Not that it ever should be an issue, but I did think that I was lucky as so many had difficulties and were in the closet.

I don't really think that now. My life path must have leaned itself to a sector of society that is far more accepting of homosexuality. Maybe I did it for safety reasons, without thinking, to enjoy a life with few oppressive sexuality factors. Living in such a large and liberal city as Manchester definitely has been a plus. I have always been gay, remembering experiences back to when I was ten or eleven, and this has never been a problem or even a hurdle in my life. I just "got on with it." I lived in the Peak District, a large area south of Manchester covering parts of Derbyshire. I lived right in the center of this, which was primarily countryside with large towns. Looking back I never saw or heard any of this "small town" mentality which so many have applied to out of city places and their attitude towards homosexuality. I am sure it did exist but yet again those sort of things passed me by.

John Frame: *Queer Radio*—the show that I've presented for the last five years was instrumental in helping me deal with my sexuality—so I know how valuable and unique it is in Brisbane. I regularly meet activists who state that the show had been crucial in developing their self-acceptance. Sometimes they've happened on the show by accident, while channel surfing—startled to hear someone actually saying positive things about being gay. I've seen the benefits of hands-on involvement with the show—not only in myself, but also especially with other long-term participants.

Alan Ross: I had an opportunity to get involved in *Gaydreams,* and it prompted my interest in gay activism. When I first came out back in 1964 at the age of nineteen, I looked around and saw the gay community as it was before Stonewall, as a kind of ragtag, motley crew where gay men were either extremely effeminate or drag queens or the other alternative was they were schizophrenic, and they could blend into the rest of society relatively undetected. I didn't see much beyond those two wild extremes. And the lesbians that I got to know were also stereotypes, and my early impressions weren't too flattering. Some of them I got to like. Then again, I didn't like myself. So I escaped the gay and lesbian community in the late '60s and sought to live a more conventional lifestyle, which was my choice. I thought that I didn't want to be that far on the outskirts of society. I wasn't willing to do that. So it was easier for me to be conventional. I was in the Wharton School at the University of Pennsylvania, and I didn't see too many businessmen in the gay world. I decided to live a double life, have kids, keep it quiet. I was fairly successful at keeping it from my wife . . . and I did, until an incriminating letter arrived at my house. It was awful. It was like dropping a hydrogen bomb on a marriage. So four and a half years later, and one son later, the marriage was over, with what had been an otherwise stable marriage. Not that I was a victim at this point. But I felt like one, unenlightened as I was. I was back in the gay community. But I was a lot more convinced that I wasn't going to turn back from being gay. I just felt that the gay community could use my talents and leadership skills in some capacity. So when I had an opportunity to get reinvolved in the gay community, it was 100 percent. And I found myself helping other people to see a new way.

Joe Liberatore: I knew I was gay from as far as back as I could possibly remember. Back in the late '60s. My dad was a weight lifter and showed me all these magazines to interest me in exercise (weight lifting, but of course I was just looking at pictures of men). But I didn't actually acknowledge it myself until I was well out of high school and actually I was gay bashed once. At this point, I was living a dual life—freshman or sophomore in college. I would go out to bars at night or on weekends. I would date women in the daytime. My major was public relations (PR) with a minor in Radio-Television and by the time I was a junior or senior in college, I actually had a boyfriend and I pitched him to everyone in the college as my best friend. We'd go to events together in college and double-date. We'd drop the women off and go out afterwards. As soon as I graduated college in 1989, I wasn't sure what I wanted to do. I knew I wanted to come out of the closet and wasn't sure how to do it. I was gay bashed and was kind of livid. I wanted to be an activist. But again, I didn't know if I'd be a perfect match—how I would come out. And a pure luck meeting, I meet someone who was gay and lived in Washington, D.C. and I was up in Pennsylvania just visiting. We became very good friends and after I graduated I moved to D.C. I was here for probably a good year, trying to get settled. I wanted to be in television. I wanted to come out but I was doing it in small levels. People I met in the clubs were very safe, very comfortable. I went to George Washington University, went through some of the programs. I took an internship in public relations for nine months. Started getting on the fast track, getting hired, and doing all these wonderful things in PR again. Completely safe, not coming out. It was a good area to be. Washington was good, to be gay, but the firm I was at was right-wing, very conservative, of course. Not every person, but if the firm had a corporate image that would be it. So I decided to see how I could fulfill myself personally outside the firm and how I could contribute to the community so I started looking through local newspapers for something that I could do, something that would fulfill me personally.

Karen Boothe: After graduating from college I took a job at a radio station in a small southwestern Minnesota farming community. Nineteen eighty-two was the year Marshall, Minnesota made national news on at least three counts. First, some farmer sold area families on a new crop called the "Jerusa-lem artichoke." Many bought into it, committing their investments to this new crop that, when processed, was not only good on salads but a source for sugar. The problem was, once all of the acres were harvested there wasn't a processing facility to send them to. It was soon a long-drawn-out legal case. Second, the farm crisis began. Third, a father and son lured a couple of small-town bankers to their foreclosed farm and shot them dead. The national manhunt, subsequent suicide by the father, and capture and trial of the son made for daily national news and resulted in a couple of novels. I certainly got my feet wet in Marshall, Minnesota. Nothing of great regional or national importance has happened in that town since the day I left for a series of jobs in Minneapolis.

Debra Chasnoff: I graduated from college in 1978, did some traveling around, had several different jobs. I produced a radio show on a public radio station, produced national conferences for the National Association of Work-ing Women, and edited a progressive economics magazine. Then I started working on the documentary *Choosing Children* in 1982. Kim Klausner and I started making this film on the weekends, in our free time. It took us two years to make. Then I moved to California and took on several different jobs again. I went to film school for a semester and dropped out, and then made the film *Deadly Deception,* which was a documentary about the health and environmental consequences of nuclear weapons production. I won an Acad-emy Award for that and, in the process of accepting that award, came out as a lesbian during the awards ceremony. I think it gave me a certain level of visibility in the gay and lesbian community that helped me launch my next project, which was *It's Elementary.* A number of people were touched by my speech that night; at least that was the significant feedback I received. After the Oscars, I decided to become a filmmaker full-time.

Karen Boothe: I came out to myself in 1984. I was twenty-four years old and my career was still young. It wasn't until 1992, when I began working in public radio, that I heard about some organization for gay and lesbian jour-nalists. I was told there was a convention of the NLGJA in San Francisco in June of that year and I had only a couple of weeks to buy my airline ticket and ask for vacation time. I didn't want anyone to know I was going but the gathering changed my life—both personally and professionally. I was grow-ing tired of the jokes about "lesbian farmers" as told by a couple of desk mates. I knew that the usual coverage that I had come to expect—yes, even in public radio—about annual pride festivals was not the most accurate and balanced coverage, and I was afraid that my ambitions in the newsroom would be squashed by managers who confuse sexual identity with a personal politics that could be wrongly seen as a compromise to my journalistic ethics. Besides, I wanted to find out if I could manage to connect with gay and lesbian colleagues—even if I was the only out person in my newsroom. I returned to my job—and gradually came out in the newsroom.

Allan Smales: By the late 1980s, I began to realize that the gay scene had changed considerably, from the underground very private and closeted (and illegal) environment of the 1950s and 1960s I had grown up in, to a far more open and legal world of the present. In Melbourne there were now gay bars and clubs, gay support groups, sporting clubs, etc. But being a typical married family man from the suburbs, I had absolutely no idea where this gay world existed, even though I knew through media reports that the whole gay scene was far more advanced and sophisticated than when I had been involved some twenty years before. By now most states in Australia had already passed legislation which abandoned the illegality of being gay, and the Sydney Gay and Lesbian Mardi Gras Parade was now an event that was more openly discussed by the general public. I began to think that perhaps there was a very vague chance that I could come out sometime in the future, but not just yet. The big problem now was that I had nobody to talk to about this. Neither was there any gay (or similar) media which I had access to where I could hear other people's stories and struggles to reassure me that I was normal. And to pick up a gay paper was a definite no-no! What would happen if my wife found it? My coming out eventually happened rather quickly in 1991. During 1990 I had finally located a couple of gay bars and clubs and was secretly visiting these for a time on my way home from the office in the evenings before going home to the family. I would just stand in the corner of a gay bar and watch . . . just to satisfy myself that the other people present seemed normal and well-adjusted. Shortly afterwards I started a relationship with a Brazilian guy who ended up being extremely important to me at the time and who saw me through some very tough times that were shortly to follow. The actual coming out to the family was a very dramatic event with a massive amount of pain and hurt on both my own part and on the part of my then wife and children. Then followed two very traumatic years resulting from my marriage breakup. But I was determined that I had come out and there was now no going back. It was at the tail end of those traumatic two years at the end of 1993 that I heard that Melbourne's (and Australia's) first gay and lesbian radio station (JOY Melbourne FM) was now on air and broadcasting.

Josy Catoggio: Knowing that there's other people out there and how to reach them and connect with them is the critical thing. I think isolation is the biggest factor in gay suicide. *IMRU* aired a weekly community calendar of events and at one point a segment called "Community Quickies," a three-, four-, five-minute interview with a local organization, about who they were, what they were doing, what kinds of people were involved. Local programming is so important because it is the only way to connect gay kids with what is available in their communities, and sometimes that may be like the only PFLAG group, Parents and Friends of Lesbians and Gays, that happens to meet in the local church; or maybe there's some sensitive counselor or therapist that they can get referred to because there's a lot of small places where, unless you have some means of communicating with them, they feel like they're completely alone out there and there's no one to turn to, and they either can't talk to their parents, or if somehow or other their parents find out, they're as good as dead. I think that gay kids commit suicide at the rate they do because they feel so isolated that they have no choice. I mean, I remember being a teenager and feeling like death was the only way out of an intolerable existence. In my case, I was a lesbian but I had no clue that I was a lesbian when I was a teenager. My best friend was a lesbian, and I wasn't anything like her so I figured I couldn't possibly be one. She was very "butch," but it was just that my life was horrible, and if I had a painless way to die, I probably would have done it. It was because there was nobody to say to me, all you have to do is survive until you're old enough to connect, and there is a whole world out there, and you're not the only one.

Cece Pinheiro: Actually, I had taken a mass media class in high school in 1975 when I was a senior. It was one of the very few and far between video classes around—one of the first around in our area. And the woman who taught it was and is a lesbian. (I didn't know it at the time. But I learned that later on. And I loved her.) You have these huge video packs—to take a camera out, it took a couple of people to carry out the equipment. One of the first people that I got to interview was Dan Smothers because I went to our Santa Cruz County Fair. Me and my friend lugged all this equipment out there, and I interviewed him. He just happened to be there—just lucky and we were high school kids—and that did it for me. But then I sort of let it go. Traveled, school, got pregnant—all those exciting things as a young person. And I didn't get back involved again until Queer TV came about in 1993 about six months after Tom Kwai had started it. QTV didn't come to fruition until '92–'93. When Kwai was working on this project, community TV didn't yet exist. The in-between time, between '75 and then, I worked for this candle factory and traveled across the country with other coworkers until the company moved. I traveled with a young man, Ed Teel, and he changed his name to Cobra, [and he] ended up being Kwai's life partner. So that's how I really got introduced to Kwai. I knew the other guy my whole life—loved him, trusted him when across country. We both came out at the same Gay Pride parade. Having a long-term friendship with somebody I loved, trusted, and had been through a lot of stuff with, and then his partner is doing this thing—so I got involved. You do things to support the people you know . . . and I knew it was going to be successful because he was great. And he knew what he was doing so I really wanted to help him. That sort of decision is political and why do you choose one endeavor over something else. Besides I loved media since high school, and I thought this was it. And that point, Kwai had taken over. And everything led me to this point that this is it—QTV.

Hilary Hamm: I wasn't really involved much in the community before QTV. I had jobs doing this and that. And when I saw QTV was in town, I just went for it immediately because I saw a medium that I could be active in and give something back to the community, to promote the gay and lesbian community in an effort to put us further out there and to give us a voice, and have it on tape. When I started [at] QTV, I had things that I wanted to do as a producer. They're like, "Oh, great! She's got her own agenda. That's the best kind of person." QTV is like an archive of our community. I am working on a Gay Games documentary, for example. Amsterdam always has its Gay Pride during the first week of August, and it just added the Gay Games into that last year. The Gay Pride celebration starts out with a boat parade. The city really treats people with respect, and I want to bring that out in this documentary. Going to the Gay Games [in the first week in August 1998], competing in sports climbing, and just being in Amsterdam was exciting. I went over there with my climbing buddy. We both competed in that. Her partner won a gold medal in her Martial Arts Forms Division. So that was really exciting for her to get a medal and for me to get that whole thing on videotape. I have actually edited that segment already. Amsterdam was fabulous. I used to live there. To go back there after five years and to know the stories that I wanted, and to go back to a place that is really rich in gay and lesbian history—it was an incredible experience.

Lidell Jackson: I'm one of the few people of color activists of my generation who is still active and/or still alive. A lot of my friends have just shut down talking to the outside world, 'cause they've gotten tired of the requests for interviews. I find it always incredibly immensely important to be part of interviews because I want to make sure that when the lesbian/gay community history is chronicled, especially the history of the '80s and the '90s, that there's significant people of color coverage. You know I come from a black community that is filled with oral tradition, which is so great and so cool, yet we don't have a lot of our history written down. There's some things that worked in my favor. One was that I was a political activist who was well known, and so I had a certain level of credibility in my favor. People were inclined to give me carte blanche to go in any direction that I wanted to go— and also being a sex positivist activist and also being a leather activist, I had all sorts of interesting connections that were happening there. The second thing, and that somehow for some reason worked heavily in my favor, is that (and I didn't realize this but people told me this) I have a good radio voice because it resonates, deep and strong, and I'm an intelligent speaker so people really liked hearing me talk. I'm also from Tennessee, you know, and like southerners Mark Twain and Tennessee Williams, I could tell stories and relay adventures of what has happened and do an analysis of what it all meant—combined with my openness. The fact that I can sit here in my office and talk about my gay life and my sex life, and the past—it's just the type of life I have lived. So, for those years, I really did enjoy being able to bring a number of significant issues to the forefront, issues for people of color and of women and inclusively into the larger community.

Marle Becker: I remember coming to New York. My first lover was a black man. I remember we were living in Washington, and we came to New York in 1966. We tried to get a hotel and, clearly, evidently they were not going to rent us a room, not because he was black, but because we were gay. Actually hotels here in New York even said to us, "We don't rent rooms to faggots." I remember saying to my lover Carl, "Where do we go? We can't go to the police and complain. We have no one to go to and say 'Oh my God, isn't this wrong? Isn't what they are doing called discrimination?' " There was no one to take our side. It wasn't really until Bella Abzug started to come out. I think Bella was one of the first politicians who raised her fist and said, "Hey, this is wrong!" I think it was probably 1988 that I got involved in *The Gay Show.* My lover died in 1987, but not of AIDS. He died of kidney failure. I got involved in a bereavement group because I was obviously devastated as any- one would be after being with someone for twelve years and losing them. At the time, the AIDS quilt was just coming to the forefront of the gay and straight community, in terms of a memorial or tribute to community people who died of AIDS. Everyone in my bereavement group had lost a lover to AIDS with the exception of me. There were four of us in the group that went down to the Washington march in the late 1980s, during the unveiling of the AIDS project in D.C. I remember how overwhelming it was and we just sort of stood there and we held each other very tightly. We just absorbed the moment. We cried and got rid of a lot of anger, and just stood hopeful. There were just so many feelings that came over us at that moment. But I remember coming back and at the next meeting of the bereavement group, as they all talked about how they wanted to make quilt panels, and I felt so left out. I felt that I couldn't make a panel for my lover because he didn't die of AIDS. That's what the whole quilt thing was about. Then they said that they wanted me to be of this experience. And they said, "It is obviously going to be a healing thing. One way or another, you will be part of this project." And we decided that we could make four panels, and each one of us would make a panel, and each panel would be a section of our own little quilt within the big quilt. So that allowed me to be a part of that process—and it was a great healer for me. It really was. It was an extraordinary experience. I never sewed before or did anything like that in my life. And when we finished making this little quilt within the quilt, I stayed on at the center and became a volunteer. Within literally weeks, I found myself sitting on Christopher Street every night after work and every Saturday and Sunday, as I collected money for the AIDS Names Project. I was almost obsessed with it. And while I was sitting out there Sunday, a gentleman named Larry Gutenberg passed by, and we chatted briefly. Two weeks later, I was in a bar, and he came up to me and said, "I would like you to be on *The Gay Show.*" I had no clue, and I said, "What is *The Gay Show?*" He said, "It's a gay and lesbian talk show. I noticed you are always on the street, collecting money for the AIDS quilt, and I would like you to come on and talk about it." I didn't feel like I was qualified, and I certainly didn't intend to be a spokesperson for the Names Project. I called up people that I had been involved with and told them I had been invited on the radio and said that I didn't want to step on anyone's toes, but do you want me to do this. Absolutely, they said, go for it and do it. I did. Two weeks later, he called me back and said one of the hosts on the program was going on vacation, and he would like me to cohost the program with him. . . . And that was it, and from that Sunday I've been with it ever since.

Joe Liberatore: ACT UP was big at the time and I didn't think a militant homosexual is where I was going. I would love to do something to participate in a march, but I thought there's got to be a way I can use my specific talents. I had a TV background, good writing skills, so I monitored newspapers for as long as you could imagine and in 1992 I saw a casting call for someone who was putting together a show out in Fairfax, Virginia, and they were doing a show called *One in Ten People,* and it was a very light entertainment show for lesbians and gay men. I went to the casting call, or some call them cattle calls, and I took the metro (our subway) as far as you could imagine. An hour or hour and a half out to D.C. Had to walk from the metro, two-thirds of a mile, maybe more. Through a muddy field, had to cross a highway with cement in the middle. I remember being in a nice suit trying to straddle this thing—skittle across a four-lane highway, made it to the interview, and as history would have it. Twenty people interviewed, narrowed to ten, and I left, shook hands, and they said don't call us, we're going to call you—to let you know whether or not we want you as a male host. You're one of ten people and in two weeks my phone rang, and they said you have not been chosen. I was totally deflated—everything pictured for myself was "You've got to come out and make a difference. You want to reach people. You want to effect change in some small way." I wanted to reconcile the gay bashing. I wanted to find a way to get even. I thought no, the best way to counter ignorance was with information. In a couple of days, they called back and said the person they picked can't make it to the first shoot. "You were our second person, and we'd love to have you come in and fill in for this person." So I went and did the first taping—turned out that my personality was vibrant and fun. And the other guy was a little more laid-back. The woman chosen for the program could not change, and I matched her pacing a little better, so I became the cohost. We did twenty-three episodes together. The show was mostly monthly and extremely taxing on the woman who produced it so she ended pulling the plug. But along the way, I had lots of fun and it was very entertainment-based—we sat in director's chairs, went out and monthly interviewed someone—Lily Tomlin was in town. She was one of the interviews we got. Jonathan Demme did Philadelphia back at that time, came back to Washington for something and we interviewed him. It was very soft, but [the program was] my first public coming out. As part of that process, I had to go to my boss because I was very close with him and he was in charge of the entire Washington, DC., operation of Fleischman Hillard, which was at the time the nation's largest independent owned public relations agency. I had to tell him not only am I doing work after hours, but I'm going on television and I'm going to tell people that I'm gay and I want you to know about this. Believe it or not, he said [he] could care less as an individual, not necessarily representing at this time the corporate view, but "do your parents know and are you cool, how do you feel about it?" And he was actually concerned, compassionate, so that gave me the energy to go on the show, and it ran about twenty-three months. I think at the time, it was on about twenty-five markets.

Nicholas Cimorelli: What I've been very excited about the last several years is *Health Action,* the program I'm doing now, and I guess I'm an example of someone who became involved in media because of my gay activism but I'm also a psychotherapist in a private practice, a transpersonal psychotherapist. My interest in health and involvement in having specialization and dealing with issues related to challenges with AIDS and HIV and transitioning is exemplified through *Health Action,* which is a prime-time mainstream program—an example of where people who are out and are gay are visible in mainstream programming and having a voice and influence in reaching a much larger audience. One of the concerns historically about having a gay hour on Sunday night is the fact that our concerns are being ghettoized—having gay listenership and not being heard by a mainstream audience. So that is what excites me about *Health Action*. When the themes are specifically gay-related, it is significant we have a gay-identified person producing a weekly mainstream program on health that is inclusive. We've developed quite a large following at this point in time, since we are aired in a tristate area within a sixty-mile radius, and that is a really exciting indication of how things have changed and opened up a door for gays and lesbians to really learn how to produce and how to really become broadcasters and take their own interests in scales beyond their sexual identities and integrate and expose those interests to a wider audience—teaching by demonstration and actually living. That type of integration is a pretty incredible thing.

Wayman Widgins: I started a cable show in Manhattan called *Mack's-Wayman News* in about '95–'96, and it ran for about one and a half years. My partner and I developed that show basically as sort of a community service type of program to highlight news and events going on in the community. Originally, it didn't start out as a gay/lesbian program, and later we developed it toward the gay/lesbian side of things. I wasn't actually a producer of radio until I came here to New York. I met someone who was working on WBAI radio on a program that at the time was called *OutFM*. He knew that I was pretty active in the gay community, and knew that I was interested in those types of things. And he just said he thought it would be a good idea if I joined the collective. His name was Bob Storm. He was a long time member of the gay collective even before it was called *OutFM*. I wasn't even a big listener of radio and was mostly involved in film and television. Bob got me interested in listening to radio. Then I would listen actually to WBAI at that point. And I realized what kind of resource it was because I had been in New York for only a few years and still hadn't really found all the resources of the city yet.

Marle Becker: I think one of the reasons why gay and lesbian broadcasting is important is because of the diversity within our community. I think we are the most diverse community that is around, if you were to sit down and make a list of all the different communities we encompassed: males and females, blacks, Asians and Hispanics, and others. And we have young people in our community. I just turned fifty-six and it is interesting because I learn from the young kids. When you have someone on a show like Barbara Cook or

Joni James, who was one of the biggest singers in the '50s and '60s in the business who supported our community, young people will write in and say "Wow, I really like that music by her. Thank you for introducing us to that." And then, of course, I'm always being turned on to the younger groups of people, the younger singers, the younger activists. I have been able to bring to gay and lesbian broadcasting some of the history of our community. It was very difficult growing up when I grew up, and it was only thirty-five years ago that I was really out. Things were very different. I wouldn't change my life for anything. However, if I had one thing that I would change about it, I wouldn't certainly choose being harassed and ridiculed through my life, or to have my life threatened. That part I certainly would change. When I hear politicians say this is a lifestyle we have chosen, oh that's a part of the lifestyle that I certainly would not have wanted, nor would wish on anyone. When I first came to New York, there were all those stories about going into a gay bar, and the bars being mixed, and if the police came in there was a red light in the middle of the dance floor. And the minute that the light came on, if two guys were dancing or two women were dancing, you'd switch partners, and it became a very straight disco or a very straight dance floor. This was in the late '60s, before Stonewall.

John Catania: I had been trying to find some way to contribute to the gay community. I moved to New York City. I was just new to the city, and I was trying to find some way of mixing my work in the arts with some sort of work with the gay community. There are a lot of ways you can contribute to the gay community, your time, but none of them quite worked for me—like volunteering at a community center or whatever. I could do all those things. But then when I met someone from *In the Life* and they explained what it was all about, I thought what a perfect way to get involved using my creative abilities. I had something that was really groundbreaking and historic to put in my time that way, so I just started to volunteer. I had no television background whatsoever, but *In the Life* needed people to work for it. So I just got interested in television, and learned how to do interviews, and produce and edit, and it provided a great opportunity for me personally—and so I've stayed with television. I love public television because of the millions of people we are reaching with our TV series. In the beginning, nobody was really watching *In the Life*. It had no advertising budget, very little promotion effort if any, so while I began producing for the show, I also was very intent upon my work being seen. No one knew about us, really. So then I volunteered to start a PR department here, and six years later we have 1,500 press clippings to show for it. We have put together a very good PR effort, and we've been reviewed by the *New York Times*, *Los Angeles Times*, and the *Washington*

Post. The word is out, and now we have a million plus viewers, hundreds of letters and e-mails. We hear from people of all ages—teenagers to people who have just come out in their forties. We're probably attracting an older audience, but that really has more to do with public television than *In the Life*. San Francisco Public Library, New York Public Library, Boston Children's Service Association, Southwest Missouri State University, Arizona State University, Loyola University of Chicago, St. Paul public schools, public libraries of Seattle and St. Louis—all we know is that these organizations and more have purchased our tapes. We have a lot of schools that have put *In the Life* into their libraries, and teachers that are using it as part of their curriculum. So we know that young people are watching. Of course we would always like more young people to be watching, but that is a constant challenge when there's so much that's grabbing their attention.

Joe Liberatore: I was able to come out of the closet to find my inner voice and a way to get out and over the trauma of being bashed back in Scranton all those years ago. I was able to come out and be proud of who I was, not just when I was in a bar or having sex with men, but in the daylight at my job. I was so confident going from *One in Ten People* to producing my own show and enjoying widespread success. At the time, I was still in the PR firm. I brought a man to our Christmas party, the first man who had ever done it, and it gave me an awful lot of freedom and self-confidence and again that's what I wanted with my show—be open and spread the wealth. There's a lot of work to go around here at *Gay News Network* so we were thrilled to spread it to field reporters.

Karen Boothe: Let's fast forward to 1999. I don't think Roy Aarons, founder of NLGJA, even saw me at that first convention. But I was among the 300 attendees who returned to our newsrooms, after drawing national media attention at the event, and began to make changes in the industry. Today, I am writing as the first elected president of the organization. Much has been accomplished since that first convention. We have grown into an organization with some 1,500 members and twenty-three chapters in the United States and Canada. We maintain an official alliance with a gay/lesbian journalists' organization in Germany that was founded based on and inspired by NLGJA. Our members in such places as Vietnam, China, the United Kingdom, and Namibia keep connected via our Web site and listservs. We have been instrumental in holding the news industry accountable for coverage of issues pertaining to gays and lesbians and have played key roles in securing domestic partnership benefits at the *New York Times*, Knight-Ridder newspapers, and other institutions. NLGJA has given voice and empowered hundreds of gay and lesbian journalists to come out in the workplace.

Nicholas Cimorelli: We all have certain gifts and talents to really put out there and we need to be seen in the communities at large. We all have roles to play and they go beyond our own community and we need to really think more globally and think in terms of how one community nurtures another community. There is such a thing as a gay and lesbian sensibility, not just for us. We have to share those gifts. We need to teach by demonstration. We need to really have our voice heard not just within our own boundaries, but to really ensure that gay and lesbian sensibility among us—and it is not coincidental or accidental that our role as artists and heroes keeps coming up.

Tom McCormack: I was sort of frustrated by that whole experience of dealing with record people and what not. So when it came time to consider doing a new recording, I just said I'm going to do this for me. I'm not going to think about the commercial possibilities of it. I'm not going to even send it out to record people. I'm just going to release it and it was just going to be for me. And I didn't really give a whole lot of thought to what it was about. I was just sort of giving myself that freedom. And in the process of writing it, it became much about hiding and self-discovery and self-identity and some of the songs were clearly about issues of coming out so that was a very liberating experience for me.

Marle Becker: I went to the Democratic National Convention when it was in New York, when Clinton was nominated and Bella Abzug was there. I had been involved with Bella's campaign from the minute I became politically active. I ran into Bella as we were leaving Madison Square Garden. I just started to cry when I saw her, and I said that it was just unbelievable for me to hear a presidential candidate use the words "gay" and "lesbian" in his acceptance speech. And Bella said, "All that time on the street, Marle, finally paid off, didn't it?" And I had not thought of it that way. And I just sort of sat down and thought, "Wow." It was like I just opened the floodgate because, at that time, it seemed all so worthwhile. All the jeers, all the people throwing Bibles at you. I remember the first gay marches, and they were threatening sometimes. So I just sat down after Bella said that. She put her arms around me and said, "See, Marle, all of that hard work paid off. This is the result of all your labor." And I guess that is how I feel about gay broadcasting. If it makes a difference, yes indeed, it is worth all that hard work.

Chapter Two

Howl of Freedom

The Rise of Queer Radio

*It is important to know how brave these pioneers and their
station managers were back in the early '70s when they were
allowing these "outrageous" queers on their stations every
week. There were many legal challenges and battles and plenty
of opposition from the general listening audiences.*

—Alan Ross, former host of *Gaydreams*

The Pacifica Foundation was formed in 1946 as the brainchild and inspiration of
poet and journalist Lewis Hill and a small collective of radio professionals, an
extraordinary group of pacifists and intellectuals. KPFA-FM 94.1 in Berkeley went
on the air on April 15, 1949, and became the first listener sponsored radio station
in the world. Pacifica's second station, KPKF-FM 90.7, began to broadcast to the
city of Los Angeles in 1959. The following year, philanthropist Louis Schweitzer
donated WBAI-FM, New York, to Pacifica. Houston's KPFT-FM 90.1 went on the air
in 1970 as the fourth Pacifica station, only to be shut down twice by bomb attacks
to its transmitter by the Ku Klux Klan. The fifth station was WPFW-FM in Washington, D.C. Pacifica stations covered the gay perspective in news, public affairs,
and literature discussions, even before Stonewall.[1]

These five stations reached out to these radio markets with the heaviest concentration of lesbians and gays, and they would serve eventually as the basis from
which to launch gay and lesbian programming throughout the United States,[2]
and eventually the world. It seemed only fitting that another poet, Allen Ginsberg,
would inadvertently lead this revolution by challenging the boundaries of Pacifica radio specifically and American radio in general. Ginsberg's life of drugs, jazz,
and no limits epitomized the Beat rebellion against the apple-pie conservatism of
the 1950s. He, like others of the Beat Generation, did not feel bound by sexual or
moral codes, and decency was merely a matter of opinion. One evening in 1956,
Ginsberg revolutionized radio, and indeed turned it upside down in a matter of

minutes, if not seconds, as he read live his poem *Howl* on KPFA[3]: This moment may have very well been the flashpoint for the beginning of gay radio, at least from the perspective of David Lamble, writer for the *San Francisco Bay Reporter*:

> Memories are foggy and the tapes may no longer exist, but let's just say that the first truly gay radio broadcast occurred whenever Allen Ginsberg first "Howled" on Pacifica Radio's KPFA in Berkeley, California, the nation's first successful non-commercial radio station. The language, rhythms, meaning, and in-your-face intensity of Ginsberg's Beat manifesto were quite unlike any message American radio had ever transmitted.[4]

In the 1960s, several noncommercial stations licensed to the Pacifica Foundation aired a series of poetry and discussion shows related to the concerns of eight gay men. Even though some listeners demanded that the Federal Communications Commission (FCC) not renew the license of one of the Pacifica stations, then up for review, the commission never reprimanded any of the stations involved in the broadcast.[5] The FCC upheld Pacifica's contention that broadcasts that involved gay issues served the public interest, as long as the topic was handled in good taste. Years later, in the 1980s, the FCC would warn Pacifica that any further broadcast of *Howl* could result in heavy fines or the forfeiture of its license. That was just one example of the FCC's inconsistency in dealing with gay programming.

Queer Radio was also challenged in 1986 by the FCC, after Reverend Larry Poland accidentally tuned into *IMRU* on KPFK. Poland became offended by the airing of "Jerker," or the Helping Hand, a radio drama about the impact of AIDS on two gay men who seek sexual companionship with each other over the phone. The story ends dramatically with the death of one of the men.[6] The FCC threatened to revoke KPFK's license in an attempt to limit discussions of gay and lesbian issues broadcast on the airwaves. In 1991, Pacifica led a successful petition along with other activists like Allen Ginsberg to oppose the twenty-four-hour indecency ban initiated by Senator Jesse Helms and the FCC.[7]

Making *Friends*

One of the first gay programs in the United States was *Friends* and it began in 1960 on Georgetown University's campus station WGTB—one of the first FMs. The daily routine of WGTB was uneventful until 1970, when a ten-person collective decided to take over the programming:

> They changed the format overnight, making a hard left turn to the rock of Jefferson Airplane, progressive electronic music, and avant-garde jazz. Announcements for campus dances were replaced with dark, subversive political bulletins. If the "pigs" arrested a member of the Black Panthers or the "liberators" held off the "imperialist forces" in North Vietnam, listeners heard about it. . . . The contemporary lexicon held that if you were "straight," you were certainly heterosexual and subscribed to the middle-class suburban ethos. You had probably voted for Nixon.[8]

Under the reign of General Manager Ken Sleeman, the station created *Friends*, a gay and lesbian program that became the longest-running gay-oriented radio program in the country. Guests included filmmaker John Waters, Allen Ginsberg, and Cheech and Chong. The deejays aired calls from listeners over WGTB and injected a bit of playfulness into their song commentaries ("Just exactly what were Paul Simon and Julio doing down by the schoolyard?") The show went off WGTB in 1976 and moved to Pacifica Radio, where it ran until 1982:

> "Friends" provided information about venereal disease and community support groups, and it challenged mainstream values, premiering, as it did, less than five years after the watershed Stonewall riot in New York, which marked the beginning of the gay liberation movement.[9]

Sophie's Parlor, one of the nation's longest running lesbian/feminist programs, also debuted on WGTB. The station was shut down for a few months in 1976 after the tower accidentally fell down. To this day, some of the station alumni believe that its collapse was an intentional move by the administration to shut down the radical programming. When the station returned to the air, it did so without *Friends* and *Sophie's Parlor*—because the new station management said that it would no longer support the homosexual lifestyle. Both shows moved to Pacifica's D.C. station, WPFW-FM.[10]

In Your Gaydreams

> . . . *was just remembering growing up in Philadelphia as a*
> *teenager, and they used to have this show, they may still have it,*
> *called "Sunshine Gay Dreams" and I was that kid in the early*
> *70's with my headset on in my room, totally connected . . . and*
> *the most important thing I could share with every teenager . . .*
> *male or female, Black or white—whatever—that are out there*
> *is that I think community is communication. . .*
>
> —Don Belton, editor of *Speak My Name*[11]

By the 1970s, a handful of public radio stations had already begun to regularly target gay and lesbian listeners—and among the first was WXPN-FM in Philadelphia. It aired *Gaydreams* in 1971. As legend stands, *Gaydreams* was the first weekly gay radio program on the East Coast and, possibly, in the nation.

Alan Ross: I went to the Christopher Street Gay Pride Celebration in 1979 in New York City, which was billed as Stonewall 10. One group had signs for "Gay Daddies." I immediately said, "I'm a gay daddy," so I ran into the parade from the sidelines. I said, "Hey, guys, how do I get a group like this started in Philadelphia?" "Well, just put an ad in a newspaper, if you can, and run and do it yourself." So I called Mark Segal, the publisher of the *Philadel-phia Gay News*, and he still is by the way, and requested, "Mark, would you please put an ad in the *Gay News* for Gay Daddies—a new group forming?" That was actually my start as a gay activist. At the time, I listened to the gay radio show in Philadelphia called *Gaydreams*. I used to call the host, Dan Daniel, who was the successor to the show's founder, John Zeh. I asked Dan to make an announcement that a new group called Gay Fathers was forming. He and I got to be friends because we would talk every week to exchange the information about the meetings for Gay Fathers. He liked me because I sounded masculine on the telephone, and I seemed to have a fairly good head on my shoulders. So when he had a fight with management at WXPN and was about to be kicked out, he asked me if I would take over his show. I said that was a fantastic idea, and my partner said he would support me. He produced *Gaydreams* for the whole five years that I was on the air. So we began to run *Gaydreams* at the station, and the rest is history.

The founder of *Gaydreams*, John Zeh, also created another *Gaydreams* on WAIF 99.3 FM in Cincinnati in the late 1970s. The show is now called *Alternating Currents*.[12]

Through nearly three decades, John Zeh, Dan Daniel, Alan Ross, Bert Wylen, and, currently, Robert Drake hosted *Gaydreams* on National Public Radio affiliate WXPN-FM. Drake revamped the program in the 1990s, changed its name to *Q'zine*, and began to stream its signal across the World Wide Web.[13] Former host Alan Ross sensed a loss of tradition after the transition to *Q'zine* and its new, slick magazine format. Indeed, Ross is only one of a handful of people who actually remember the story behind the show's original name. During his five-year stint as host (1995–1990), he had an opportunity to interview *Gaydreams* founder John Zeh.

Alan Ross: Initially, I was uncomfortable, myself, about the name of the show. I didn't understand the "dreams" part. But then I came to find out the historical significance behind the name. And the fact that it did have the word "gay" in it really helped us get people to listen to that show. And nowa-days with *Q'zine*—maybe it is really up-to-date and it is probably a profes-sional show and people like it for its own merit—but they still have to explain what the name means. John Zeh related the show's history to me during an interview and described his odyssey through the Midwest where he went on to establish other *Gaydreams* programs in Cincinnati and a few other cities. The program was named as a tribute to "Sunshine Daydream" by the Grate-ful Dead, which was subsequently coined as *Sunshine Gaydreams,* the title of a collection of interviews by Allen Ginsberg. It's sad that there is no longer a radio program that bears a name with "gay" in it on WXPN. Every time a person looked at the radio listings and saw that there was a program called *Gaydreams,* they had an immediate understanding of the program's content.

However, if you look in the paper and see a program called *Q'zine* or *This Way Out* or anything else that fails to flaunt the word "gay" in its name, you would not be inspired to turn on the radio to listen to that program unless someone first told you the specific gay nature of the program. I did an interview with Lily Tomlin when she was in town doing her one-woman show. Essentially the way I approach people like this is to remind them that I'm interviewing them for *Gaydreams* and that this particular audience is going to be sitting on the edges of their seats wondering what this particular person is going to say. I really wanted them to make our audience feel as welcomed and as self-actualized as possible, and this was also evident when I made the music and interviews come alive and animated with openly gay singing groups like the Nylons, the Flirtations, and Romanovsky and Phillips. Indeed, on October 11, 1987, it was my honor to host the national satellite-feed radio broadcast of the March on Washington for Lesbian and Gay Rights with the staff of *This Way Out*.

In 1989, the Gay & Lesbian Press Association held its annual Lambda Awards and *Gaydreams* won an unprecedented three Lambda Awards out of the four radio categories. The program took top honors for Best Gay Radio Show, Best Interview, and Best News Radio Broadcast. It was during those years that shock radio began to sweep across the nation.[14]

Alan Ross: When I hosted *Gaydreams* and other radio shows, I was appalled with the right-wing hatemongers and other shock talk shows that were coming on the air. But since I am passionate to defend free speech, I realized that the only option I had was to be responsible myself and to encourage responsible journalism whenever I had a forum for advocacy. Since my show was the only gay show in Philadelphia at the time, I also recognized that I was the "Voice of the Gay Community" to large numbers of people who listened and who may never have known anyone in their life who was openly gay. Thus, I felt a responsibility as an ambassador to gays, closet gays, and to the general public who might tune in. Our station was giving us the line (i.e., the infamous seven dirty words) that we couldn't say this or we couldn't say that. And I'm saying, whatever you tell me I can't say, I'm going to go over the edge of that and step my big toe over that line just a little bit because that's just the personality that I have. I have always been one to push the envelope just a little bit. Now, I've never been one like Howard Stern to push the envelope three miles beyond that or Lenny Bruce. Bruce established a whole new set of guidelines by exceeding them so blatantly. I think Lenny Bruce was stepping over a line that was at least ten years ahead of his time. What I was doing was stepping slightly over the line. I was a little more conservative than Lenny Bruce or Howard Stern, and anyone who is drawing lines of censorship as far as I'm concerned is absolutely an enemy to freedom. The only remedy for bad speech is more speech, as far as I'm concerned. You just can't stop speech.

Robert Drake: I agreed to *Gaydreams* on one condition, that the show, which had worked hard to help those listening come out, would change its focus a little and simply celebrate the feeling of being out. That meant exploring the arts and culture that makes up our diverse community. Additionally, it meant broadening the scope of listeners—from a core gay male audience to a mix of all kinds. Being able to take the reins of WXPN's gay programming back in 1996 was a successful moment for me, since the first gay person I ever heard was Dan Daniel—host of *Gaydreams* (the show that started it all on WXPN, twenty-five years ago). It was in 1978 (or so) and once I heard him and the program, I knew that I was not alone. That powerful feeling has fueled my passion for hosting and producing *Q'zine* each Sunday night since May of 1996.

Robert Drake began his media career by volunteering at the *Philadelphia Gay News* in 1981. He worked in print media exclusively through 1986. Soon after, he began to dabble in noncommercial radio. When Bert Wylen left WXPN in the late 1990s, Drake was approached by station management and asked if he would be interested in taking over the program. Drake had already been hired by WXPN in 1998 to produce the *Kid's Corner,* a locally originated children's program now in its eleventh year; and within his first year it won the George Foster Peabody Award for Excellence in Broadcasting. All Drake's experience had prepared him to take over the reins of the long-standing, legendary *Gaydreams* program in 1996. *Gaydreams,* with its new title and format, began to reach out to the entire queer community in arts, culture, and information, reflecting the changing needs of the LGBT listeners—many of whom were now out and celebrating life.

Robert Drake: I was able to understand the political issues that faced a community that I was slowly realizing was my "real" family. I developed friendships with the coworkers at the *Philadelphia Gay News* (PGN) and slowly began casual conversations with some people to begin a new weekly paper (the *Au Courant Newsmagazine*) that would supplement the PGN and offer more arts and culture coverage as well as explore the factions within the overall gay community, smaller communities that were just beginning to identify themselves—bisexuals, transgender, etc. The *Au Courant* is still around today, seventeen years later, although I left the paper in 1986. As of today, I am the only living member of the founding partners; the others have died of AIDS. I was the general manager of *Au Courant* from 1982 to 1986, and during that time the paper was proactive about the growing health issues surrounding the gay male community. Although we had originally developed a mission statement that was to focus on the "lighter" side of the community, we quickly became the town crier in all things HIV and political. This drew me deeper into the gay community, both locally and nationally. By 1986, I was burnt out and needed a break. Having taken a year off from all things media, I started volunteering at a small public and community-based radio station in Philadelphia. In 1995, I launched *ThiNG Magazine*, a guide to gay nightlife in Philadelphia. Although it did not have the success I would have wanted, it did force both the *Philadelphia Gay News* and *Au Courant Newsmagazine* to revamp their stale formats to include coverage of a market that was sorely missed.

I Am, Are You?

> *This is a little backwater public affairs lesbian and gay show that's been on the air for twenty years, and I don't think it got any recognition anywhere for anything. If you say it in a sentence, "I am, are you?" you will get what it means. The show had the same theme song that it had for almost twelve of those twenty years. The theme song was kind of embarrassing, sort of '60s, '70s.*
>
> —Jon Beaupre, former *IMRU* producer

Six months after *Gaydreams* debuted in Philadelphia, *The Great Gay Radio Conspiracy* made history in Los Angeles. The program became known as *IMRU* in 1974. It is a locally produced lesbian and gay radio program, still broadcasting today on Pacifica's KPFK 90.7 FM. One of the early *IMRU* founders, Greg Gordon, and the collective that he inspired would plant the seeds for other gay and lesbian shows over the next two decades. Gordon was the production coordinator for *IMRU*. It was during his stay at KPFK that he envisioned the now internationally distributed Los Angeles–produced news magazine radio program *This Way Out* (TWO). Gordon has been the driving force behind TWO since its debut in 1988.

Lucia Chappelle joined KPFK in November 1973, and shortly afterward, she became a significant contributor to *IMRU*. From 1987 to 1995, she was the program director for KPFK. Chappelle and Gordon have worked on several radio projects over the past twenty years. She is the associate producer and cohost of *This Way Out*. She has also served in the clergy of the Universal Fellowship of Metropolitan Community Churches (MCC) for ten years, and continues her ministry to the gay and lesbian community on Planet Out. The joint credits of Chappelle and Gordon also include producing and anchoring live, national satellite broadcast coverage of the rallies following both the 1979 and 1987 March on Washington for Lesbian and Gay Rights.

Another former *IMRU*er, Cindy Friedman, alongside Chappelle, is involved in producing the daily news for Planet Out, and that is actually Friedman's major paid job at this point. Friedman has a long history of producing—both for *IMRU* and TWO. She has also worked extensively for a variety of women's and feminist causes for almost fifteen years, including a stint as acting executive director of Haven House, a battered women's shelter in Pasadena, California. Her partner, Josy Catoggio, worked alongside Friedman during the *IMRU* years, and has earned national recognition as an interviewer of gay and lesbian authors, activists, intellectuals, politicians, and celebrities since her radio debut in the 1970s.

The following is the story of one of the earliest queer collectives in America, from some of the people who shaped *IMRU* programming for the gay and lesbian community—Greg Gordon, Lucia Chappelle, Josy Catoggio, and Cindy Friedman. Independent producer Jon Beaupre came aboard KPFK in 1991 during *IMRU*'s transition into a slick magazine format. Beaupre became chairman of the board of Overnight Productions soon after his departure from *IMRU* in 1998.

Jon Beaupre: I think like most of my contemporaries, I moved to southern California with my partner. At the time, he wanted to attend graduate school. I had long since graduated. When I heard a call for volunteers on this local Pacifica station KPFK in 1991, I thought, "I don't have a lot of friends, connections, or family here in southern California." I was sort of floundering or kind of desperate to make some sort of connection with somebody so I went to the volunteer orientation for the lesbian/gay radio program *IMRU* in January 1992 and sort of found a home. I found people that I really liked. The show was amateur, to put it mildly—well intended, but not terribly technically proficient. The content was always limp and sloppy and not really thought out. I thought that I could really make a good contribution here. And within two sessions of volunteering, I was on the air, and I was doing pitches at fund drives. I was writing and suddenly trying to bring some discipline (I mean that in a good sense) into a group that had been casual and not very committed. They were committed philosophically, but there weren't a lot of hours that people were available.

Greg Gordon: I will tell you how I got into KPFK in the first place. The then called L.A. Gay Community Center had started a few years before, and we're talking about the early '70s now. I was volunteering as a rap group facilitator. And at the time, KPFK here in L.A. had a once-a-month gay men's radio club called *Gay of Heart* (GH). I think Tuesdays at 11 P.M. was sort of a sex hour at KPFK. The first Tuesday of the month was *Lesbian Sisters,* the third Tuesdays was GH, and I'm not sure how they filled out the other sexual variations on the other Tuesday nights. Anyway, it was a one-person show, from what I understand. All I know is the host went by the name "Morning

Glory," and apparently he was moving to Georgia with a boyfriend. KPFK posted notices at the center about needing people to take over the show, and me and a couple of other guys from the center contacted that station. There were three of us (Colin McQueen, Enric Morello, and Greg Gordon) at the time that decided to come aboard. And my background up until then was a bachelor's degree from Radio/TV at UCLA, but I hadn't really done, other than working on the campus radio station, any other kind of radio. *IMRU* grew from that. One of the positives of this experience was the growth of the collective that evolved from producing *IMRU*. The first show was just a live open phone show—a discussion on the myths about homosexuality, really a kind of Homo 101. I do distinctly remember because I debated in my mind whether to use an on-air alias or whether to use my real name. I used my real name and I remember driving home and thinking about what this meant. It was 1974, and I was a little bit concerned, yet I remember feeling really liberated on the drive home. I know that sounds really cornball, but that was a very freeing experience.

Lucia Chappelle: I first came to KPFK in Los Angeles in the fall of 1973. I started producing more public affairs work, including my first little minifeature on a gay and lesbian demonstration in Hollywood, which had been called to boycott local businesses. As it turned out, the demonstration had been canceled at the last minute, and the boycott had been canceled because some of the gay and lesbian leaders had held a meeting where they had come to some settlement, but a number of people turned up for the demonstration anyway in the pouring rain and decided to go ahead with it. They didn't feel like the leadership was speaking to their needs and their concerns, so they had a march. They marched down Hollywood Boulevard and I recorded that demonstration and some interviews with some of the people who had been involved afterwards to fill in some of the blanks and produced a twenty-minute piece called the "Tinsel Throne"—the name was taken from one of the people who said that we had to take these gay leaders off of their tinsel throne.

Greg Gordon: Anyway, other people got interested in what we were doing. We had a bunch of people at the time. Our first really professional production show was in February of 1975 and we really did something that I'm still proud of. We had an hour-long show about gay men's romance. It was all prerecorded. We had a subcommittee, so to speak, that dealt with gay men in long-term relationships, another one that dealt with gay men who were single and wanted to stay that way, and another group of gay men in open relationships. And it was mixed with music and it was really slickly produced. Lucia was a volunteer at KPFK at the time. I don't even remember the specifics of how she became involved, but she was the first lesbian on *IMRU* then, which happened kind of naturally, both from the political consciousness of the men who were doing the show, plus the fact that we were finally attracting some women. At one point, *IMRU* had maybe twenty, twenty-five volunteers and it was run as a collective. Needless to say, my experience and my contacts with many of the local community were limited before doing *IMRU*, but they obviously expanded.

Lucia Chappelle: I went down to volunteer at KPFK, because quite honestly as a drama major I couldn't find a job. I had been listening to Pacifica radio since I was about twelve, I think. Back in New York, I was listening to WBAI and then continued listening to a Pacifica station when I came to L.A. to go to school. And you know, I mean, it had opened up my world politically. After volunteering to help during the Christmas fair, I landed a switchboard job at the station, and of course anybody that gets involved in that kind of community-based radio ends up moving into programming. I coproduced a documentary on the history of Metropolitan Community Church, and it won an award from the Southern California Associated Press. We talked to the Reverend Troy Perry, the founder of MCC. We talked to the pastor of the local church at that time. I was a member of MCC, and along with KPFK's public affairs director Mike O'Dell, who was teaching me the ropes of radio production, we just talked to a lot of people and did a documentary, the spine of which was the dedication service for the new church that was replacing a church that had been "arsoned." And a number of churches had been "arsoned" from late '73 to early '74. A number of MCCs had been burned, so that was kind of a running theme through the program. Some excellent producers took me under their wings so that when *IMRU* started at KPFK, I had already been there and I had done a little bit of production work. I naturally joined in with the people that were working on *IMRU*. And that's how Greg and I met. I pretty much knew my way around a studio, which end of a microphone was which. When we started working together, it just opened up a whole other aspect of what the community radio thing could be.

Greg Gordon: It was the early '80s, when the women in the collective— and this is going to be from my perspective obviously—wanted their own week. Their one week of *IMRU* was to be lesbian only, the irony being that I don't believe any program they ever did was produced strictly with women. There was one guy who was the engineer, you know, a board operator type person who was wonderful. I think he wound up engineering almost everything they did because they simply didn't have enough women to do all the tasks that needed to be done to produce a program. There was a lot of conflict and tension, lesbian separatism versus lesbian cooperation with gay men, and so what went on in that area with *IMRU* is probably no different than what went on with most other cogendered queer groups. I think that in some ways it was just one of those instances that exemplified the tension that existed probably in many gay and lesbian organizations at the time. And certainly, *IMRU* continued. The problems were resolved and everybody lived happily ever after, so it wasn't a major turning point.

Josy Catoggio: Originally the only program at KPFK for me to work on was *IMRU* because at that point Helene Rosenbluth produced *Lesbian Sisters,* which was a once-a-month separate show, and *Feminist Magazine.* There weren't very many women involved in *IMRU* in the beginning. So I pretty much had no choice but to get involved with *IMRU* because that was the only place there for me in the late '70s. There were a couple of other women involved, but mostly it was pretty much male stuff—so I thought "Well, I'm needed there. I'll do that."

Greg Gordon: From my perspective, the feminist consciousness of the gay men in the *IMRU* collective was good, but I felt that in some ways we were sort of being crucified for the sins of our gender so there was a lot of tension there. We really wanted *IMRU* to have a cogender rather than a separatist kind of program. These issues were resolved, not openly, but on a personal level in terms of Josy and some of the leaders of the lesbian pact. I felt like we were being criticized and we were automatically the enemy in their minds to some degree, and that really hurt. But like I said, it has since been resolved and Josy and I are the best of friends and close so it is all ancient history.

Josy Catoggio: We also thought it was really important that we involve Gay and Lesbian Latinos Unidos (GLLU), which is an organization out here, and we even invited them to do their own program at one point. I realized, having been an activist for a number of years, that it was really uncomfortable when a person or two of color would come into this largely white group— 'cause I know I felt that way as a woman when I first came in—they would feel like they just didn't fit. So I actually went to one of their meetings and said we will do anything we can to facilitate your doing this, even if it means giving you the training and the technical support and you can do whatever you want with the time. And so in fact, for a number of years, while *Lesbian Sisters* was still a separate show, you had this other separate show [*Radio GLLU*—Gay and Lesbian Latinos Unidos] on the fourth Sunday of the month. We gave them as much support as they needed until they were able to do it on their own, and in fact, Rita Gonzalez, one of the women that got involved at their very beginning, is now like the coanchor of *IMRU.*

Lucia Chappelle: I remember the night we did a program on the Christopher Street West Association, which just had some trouble. When we opened the phones afterwards, about half of the members of the board called in and resigned live on the air. We had another very controversial program when we had gay Nazis on the air—live with open phones. There were those kinds of shows, but then there were the shows that got to the heart of people trying to come out and just trying to live. There were all kinds of people that we interviewed that we brought to the air and let the community talk to them. An amazing array of people came on the show—Harvey Milk, Christopher Isherwood, and Jim Kepner, the great noted gay historian who was a regular volunteer and who just died recently. There were those shows, and then there were the documentaries that we produced. Greg and I did a documentary on the first march on Washington in which we had participated in a live broadcast that was carried on public radio, and it really stands up as a document of that moment in queer history.

Josy Catoggio: One of my first major projects was a tenth anniversary Stonewall retrospective highlighting some of the milestones of the decade that aired in 1979 as part of Lesbian-Gay Day on KPFK. I borrowed every back issue of *Lesbian Tide* that I could find and I just sort of went through them and sort of pulled out all the highlights of what had happened to lesbians in the ten years since Stonewall. And so that was the first show I worked on, and I basically compiled the women's half of that show and coproduced it with a guy. He went through back issues of *The Advocate*, and there was a lot more men's stuff. There was a lot of proposals to get rid of the antisodomy legislation and stuff like that.

Cindy Friedman: I didn't have a clue that radio was in my future until I hooked up with Josy. When I came to *IMRU*, I was basically coming in with Josy—that was how I started in 1983. Shortly after, the *Los Angeles Times* did a nice last-page piece in the calendar section on my involvement, and I hold that as solely responsible for my not becoming the director at the battered women's shelter where I had been number two for a thousand years. There were certain people on the board who, after that article, suddenly started making remarks that I didn't dress right, and who had just suddenly determined I wasn't going to run that place. A number of years later, of course, I did. As far as when I began to program to lesbian audiences, that was kind of instant. I had already worked as a social services person working at the battered women's shelter and hung with the people who were working on violence against women, and a lot of them, strangely enough, were really cool political lesbians so that was kind of a community for me and an area of interest for me until I got into *IMRU*. After a short stint working with community calendar and paying the typical radio dues, I fell into news, sort of the next station task, but one that I took seriously, first at *IMRU* and later at Planet Out [an Internet-based news and entertainment service].

Josy Catoggio: And it's funny how we met because we actually met in a lesbian bar where we both used to go to play Ms. Pacman, and she asked me when the Christopher Street parade was because she thought I would know, being as how I was on the radio. Once a year, *IMRU* would broadcast a fifteen-hour marathon, from 9 A.M. to midnight, typically the week after the Christopher Street West Gay Pride Parade in June or early July. We'd pass out flyers at that, and that would remind people to tune in. I mean we did all this on our own money. Can't tell you how much money over the years we spent on printing flyers and sending out press releases and long-distance phone calls and all that kind of stuff. I've always been a volunteer. Most of us have been volunteers and spent our own money doing it because we're really passionate about it. Well, it has been my major career. I was a bookseller for many years. That's what I did to support myself once the money dried up for social service stuff because before that I worked at the gay and lesbian community services center when there wasn't even "lesbian" in the name yet. It was the Gay Community Services Center. I was one of the people who fought to put "lesbian" in the name. Anyway, there were some CETA jobs—you know, the Comprehensive Employment and Training Act. So an awful lot of social service agencies got hooked on this money that supposedly trained people to work, but a lot of us already knew what we were doing; we actually did get paid for doing the antihomophobia workshops for a couple of years. That was '79.

Lucia Chappelle: In the early days of *IMRU*, there was barely a hotline at the gay and lesbian center. I mean these things were just starting. We would spend two, three hours sometimes after the show taking phone calls from people off the air—many times from people who were in crisis. I was working in a collective of people, smart people. We were fortunate enough to have a group of volunteers who all had some radio experience or news-gathering experience of some kind, and we just sparked each other and learned from each other and created a way of covering the community as we went along. I was with people who were hearing these things for the first time, and quite honestly their minds were blown, just because here were the sounds of our movement, our history. Well, I guess that's when we really got good at what we were doing.

Cindy Friedman: One of the *IMRU* news features that we produced was about battered lesbians, and that was cutting-edge journalism in 1983. Josy and I both went to the first national conference on the subject so that was a proud thing to put out there. What was peculiar was that I really wanted to do a companion piece about domestic violence and gay male relationships, and I'm not sure that's happened yet because nobody's been able to talk publicly about it. There are a couple books about it now and even a program out there somewhere, but for some reason that was much harder to get informants to talk about. I also did a big feature early on about youth suicide in '84–'85—dozens of segments, an hour and a half, two hours, that sort of thing. That had always been a really important subject to me. I also taped in 1984 what was really the first big conference on HIV. I think it was the AMA [American Medical Association] conference. They had a session on AIDS. Later, about 1989, I did the technical work on the radio drama *AIDS US 2,* the real-life stories of a number of people, either with AIDS or connected to people with AIDs.

Josy Catoggio: When Cindy and I got really bored with doing the—pardon the expression—straight radio, we decided we would do parodies of our own stuff, and Cindy would fake news items and we would even write a fake community calendar at the end that would have like silly little events, and we did this parody of a talk show in a reverse world called "Straight Talk" where heterosexuals were the oppressed minority and Cindy played this straight woman with this very meek quiet little voice and she was with her husband and I played this radical straight activist who was advocating for straight rights. We did silly stuff like that.

Cindy Friedman: In those years, *Saturday Night Live* was our inspiration for the numerous comedy bits that we produced.

Josy Catoggio: I stayed involved as a volunteer with *IMRU* for close to twenty years. For many of those years, I was primarily focused on author interviews at *IMRU* because I'm passionate about books and eventually became a bookseller and worked in bookstores and managed briefly before I got too sick to work. I like doing the real big-picture stuff. I mean, pretty much any, almost any, gay writer you could come up with I've probably talked to at least once, and some of them four or five times. That's been my primary passion for this work and the reason I kept doing radio. The *IMRU* collective decided to cut author interviews to a maximum of five to six minutes. I felt like that was a total insult to authors. I didn't want to talk to people that could say what they had to say in five to six minutes.

Jon Beaupre: I went to the station manager and the program director and explained what the situation was. That I was one of a number of volunteers who was really committed and connected to reformatting this show that had a long history, but had become kind of fallow and contentious. And they basically gave me their blessing. I realized that the real barrier was one woman with *Lesbian Sisters*. She was unfortunately the woman who had been with the show the longest—Josy Catoggio. Josy had a reputation and recognition in the community that was rather spectacular. She and her work were very well known. She was a very, very fine interviewer, very knowledgeable on literacy topics.

Josy Catoggio: I wanted to talk to the big-picture thinkers and the philosophers and the anthropologists and the psychologists and the people that had like major stuff to say that would really change people's lives. We won a bunch of awards over the years, and one of the ones that I got to do the acceptance speech for was a GLAAD award, and everybody was giving awards to the tiniest little thing that any straight mainstream media person could do. In the thank-you speech, I said that *IMRU* is the one place where we talked to each other as a community, where we weren't doing sort of Homophobia 101 for the straight people, but where we could talk about anything. We talked about gay hookers and we did features on anything we could think up. Somebody did a feature on gay homelessness at some point. And we covered the conference of the Black Gay and Lesbian Leadership Forum held every year in southern California.

Jon Beaupre: Josy, as a lesbian interviewer, is a literary voice that has had quite a following. She's fairly well known. I knew this was going to be a difficult battle. I didn't want Josy to think that she was being kicked out. In fact, I wanted her to produce more, but I knew the survival of *IMRU* depended on this reformat. There finally occurred a historic and momentous meeting on October 12, 1996, in which the people from *Radio GLLU,* and Josy Catoggio from *Lesbian Sisters* all sat down at the table with the program director and the new volunteers who wanted to reformat the show. The idea of supporting these groups was always high in our minds, but when you reserve that time, we have considerably much less time to cover disabled lesbian and gay people, gay and lesbian Asian Americans, etc. We had almost no transvestite coverage other than what was in a couple of *Lesbian Sisters'* pieces and in a couple of other cases where there was some coverage of transgender issues. I laid out the situation and the fact that we had every intention in the world of making these changes, that we had gone as far as to commission a new theme, a nonlyric theme, a theme that was just instrumental, and restructured the show so that it would have anywhere between four to six features a week. There would be a much quicker—fast-paced—newscast at the bottom of the hour and international gay and lesbian news at the top of the hour. We would self-produce the local newscast at the bottom of the hour. So you wrap around those two things the five other features of the hour and we would have a considerably more lively and considerably more listenable show, with good music segues and good continuity writing. No one had ever written with continuity. We'd just kind of sit down in front of the microphone and start talking.

Josy Catoggio: We were really disappointed, at least some of us, and that was when I quit, when the program director at KPFK decided that she didn't want these so-called balkanized slots. So she eliminated essentially *Lesbian Sisters* and *Radio GLLU,* and decreed that *IMRU* would be just one show, the same from week to week, and the format would be this magazine format that is largely entertainment-oriented. That was when I quit.

Jon Beaupre: What happens in nonprofit radio is people have a share of the clock for long periods of time and sort of believe they own that clock. So people at *Lesbian Sisters* really believed that the first Sunday of the month should be theirs and that fourth Sunday was the *Radio GLLU*'s. We knew in order to be at all successful in reconfiguring the show and reformatting the show, we had to streamline. We had to strip down; we had to remove ourselves from the outside obligations. I did not want to be on the record as trying to kick *Radio GLLU* off the air or to kick *Lesbian Sisters* off the air. I wanted it clear from the get-go that not only were they not going to be limited to their one slot each month, but if either of these groups wanted to produce more in the new format context—that is five- to seven-minute pieces—we would help them do that. They could even keep their brand: this segment was produced by *Lesbian Sisters* or the segment was produced by *Radio GLLU.* But we knew there was a battle looming and it was going to be difficult. When I say we—there were three other volunteers working with me—Christine Wilson, Pam Marshall, and Christopher David Trentham, who was the senior volunteer at that point. Christopher had been with the show for eight or nine years at that point. It was with Christopher that I won the first Golden Mic award as well as one from the Radio & Television News Association. The program director said, "You've got until January 1, 1997," which was two and a half months away, to get the new show in order. Furthermore, she said, "You're going to move from 10 o'clock at night to 6 o'clock at night on Sundays." We went, "Ahhhh! What have we done?" We scrambled like crazy and did a couple of test runs and they failed miserably. The show—by that time—was twenty-two or twenty-three years old—and had never undergone any type of reformat or redoing. We went on the air in

January of 1997 with the new format. By the middle of the year, we had a show of which I was really proud. We had recruited correspondents from Berkeley and San Diego to do stories occasionally from there for our news segment. We commissioned a couple of pieces from writers from major gay and lesbian journals, and we had interviews from just an amazing cast of people.

The Gay Show

I first met Larry Gutenberg when he came to WBAI in 1983, when I was coordinator of the WBAI Gay Men's Collective. Larry had worked his way up through the ranks of commercial radio in the Midwest over many years, and the entire collective was impressed with the wealth of radio knowledge and professionalism that he brought to our program Gay Rap. *When Larry became coordinator of the WBAI Gay Men's Collective in 1984, he had many chances to display his excellent skills in dealing with people. Larry had also had a column in a gay newspaper in New York for some years, and he had developed a keen understanding of the political and social goings-on in this city. Whether he was interviewing gay or lesbian politicians, militant drag queens, public officials, movement activists or even antigay bigots, Larry's professionalism always shone through. By immersing himself in his subject he had a talent for coming up with the probing questions that revealed the sometimes hidden workings and motivations of people and institutions.*

—R. Paul Martin, WBAI producer[15]

Another Pacifica station, WBAI-FM in New York, was among the first stations in the nation to air gay and lesbian programming, yet it was not until 1982 that it would do so on a regular and predictable basis. Originally there were two collectives—the Gay and Lesbian Independent Broadcasters (GLIB) and the Gay Men's Collective, with both groups finally merging in the late 1990s. The Gay Show was the creation of the Gay Men's Collective, which had already experimented as early as 1982 with a show called Gay Rap. GLIB produced Outlooks several years later, which alternated with The Gay Show every other Sunday. Then, in the mid-1990s, WBAI management decided that both shows, Outlooks and The Gay Show, should be united, and OutFM emerged as the product of two diverse formats.

Nancy Kirton: I began about twelve years ago with the Gay and Lesbian Independent Broadcasters. We were around for about seven and a half years, and along with that group was another one called The Gay Show, which aired on

WBAI Radio. Each of these two groups had programs that alternated Sundays. There was one or two other lesbian and gay programs on WBAI. But *Outlooks* and *The Gay Show* were the dominant shows airing all queer programming on WBAI. The difference between the two groups was very sharp. *The Gay Show* required a lot of ability to pull known individuals and was concrete in a way that GLIB was not. The personalities were consistent, but much less comfortable and therefore awkward in reflecting the concerns and intimacies or nuances of the diverse melting pot within the queer community. So you couldn't just go in and out of that program. There were about three to four leading people on the show for many, many years, while GLIB had three consistent and many more people in and out throughout its many years on the air. *The Gay Show* certainly outlived GLIB. I'm not sure of the transition, but it probably happened about four years ago. At one point in time, the head honchos decided it should be one show united with *The Gay Show*. That was very difficult. The old GLIBers—including myself and Nicholas Cimorelli, who invited me to come back—and then Tony Glover and the guys from *The Gay Show* who came aboard—had these very different styles in radio. *The Gay Show* was very news-oriented, very serious and political, and at a very different level from GLIB. In fact, I'd say that GLIB was much more grassroots-oriented radio. We've interviewed people on a very different level. I think, at one level, GLIB didn't have as much access as the producers of *The Gay Show* to people in the upper political arena, such as the Barney Franks of the world, or to notable mainstream network broadcast correspondents. *The Gay Show* seemed to have plenty of that going on, but GLIB was where the real work was happening in terms of community activism. So here you have the convergence of these two very different groups. *OutFM* was very difficult to get started, but eventually it did.

Lidell Jackson: Particularly since being such a major political activist person of color at that time, and I guess, perhaps still, I had my finger on the pulse of a lot of what was going on in the community. Always, whenever anyone asks me to do anything, I'm always satisfying a demographic. Always, because you know, I'm a black, openly gay male, political activist, sex positive activist, so I sort of push every button people have, except I'm not a woman. That's the only thing—if I was a woman then I would satisfy everybody's demographic, all the time. And to this day still, you can go to the Community Center in Brooklyn and see a plethora of relatively young people, color activists of all different races bopping through there, doing their stuff, and getting involved and having their functions and meeting with their groups and everything, and you think, this is so cool. This is really cool. Well, the show, *The Gay Show,* when I was there embraced a lot of that, so that's what I brought to the show.

Marle Becker: My involvement really began 1988. That was the beginning for me. I spent every Sunday evening at the radio station, and even before I realized it, I was part of the collective. "Well, you are part of the collective now." That sort of just happened. I wasn't aware of it. I had mentioned to a friend that I didn't know if I should stay with this or what I should do. And she said, "You've been an activist for so many years, and you are getting older now. This may very well be another form of activism for you, in a different way for you to do basically the same thing you've been doing—shake your fist and march all over the country for gay and lesbian rights." So I think that was good encouragement for me and good advice. It was awfully difficult to get people to come onto *The Gay Show* in 1988, even people who were out of the closet. You were really hard-pressed to get a guest, not because they didn't like the program, but because things were so closeted back then. It was eleven to twelve years ago. If there was anything that AIDS did for our community, it brought gays out of the closet. And initially, it was like pulling teeth to get people on the show, even straight people who represented gay organizations such as the AIDS organizations. People just felt funny about it.

Lidell Jackson: My background is really an activist, which is how I got involved with *The Gay Show*. I have been an activist since 1989. And then there was a woman working at WBAI in the gay department, who has since moved on to be a conference coordinator. I respected her a great deal and really liked her. She, along with Nancy Kirton, asked me to attend a story meeting at one point, and I was asked to consider being cohost. And I had never done that before, but I thought, well, how difficult could it be? I mean I used to—before my political activism—be a Broadway dancer and singer, so I've never been one to shirk, you know, stay away, from the limelight. So I said okay and decided to go ahead and cohost *The Gay Show* with Larry Gutenberg, and I did it for quite awhile. I was always taking my responsibilities seriously about making the show diverse whenever possible, you know. I was always bringing in people who I knew were other political activists, who were people of color, who were women, and bringing their issues to the forefront. And, and there were times when I was doing it with sort of a fervency, almost a ferocity, so that all the other people who were involved would just sit back and watch. I actually didn't mind that. Nowadays I would be more inclined to go, "Wait a minute, white man, you have to be as responsible for doing this as I am." What did happen, as time went on, was that some of the other guys, who were white men, involved in the show became more savvy about being more diverse—Larry Gutenberg, Rick X, Nicholas Cimorelli, etc. They really got the idea into their head, making sure diversity was part of every show's programming, to the point that it became almost a given.

Marle Becker: My interest in *The Gay Show* really came from Larry Gutenberg. I didn't know anything about it until Larry told me. Allen Ross sort of came to *The Gay Show* roughly the same time as me. I think that he might have begun two to three weeks after I did. He was a listener. Allen knew a lot about *The Gay Show*—I didn't. Allen Ross was one of the cohosts. It was Allen, Larry, Bob [Storm], and myself. Usually we took turns. There were two cohosts each program, and we alternated with each other. Larry Gutenberg worked in broadcasting. That was his job. I believe he actually worked in Chicago, if I'm not mistaken. Then he came to New York and got involved in the Gay Men's Collective there. So those were my three buddies. I learned something from all of them. Allen was very understanding and helpful in the fact that we were both new. There were many times I just wanted to throw in the towel because I didn't think that I was good enough to do this or I didn't think I was qualified to do that. And Allen sat down and sort of held my hand and said, "You can do this. You are getting better at it." I appreciated that. And Larry was certainly responsible for me being in radio. I wouldn't be in radio if it weren't for Larry Gutenberg. So they all taught me a great deal about life, and certainly Bob and Larry did about living with AIDS. What it must have been like, I can only imagine from being with them. I guess if I had a hope it would be that they took something of me with them as well. I certainly have been left with a lot of their beliefs, ideas, and thoughts. So if I gave them half of what they gave me, I'd be happy.

Nancy Kirton: *The Gay Show* was primarily a men's radio program that was perceived predominantly and formed by gay white males. One of the few exceptions to that is the involvement of Lidell Jackson. Lidell subsequently left the group amidst many disappointments, one being that he felt the men of color culture were not being fully endorsed and spoken to by *The Gay Show.* He couldn't deal with being the "only one" in the program.

Lidell Jackson: There was a point at which I didn't want to continue because it was taking up too much time, and that was the line for the record. Deep down I was getting tired of working with white people, and I was getting to the point of thinking, well, you know, the only reason why you really like this show is because you can bring the people of color element to it. If anything, you should just go ahead and do your own people of color show. And I didn't want to do that. And somehow, even though it would have meant not necessarily reinventing the wheel, it would have meant having to go and create a whole sort of thing on my own, and I actually could have done it, but I was too busy doing all my other political activist stuff to really continue. It was becoming burdensome to fit it into an already overburdened schedule, and I had actually got to a point that every New Year's Day my resolution was to drop one thing per year, and one year it came up that the thing that mattered the least to me was cohosting *The Gay Show.* I was getting increasingly tired of having to negotiate people of color issues with a group of white men. Nowadays, especially nowadays, I am part of a community that is so diverse and inclusive that I don't have to maneuver and negotiate or do whatever to include the issues of people of color. Another thing that happened was that I seroconverted from being HIV-negative to HIV-positive, and that was in '91, and so that was a real change year for me. So I dropped the show. It was shortly before Larry Gutenberg died. [See Appendix 2A.]

Marle Becker: One of the cohosts of *The Gay Show* had a nice collection of our programs, but sadly and tragically died in a house fire. The tapes and all went along with him in that fire. Larry Gutenberg, the granddaddy of *The Gay Show,* was really the person who held the program together. He had a nice collection. Unfortunately, he died of AIDS. Of the people that I started with, Allen Ross is dead, Larry Gutenberg died of AIDS, and Bob Storm died of AIDS. [See Appendix 2B.] So there were four of us. And right now, I'm the only one that is left of the initial group that went on WBAI in the '80s. I suppose of the three of them, I felt closest to Bob Storm. Bob and I didn't know each other before *The Gay Show,* but we were certainly involved in many of the same organizations long before Stonewall. I started out basically in the civil rights movement. I guess I didn't know it at the time, but as I was marching for civil rights I was also marching for myself. I wasn't really quite sure of my sexual orientation back then. My involvement in the civil rights movement was a way for me to get out there and march. It was boot training for me. It was sort of my boot camp so that when the gay rights movement really started to become apparent, I was really prepared to take part in it. Bob and I had a closeness because of that.

Lidell Jackson: In a couple of instances or maybe three instances, I was the host completely and I loved that. That was thoroughly exciting. When I was doing it with Larry, I was always the cohost. I was always second in command, and sometimes I felt even less than that because they had a sort of old-boy network that they were all a part of and I was kind of new—and they were all white and I was a person of color—so I would put myself in where I could. But on times when I did it all myself, I really, really enjoyed it immensely. I talked about issues of the leather community and how they interfaced with the rest of the community, and issues of racism certainly—and also issues on the negative side or on the positive side of how certain aspects of our community are becoming more diverse, and how it is happening, and here are some examples, and here are some people speaking to that. That sort of thing was on my shows, and I did so in a counterpoint kind of format, but I'm not about having one of my progressive friends duke it out with a white supremacist on the air. That really wasn't my sort of thing. Instead, I sort of heralded the good things that were happening in our lesbian/gay, two-spirit, bisexual, transgender community, and made certain that, whenever possible, the gap got included because the show was gay male predominantly, with lesbians thrown in every now and then. And then also whenever possible, I would bring in a sexual context, rather than try to present this sort of homogeneous mainstream picture of us as a sort of a sweet gentle society, community, that's mostly in and we're like everybody else. We're not like everybody else. Many of us, as gay men and some lesbians as well, who embrace sexual freedom and sexual diversity have no qualms against talking about it and whenever possible exhibiting it. So that to us is a strength. I remember one show when I had some of the guys who work at my sex club come and talk about sex and sexual freedom and what it means in the people of color community, and how sometimes it resonates differently than it does in the white community. I loved that show. That was [laughing] a great show. And the reason that it was a great show was because you heard from voices that you'd never hear from—people of color, different ethnicities, talking about their history, how their histories intersect with the concept of sexual freedom in their own societies. One of the guys, I remember, was Native American, and he was talking about how, you know, there are some Native American tribes that embrace two-spiritedness as a concept, you know, having both male and female parts of their personality, and are seen as shamans and are given the children to raise and things like that. The other part was also the idea of embracing sexual freedom by some of the tribes, and how that made it so difficult to come into a white society that was so sex negative, or to hear from some of the black men and women who were sitting there talking about how family means a lot to them, and in black families, you don't really talk a lot about sex. You just do it. So being conditioned not to be honest about the sexual freedom of expression, and then suddenly changing that by becoming gay or lesbian, and then having that turn the whole thing on its ear, because in order to come out, then the rest of the family had to recognize that sex was a part of what it means to be lesbian or gay, and because it's the crux of why we're different and whom we have sex with and are attracted to—all those things were exciting to me. I never heard panel discussions like that on other shows. And I had a chance to do it, and that along with the discussions about lesbian and gay political activism and all of that and people of color activism—these were all things that really, really worked well. Some of the feedback that the show used to get—and that I used to get when I was bopping around talking to people—was that it was great to see, to hear, people of color being taken seriously, and that people of color didn't just mean black, but there were always Latino, Asian, Native American, and Arab people, and all these different nationalities/ethnicities coming through the show. I mean this is New York, one of the few cities where so many of the different people of color/ethnicities actually interface with each other.

Marle Becker: I think, for me, probably the most moving show as a member of *The Gay Show* collective was a program that we aired on Mother's Day. We had three mothers on the program—one who was a lesbian, another who had a son who was gay (and if I'm not mistaken, I think that she had two children—a daughter and a son and both happened to be gay). The third mother that we had on was a mother who had just lost her son to AIDS. It was one of the most important programs and I was proud and pleased to be a part of it because it finally put a face, I think, on families and that was some-thing that had been missing from the gay community for such a long time. I don't think that people connected us with mothers and fathers and sisters and brothers. And this woman who was the mother of the young man who died of AIDS was without a doubt one of the most extraordinary guests that I've ever had the pleasure of interviewing on the radio. Her son's lover had AIDS. And the son cared for him until he died, with the mother's help. She nursed her son until he died, and she became a full-fledged activist. She was out on the street at every single demonstration for ACT UP. And this was a woman who literally lived the existence of the Long Island housewife with three to four children. That program for me was a real turning point. I really thought that we made a difference. Not only did I think that, but we obviously did because we received an extraordinary amount of mail from listeners on that program.

The GLIB Collective

In the late 1980s, several WBAI volunteers decided to form the Gay and Lesbian Independent Broadcasters (GLIB), and as a collective they produced a separate independent radio show that aired every other Sunday. It began with a proposal to WBAI management, and upon acceptance it brought together a diverse group of people—some of whom had never been on radio before. Nicholas Cimorelli, a former member of *The Gay Show,* led the collective.

Nicholas Cimorelli: Well, I started back in 1985. I was involved with GLAAD and actually that came about when the organization was in its infancy stage. I was one of the early members of GLAAD before GLAAD was a national organization. It was just basically being developed out of a brownstone down in Brooklyn. As a result of working with them and serving on their board for two years, there was a notice—requesting proposals for WBAI—put out to the community of gay and lesbian organizations in the winter of '88. They wanted to expand gay and lesbian programming. At that point, people from a number of different organizations, like the Coalition for Gay and Lesbian Rights among others, pulled together a group of people and, out of those eventual meetings that took place, a handful of us submitted a proposal to WBAI. It got accepted and we did our first program on the air in May of 1988. We called the organizing collective GLIB. The original name of the program was *Outlooks,* sponsored by GLIB, and those were the people who went through the initial process of submitting the proposal. Some years later, it became *OutFM,* which is still produced as a gay and lesbian broadcast on Sundays.

Lisa Winters: The lack of an identifiable place for lesbians and gays to meet in the Bronz was our biggest challenge in organizing. The Bronx is a large borough and not easily accessible from outermost points by public transportation. Many queers traveled to Manhattan for socializing where there were identifiable places to meet. Thus, our challenge first was to find each other in our big borough. Not quite sure of the right medium to reach lesbians, I took out an advertisement in *Woman News,* a weekly New York City lesbian/feminist newspaper, hoping that some would read the paper and see my ad. This proved to be a good decision—I got over thirty-six phone calls in the first week! I was pleasantly surprised not only because of the response, but because there was the potential to really begin organizing in a borough outside of the visible areas of Chelsea, Greenwich Village, and Park Slope, Brooklyn.

The concept of "we are everywhere" became the pivotal driving force in Bronx community organizing. In the summer of 1988, Bronx Lesbians United in Sisterhood (BLUES) was formed in my living room and became an important organization not only for dykes in an outer borough but also for the larger queer community. Our issues, as Bronx dykes, were also different, perhaps more complex, making us unique in what we were trying to do. We were trying to organize, without resources or an infrastructure, a racially, economically, and culturally diverse group of invisible lesbians compounded by serious transportation issues.

BLUES gained nonprofit status in 1990 and has had many important successes over the years, including three political Bronx conferences raising issues of race, class, and outer-borough organizing; successfully lobbied to have appointed several out lesbians to community planning boards; met with two senators to lobby for the passage of a state-wide hate crimes bill; and met with several appointed and elected officials about funding, lesbian visibility, and domestic partnership. We made solid relationships with many leaders, including the Bronx borough president and various community leaders. BLUES became an organization to talk to when service providers were seeking to become more "inclusive" or political leaders wanted "support." BLUES became a model for grassroots multiracial organizing and, most important, had lasting effects on the women that helped to create and nurture an organization and a visible community. Radio became an extension of these organizing effects.

Nicholas Cimorelli: GLIB grew from a grassroots effort and a call from WBAI specifically to a coalition of gay and lesbian organizations that was historically more diverse in terms of gender parity. There were many women involved in that and that actually remained the case throughout. Meetings were held to write the WBAI proposal in early 1988 and the first program was produced and aired by GLIB in May of '88. Back then, we were given time on alternate weeks with *The Gay Show,* which was still on the air. You see, GLIB was separate from *The Gay Show*—and both alternated every other week—the same time (6:30–7:30) on Sunday evenings for an hour. We got two hours a month. People in the community knew that if it was 6:30 Sunday on any given year it was gay time, whether or not it was *Outlooks* or *The Gay Show. The Gay Show* had more men so it was more male-oriented but that went through changes too over time.

Nancy Kirton: GLIB advocated "Your Voice Is Our Voice" and was distinctly a multiracial, multiethnic, cogender group. GLIB was conceived by about thirty people who met and hashed out, trashed out, who, what, and where to give it birth from paper to the microphone. There were anywhere at a minimum four to six members typically, and at one point I think we actually had more than thirteen members, which is a pretty huge collective—lots of fluctuating energy. But what is interesting is that GLIB also had a lot of problems when it came to doing work across racial lines. And the very common thing that seems to happen at times—as more people of color infused themselves into the group, the white men/women felt the need to leave. And this was a pretty difficult time. GLIB operated on what seemed to be a revolving-door membership.

Lisa Winters: The collective was brilliant and brought together a diverse and unique mix of talented volunteers. I mean, where else could we do this kind of innovative magazine format style, basically topic-oriented issue programming, except on public radio. It was a very diverse, energetic group of gays and lesbians, mostly young and interested in doing gay and lesbian programming. It was thrilling then because nothing like this had been done before on public radio. There were newspapers, women's news, and other print media, but we didn't have access to the airwaves like we did with WBAI. We began taking classes on how to actually work the sound board and how to produce canned pieces and live pieces. And this gave us access to all these terrific skills, technical skills, and access to the gay and lesbian community in an important way. I had no idea that I would ever have access to radio in the way that we did.

Nicholas Cimorelli: There was a real infrastructure that we developed within GLIB where members of the gay and lesbian community had access in approaching us. Training was offered through the station to develop media skills. We trained each other, and the people who had been with the station for a number of years became more seasoned, critiqued each other's programs, and we tried a number of different radio magazine and thematic formats, alternating in-depth programming and menu magazine formats.

Lidell Jackson: GLIB started very shortly after I left. I was in one of the first GLIB meetings. There were a number of reasons why GLIB started, but one of the reasons why it started, I was told, was because I left *The Gay Show*. Once I left the show, there actually seemed to be a vacuum of people of color and women coverage. Yet what had happened was people had just gotten used to *The Gay Show* just being this cool, savvy, multiracial, really with-it, on top of things, "got the buzz" type show and it went back to being, you know, the good old white boy network, and that annoyed some people. At least that's what I was told because I was invited to one of the first GLIB meetings and it came up in the meeting and everyone turned and looked my way. I was like, "Oh no, so now I'm being blamed for leaving the show. I go and this whole concept of multiracial, multiculturalism goes with me, and so it was all my fault. It's like wait a minute, wait, wait, wait." Particularly in the people of color community, you so seldom see anything that embraces your philosophies or your political and personal realities and identities that, when you do see something, you embrace it. You claim ownership of it. It was all my autonomous decision to join it and be there and then to leave once I wanted to stop. So it occurred to me as I sat in the GLIB meeting and everyone looked at me—they didn't look like they wanted to kill me, no, but they were looking at me like "It's all your fault that we have to resort to creating our own show," and I'm like, "Is that a bad thing? You know, you should be creating your own show. Why should there only be one show? There can be more than one show." So once we had got to the point of being able to pull together a show, then *The Gay Show* felt challenged, and once

The Gay Show found out that I was involved with GLIB, in whatever advisory capacity, then I get calls, "This is all your fault that they created this show." And I'm like, "Wait a minute, wait a minute, wait a minute, fellows, whatever people want to create, they should be allowed to create, and, if anything, this should challenge you guys to pump up the diversity on your show because it has been kind of sinking you."

Lisa Winters: Producing a weekly radio show was like community organizing in a sense that we were constantly doing education and outreach to people, not only to join our collective, but to keep tabs on how we were doing in our roles as broadcasters. We had lots of people who were doing extremely courageous and important work all over New York who would never have gotten a voice had they not been invited as guest on our radio show. We prepared a show on outer borough organizing, which had a fine response from queers in Queens, Staten Island, and the Bronx who had been unaware of how to successfully reach their communities. Media is an incredibly important venue for getting our issues out in a big way. Radio was really one of the only ways that I was able to see that happen in a very real way. I remember sometimes going to events and running into listeners who would say, "Gosh, I heard your radio show on WBAI the other day, and I took down that phone number and called that organization." Or others would say, "Thanks so much for that interesting piece on "Butch Femme dynamics." All that was very encouraging. Media as an organizing tool was one of the greatest things about the Gay and Lesbian Independent Broadcasting collective. The people who were involved in the collective had a social vision of change, and as social activists that vision came across the radio to help people get involved in changing their community and their world, but we also helped others and ourselves learn these really incredible communication skills—which were basically free. And I think we gave terrific information to lesbians with AIDS, what kind of resources were available, health resources in particular. I don't know if I can speak to any one show that I can remember, but I think almost everything that we did was terrific. Nick Cimorelli had a wonderful health and healing show—shows that really spoke to all kinds of issues that the community was dealing with. Everything from emotional to physical—not just on AIDS, but on health in general.

Nicholas Cimorelli: I got involved, as a result of being at WBAI, when all of the intensity of multiple loss surrounding AIDS was going on in the late '80s. In terms of concerns with alternative treatments, WBAI had put out a request for programming—AIDS specials. A coproducer of mine, Bob Lederer (senior editor at *POZ* magazine), did a four- to five-hour special on alternative treatment for AIDS and an update on the treatment protocols that received a lot of good press. As a result of that, the station thought it would be good to have programs devoted to AIDS and alternative voices around AIDS treatment. Bob spearheaded that and invited me to join him and Betsy Lenke in a program called *AIDS: Paths for Self-empowerment and Living*. There were some other people involved too. In the end, we were the only ones left by the time the program got on the air. We were producing it and it ran for about four years. Then as treatments changed and things shifted in the media away from AIDS as an exclusive focus, the station realized there was an interest in health and a deeper understanding of the immune system as well as the mind and body correlation that came from that research. The station invited Bob, Betsy, and myself to develop a more expanded format for a health show and Betsy invited another woman to join us, Kathy Davis. Now for the last seven years, I've been producing *Health Action,* which is a prime-time weekly program. So *Health Action* evolved from *AIDS: Paths for Self-empowerment and Living*. Bob and Kathy are my coproducers. It is an hour every Tuesday from 2 to 3 P.M. and it is really a holistic health program where we're looking at the connection between our physical health and our mental and emotional health, and we take a multidimensional and transpersonal approach to proactive health and well-being. We recently did a whole piece on the intersection of science and modern medicine.

WBAI-FM Is the *OutFM*

Over the years, *OutFM*[16] has evolved into a news magazine format devoted to entertainment, life, and theater, as well as political issues and coverage of grassroots involvement in the LGBT community. It is still carried by Pacifica station WBAI-FM in New York. Like its predecessors *Outlooks* and *The Gay Show, OutFM* has relied on volunteers and donations to survive as one of the oldest and longest-running queer programs in America.

Lidell Jackson: Nicholas [Cimorelli] was one of the more progressive white men, gay white men, who was involved with *The Gay Show,* and he carried that attitude over into GLIB.

Nicholas Cimorelli: There was a significant number of people who had passed away both in *The Gay Show* and *Outlooks* as well as at the station—hosts, producers, and others, so that the programs somehow ended becoming one show. (That's not the reason, and there were a series of other reasons that I'm not really clear on.) The transition took place over a long period of time with a number of things going on, some to which I'm not even privy. But the bottom line is *Outlooks* became *OutFM. The Gay Show* had ended.

Marle Becker: *OutFM* is a collective of about seven to eight people and obviously when you get that many different people with different agendas in a collective, there's always a problem. I would like to see the collective really put itself together. I have always believed from the time that I went on the radio, people don't tune in to hear Marle Becker, they tune in to hear who I have on the radio program as my guest. And I am only as good as the guests on the other side of the microphone.

Nancy Kirton: So the collective now, although I'm not involved with it at present, per se, has evolved into a very news magazine type of format. It is dwindling as far as membership and those left are trying to keep it together. I think that one of the problems has been outreach and that supportive grants have not been focused on. And you really have to be very much in the community and travel in certain circles, and not be terribly concerned with making a living per se. So when you have these many competing forces, the work, its development for the short and long term, varied personalities and interests levels always adjusting themselves to one another, it is difficult to do a volunteer show that's top-notch when you also need a focus on PR, and paying the bills through the equally arduous tasks of fund-raising, grant-writing, etc. . . . The focus of the creative energy and overall vision becomes quite jumbled. And as a new collective . . . well, you can only imagine how the struggle continues.

Wayman Widgins: *OutFM* has gone through several permutations. I came two years into the term of *OutFM*. Actually my partner joined first because I wasn't really interested in doing radio per se and I would help him out. That's how I got involved. I would help produce his segments because I have more of a technical background than he has. I would do the producing and help him do interviews and record them for him and things like that. And then I was asked by the current members of the collective to join as the *OutFM* coordinator because they saw that I had some administrative skills so they wanted me to actually keep the collective in order.

Nancy Kirton: I left the collective in 1998, but I continued to watch from the sidelines. A couple of the key figures of *The Gay Show* left, and in fact, to this day, only one of them remains on *OutFM,* and he's Marle Becker—an incredibly mature middle-basso voiced radio announcer. He's just phenomenal to watch and listen to. From all this, we now have a show called *OutFM.* It's changed a lot, and it shows the spirit of two collectives that have merged. But what has happened now, *OutFM* has converged with the defunct GLIB, and it is comprised primarily as a people of color collective, with more male involvement than female participation. Gender parity has always been a struggle. Although a departure from the old days, I think the figures that have come on to the shows are a little more mainstream, and that is probably because of the gay and lesbian community in and of itself. Queers have positioned themselves more mainstream. The show has in some ways detached itself from grassroots energy, which is reflected in the programming.

Marle Becker: We've had singers Joni James and Barbara Cook on the show and just about every out singer. Joni James, Barbara Cook, and Judith Light are straight but they have a large gay following. It's nice to know that they are willing to come on the program and say thanks for buying my record, thanks for buying tickets to come to see me. I'll support you and you'll support me. That's the way it will be.

Nancy Kirton: I have watched them excel in and really push showcasing people in entertainment. We did programming with people who were primarily making their living as artists. I did an interview with comedian Reno, who was just doing an HBO special at the time. It didn't particularly reflect her lesbianism, rather more of her need to find her biological mother. So, there's been a mirroring of how gay and lesbian people have become part of the general genre in life through entertainment. When we had Sapphire on *OutFM,* it was incredible because the phones lit up and money came in. We had her on for a fund-raiser marathon. She was at the height of her career in the mainstream. Her book *Push* went international into seven languages. Sapphire is reportedly an out lesbian, who's written a powerful narrative about an abused black teen who is struggling to find herself. These highly profiled people have given the show flavor and credibility. The radio shows I've worked on at WBAI included many straight listeners because they found it instructive, educational, and interesting. That's a real plus.

Wayman Widgins: There's been some really heartfelt interviews with people from PFLAG. That was one that was very important to me. We had a pretty good discussion on the difficulties of what some of the parents were going through. Quite a few of them had lost their children to AIDS. I thought those kind of interviews were the types of shows that I most liked. And we did another interview with a woman from the New York Gay and Lesbian Community Center. She talked about her program on alternative insemination. I think that interview was very informative to the audience at large, especially to people who were considering developing families in our community. And our marathons are always fun too—fund-raising drives. We had people like Robert Penn, author of *The Gay Men's Wellness Guide,* on the show, and it was a very successful fund-raiser for the station.

Marle Becker: I would like to see *OutFM* as a more cohesive collective. AIDS really brought us out of the closet and for once brought the community into a strong family unit. I think that allowed us to fight the disease of AIDS the way it should have been properly fought. And certainly, we've made mistakes. I think I'd like to see the *OutFM* collective as strong and as vibrant and powerful as the gay community can be. So when the chips are down, we can really stick together and pull together, and say "Yes, indeed, we can go forward with a program that will have an appeal to everyone." I think the collective is one of the benefits of being involved in *OutFM,* and as far as I am concerned, for *The Gay Show* too.

Wayman Widgins: One of the strengths of the collective is that we have a very broad way of approaching our community. Some of us are more interested in the arts and entertainment field, and some of us are more interested in political things. My interest personally was in bringing up the underdog to get some recognition. There have been lots of people. Earlier this year, we interviewed author Christian de la Huerta, who just released a book on spirituality. I have interviewed organizations and services like the Immigrant Program at St. Vincent's Hospital and it dealt with issues of how immigrants are handled in the gay and lesbian community, revolving around HIV and AIDS issues. I thought that was a problem that had been around for awhile, but that didn't really have much recognition or press so I decided to feature it on the program. Some of the other producers, like Nancy Kirton, the late Bob Storm, George Reilly, Mack, and Marle Becker, tend to focus on the heavier hitting people. Marle just interviewed Judith Light on the show last week. It was a really impressive interview. The phones lit up like you wouldn't believe. People were very interested in talking to her and finding out some personal things about her and her advocacy work.

Marle Becker: I think the biggest change that I have certainly seen is how easy it is now—now I have people calling me, wanting to be a guest on the program. The difference then and where we've come now is just incredible. It's extraordinary. I suppose the biggest change that I am aware of constantly is the present quality of our guests. We just recently had Judith Light of *Who's the Boss* on the program. The minute Judith Light sat down behind the microphone, the switchboard lit up like it was Christmas and everyone wanted to talk to her. A friend of mine left a message afterwards and he said, "It really shows that this program has improved so much; not only have you improved but the quality of your guests has improved. It is amazing how interesting it can be when you have someone who is so well-spoken, so articulate, so concerned about the movement that she believes so strongly in everything she said." Judith Light was one of the highlights of my tenure with *OutFM* and *The Gay Show.*

Nancy Kirton: Some people went on to make a name for themselves or did professional work way beyond what the collective could have given them. WBAI is a great training ground for such. So what is kind of neat about these venues is that they really are a great platform for going into more professional work. But in and of themselves, they only grow up to a certain point, it seems. That's the bridge that needs to be gapped. Lesbian and gay people have an opportunity to become part of the mainstream. We see people like Lily Tomlin and her lover of many years, but other people we know are to remain nameless, which is really sad. Even with performers like k.d. lang and Melissa Etheridge and such, we still cannot access these people, and that would make a difference. Rather than to just hear their CDs and such, it would really make a difference for them to come out for a fifteen-minute interview.

Marle Becker: We've had a lot of politicians. Bella Abzug—one of the greatest women who I think I've ever met in my life. Bella played a tremendous part in my becoming an activist. I met her long before I went on the radio. I worked on every single campaign that Bella ever ran. I learned a lot from Bella, and she was certainly one of the most articulate, exciting, and interesting people that we had on the program. Others have included Congressman Jerry Nadler, Congressman Barney Frank, and probably every AIDS organization that you could imagine.

The quality of the guests has really improved. Initially, the people who came on were people that maybe had their own agenda. And certainly it [has] improved to people whose agenda really includes everyone.

Nicholas Cimorelli: With *Outlooks,* we did so many magazine programs— we had an art section, political section: we did pieces on most outstanding works. There was also a program that focused on the weekly magazine called *Out Week* here in New York. In fact, Michael Signorelli, who has published a number of books since then, was one of the cofounders of that magazine. We did a number of programs on sexuality and quite a bit of programming on AIDS. As for myself, I had attended the International AIDS conference in Florence, Italy ('91) and Amsterdam ('92)—and I did coverage for the program and for the station during both conferences along with my coproducer, Bob Lederer. Through the series we had done on AIDS and the international conferences, as well as the series on sexual identity, there was this whole issue, which I guess is still going on in the gay community, that centers around what would be considered a positive gay identification or a sex positive "identity or lifestyle."

We had some people come on and have some debates at the time when the community was transitioning from a gay and lesbian community to the lesbian, gay, bisexual, transgender, and two-spirited communities. So there was a lot of expansion around those transitions that were developing. For me, a lot of highlights were around the AIDS programming that we had done and around issues that were coming off in the community with respect to our evolving identities and lifestyles.

Nancy Kirton: In politics, *OutFM* continues to report what is happening in grass-root efforts, but does little follow-up on political issues. Our strongest political and grassroots producer is Jesse Heiwa. But really innovative programming, like coverage of the Pride parade here in New York every June, the last Sunday of June, is quite stellar. In fact, in 2000, I returned to *OutFM* as an associate producer doing mostly fifteen-minute segments and covered the Dyke March of 2000 and some borough pride events. I have also gone on to help the collective with outreach by killing two birds with one stone through my work with Identity House, a counseling and psychotherapy referral organization of thirty years. This is part of the grassroots community effort that was very much part of GLIB. The collective currently has little revolving door membership, and this kind of commitment has helped the program's presentation become more polished. Marle Becker, Jesse Heiwa, and I, from the older shows, remain involved with *OutFM,* but not at the level at which we served ten years ago.

Wayman Widgins: I think the biggest shows that I was personally part of and have been the most successful and have had the most impact are actually the Gay Pride Day shows. And I have done two so far and they tend to be very successful, mostly because they are very long shows, at least the last two years. This year's show was nine hours long. And the year before, it was a twelve-hour program. We basically covered just about everyone in the community. We got interviews from major people involved in the community and had a lot of music programs. Basically we kept our listeners in touch with what was going on that day at the actual march.

Marle Becker: I think our listenership has changed. Also, perhaps I am more aware of who listens to our program. I wanted to tell you one of the great things about WBAI is what happens during Gay Pride Week. They usually give us the Sunday before Gay Pride Day, which is when we have our rally here in New York. On Gay Pride Day, we have coverage from 9 A.M. to 6 P.M. and it is really solid gay and lesbian programming for the entire day. On those days I have been in the studio, we have had people in the field, we do phone-ins and air guests that we prerecord, and we play a lot of music. And it's really a celebration in the gay and lesbian community. When I've been in the studio and we've opened up the phone lines to the callers, it has always been amazing to me as to who would call into the station. From the very beginning, we'd get a lot of crank calls, and then three to four years down the line, the crank calls started to be fewer, really less and less. And then we'd have people like a seventy-eight-year-old woman—who called in to say, "I'm a straight grandmother. I just wanted you to know I support you guys and I think what you're doing is terrific. I hope that all the politicians come out for the gay and lesbian community." We would also get people calling in from prison, saying, "I listen to you" or they would write to us: "I listened to the Gay Pride program. I'm in jail, and it is my only connection to the world and the gay and lesbian community." Then there were calls from people who were just mind-blowing. I had a phone call from a sixty-eight-year-old man one year during Gay Pride Day, and he said he listens to us in his bedroom with the pillows over his head because he lives in a Bronx housing project and he didn't want anyone to know he was gay. He puts the covers over his head and listens to us that way. And I thought, imagine being that frightened that you were afraid of even having your neighbors hear you listen to a gay program. It is just a continuing process of extraordinary people that you become involved with by doing this. And that's really the blessing from being involved in all this. The listeners are really wonderful. God bless them. They're the best.

"Other" Collectives

In January 1989, *The Tenth Voice*, Kansas City's first queer radio program, made its debut on KKFI 90.1 FM. The community station also aired *This Way Out*, *Aware: Positive Health Talk Radio*, and *WomanSong* (music by, for, and about women).[17] For the next decade, more than 500 individuals would be heard over KKFI as its hosts discussed a myriad of gay, lesbian, and transgender issues. Over the years, a number of other radio collectives have formed (and some have disbanded) in cities across the United States. Winter Park's WPRK-FM started a lesbigay program appropriately named *Family Values* to counterattack right-wing gay bashing in Florida. In Dallas-Forth Worth, KNON-FM's *Sin Fronteras* is a Spanish and English bilingual radio program that has served the diverse Latino community, particularly lesbian and gay listeners, since July 4, 1993[18]; also on KNON, *The Lambda Weekly* is a news and entertainment show for the larger gay and lesbian community in Dallas-Fort Worth.[19] Another program, that made an impact in St. Louis was *Coming Out of Hiding*. Its final show aired on December 29, 1999. *The Lambda Weekly* and *Coming Out of Hiding* are merely two of the many radio collective efforts of the LGBT community in recent years.

Lambda: Voice of the People

> *Radio is such a wonderful and powerful medium. And I find it incredibly exciting to know that at any given moment, ANYONE could tune in and hear us talking about gay issues. Now THAT's power! We really ARE everywhere!*

—Steve Walters-Dearmond, coordinating producer for *Lambda Weekly*

Lambda launched after a small group of people met in a New York City apartment and decided that they needed to create a legal defense organization for the lesbian and gay community. In 1972, a New York court denied Lambda's application to become a nonprofit legal organization, but this decision was overturned by the New York Supreme Court in 1973. Lambda was the first organization in the United States, and perhaps the world, to establish itself principally to fight for lesbians and gay men in the courts.[20] Twenty-eight years later, the Lambda Legal Defense and Education Fund is a "queer" institution because of its willingness to fight for civil rights on behalf of lesbian and gay youth, parents, workers, military members, those with HIV/AIDs, and many others.[21] LambdaCom Corporation produces *Lambda Report,* the communication arm of *Lambda Report Connection* and *Voices of the Rainbow,* and has been creating gay and lesbian radio and TV programming for more than a decade. A number of radio stations have since created their own local spin-offs of these shows.

In 1983, *Lambda Weekly* debuted on Dallas community radio station KNON 89.3 FM—"The Voice of the People." Bill Nelson was the first host of the program, but he left in 1985 to run for Dallas City Council. The Nelson-Tebedo Clinic in Oak Lawn, which is a predominantly gay neighborhood in Dallas, was named after Nelson and his life partner, Terry Tebedo, after their deaths in the early days of the AIDS epidemic. Alonso Duralde, one of the hosts from 1985 to 1991, is presently the artistic director of the USA Film Festival. In 1991, Steve Walters-Dearmond became the host of *Lambda Weekly.* His coproducer is David Taffet, who is a business owner and the former vice president of the Dallas Gay and Lesbian Alliance. Walters-Dearmond is the coordinating producer of *Lambda Weekly,* and has a long history in radio. In the 1970s, his first radio job was as a religion news reporter in Evansville, Indiana, during his studies at a Catholic seminary. In 1991, Walters-Dearmond became the third person to host the show since its inception. After college, he moved back to his hometown and became an all-night on-air personality on Country KC95 in Kansas City, Missouri. He moved to Dallas, after KC95 was sold, to work for a major telecommunications company.

Walters-Dearmond became involved in community radio in the early 1990s when the previous hosts of *Lambda Weekly* left Texas and asked him to take over the show.

Steve Walters-Dearmond: The Dallas/Fort Worth media market is the sixth largest in the U.S. We have about sixty radio stations; most of them broadcast on FM frequencies. Collectively, those sixty radio stations broadcast over 9,600 hours of programming in any given week. Of those sixty stations, only one broadcasts GLBT-targeted programming. Of those 9,600 hours of programming, only two are targeted for the queer listening audience. They are heard on Sunday evenings on a 50,000–watt community radio station. That pretty much tells you where the gay/lesbian community stands in "the Buckle of the Bible Belt." There are, however, four hearty gay souls who keep coming back to the ramshackle KNON-FM studios each and every Sunday evening. We MUST! *Lambda Weekly* has been on the air for nearly sixteen years. We must be there on the air for the gay man who mistakenly married a woman to save his family name as he takes a drive for the purpose of pushing that special button on his car radio to hear his only safe contact with his community. We must be there on the air for the lesbian who needs to find safe places to socialize with other women like her. We must be there for the really young gay people who need to hear that it IS OK to be gay. We must be there on the air for our community members who are now too old or too sick to join us in person. We MUST be there to rebuke anyone who attempts to say that gay people are any less important in the grand scheme of humanity than anyone else. For Mike Hathaway, David Taffet, Kathy Tipps, and Steve Walters-Dearmond, *Lambda Weekly* is not a job. Apparently it is a purposeful mission. Some of us have been doing this for nearly eight years.

Lambda Weekly's mission is to educate the general radio-listening public and to empower the gay and lesbian community. The show is also dedicated to reporting news and information about HIV/AIDS as it affects every person—gay, straight, female, male, adult, or child. It was one of the first continuous radio programs in the United States providing news, information, and interviews targeted toward the gay and lesbian community. Some of the events have included broadcasting live from the top of a roller coaster at Gay Day at Six Flags Over Texas. Other events covered include:

> the only live local coverage of the 1993 March on Washington, DC; the only live local coverage of the 1994 March on Austin, Texas; annual live coverage of Oak Lawn Community Services' AIDS LifeWalk by reporters walking the route; the only live coverage of From All Walks of Life in Ft. Worth, Texas; annual live coverage of the Alan Ross Texas Freedom Parade; Chastity Bono's first live radio interview—as a gay rights advocate; the only local live coverage of Candace Gingrich's appearance at National Coming Out Day at the Great State Fair of Texas; the first interview with Craig McDaniel, Dallas' first openly-gay City Council member; the only live coverage of "The Bus Ride Through East Texas"; and the anti-gay melee in Gilmer, Texas which was later reported by national news outlets.[22]

Weekly programming consists of local news, women's issues, the weekly calendar, music by gay and gay-friendly artists, and humorous segments like "Those

Darn Heterosexuals," originally inspired by the Lorena Bobbitt episode.[23] KNON also airs *This Way Out*, the international LGBT news magazine show.

Meet Me in St. Louis

KDHX reaches an eighty-mile radius. We were voted St. Louis's number one radio station for 1998, beating out every other commercial radio station in St. Louis. KDHX is a noncommercial, membership- and volunteer-supported radio station. KDHX has over 150 volunteers and only six paid staff. It is one of only eight stations of its kind left in the United States. What a wonderful station.

—Michelle King, KDHX producer

On June 15, 1989, *Coming Out of Hiding* aired on KDHX 88.1 FM in St. Louis. *Out and Open*, a locally produced LGBT talk program, was added into the KDHX programming mix a few years later. *Coming Out of Hiding*, which challenged the mainstream's disregard for lesbian, gay, and transgender audiences, was the collaboration of Michael Ford, Karl Hawkins, and Chris Beutler. When Michael Ford moved from Houston to St. Louis in the late 1980s, he became involved with KDHX's *Morning Show*. He had been an engineer for *After Hours*, a gay variety program on KPFT in Houston, and wanted to hear a similar program on the air in St. Louis.

Denise Hill: After putting in a proposal to the station, the program committee suggested that Michael team up with Karl Hawkins and Chris Beutler, two people from the community who had proposed a lesbian and gay talk radio program after visiting the station on a house tour. Michael's intention was to create a radio program similar to the one he'd worked on in Houston, but he worked with Chris and Karl to create something that would include elements of both proposals. As Michael, Chris, and Karl were preparing for their first program (which aired June 15, 1989), Michael Ford and I met at a Pride committee meeting. He was very excited about the project and when he learned that I had a background in radio, he asked me to come and work on the show with them. I agreed to help however I could be of use but was unable to make the first program. Initially I produced and read a weekly calendar but, after hearing me on-air, the station manager requested that I take a more active role in announcing and hosting. Karl left the show a few weeks later because he wasn't interested in the format and Chris left in February 1990, but there were many others who contributed to the program over the years.

Denise Hill began working in radio at an on-campus radio station at St. Louis University in the late 1970s and was the only LGBT person to run for a political office in St. Louis. She was the executive producer and host of *Coming Out of Hiding* on KDHX from 1989 to 1998 and the executive producer of *The Other Voice* from 1991 to 1992.

Denise Hill: Michael and I shared the belief that the program could only give voice to our community if our programming reflected the diverse voices of our community. To that end, as executive producers of the program, we believed that anyone in the community was welcome to participate, and we worked to ensure that the program featured a wide variety of music, news, commentary, shorts, and interviews. Our primary concern was producing quality radio; we didn't edit for content (within the guidelines of the FCC!) and were known to air opinions that we didn't necessarily agree with. Our rule of participation was that you couldn't appear on-air in a show called *Coming Out of Hiding* and be in the closet yourself. When we lost Michael to AIDS in 1992, I continued producing and hosting the program until the end. Over the years there were many people involved both on-air and off and I am proud that our program gave a voice to the LGBT community for as long as it did.

Michelle King met Hill near the end of the program's run on KDHX. King had worked in the music industry for several years, and with the help of Hill and the station's support, she would eventually add radio producer, programmer, and host to her list of credits.

Michelle King: I have been in the music industry for around eleven years, starting out when I met Melissa Etheridge when I was in high school. I worked at various music stores throughout the beginning. Then went into deejaying. I deejayed for a little over two years at a lesbian club in St. Louis. Then switched gears completely and became a stripper. Yes, a stripper. For three and a half years. The thing is I still stayed in the industry of sorts. Instead of the dance scene, I got involved in the alternative rock, heavy metal scene while dancing. The funny thing is that when I started I hated that style of music. I learned to totally enjoy and appreciate it. I found that good music comes in many forms. I married a woman I was in love with, quit dancing, and became a nine to fiver. I hated it. The marriage lasted two years. But I learned a lot from it. While I was married I was introduced to a lady who did the *Coming Out of Hiding* show on KDHX 88.1 FM in St. Louis. She heard I used to deejay and asked if I would engineer. So that was the beginning of where I am at today. I started as the engineer, moved to music programmer to programmer to producer! In about a span of two years. The show was a music show geared toward the gay, lesbian, bisexual, transgendered, and straight allied community. Music from "our" community. We also had news, updates, etc. It was just once a week for one and a half hours. Such artists as Melissa Etheridge, Indigo Girls, Michelle Malone, Wendy Bucklew, to name a few.

Denise Hill: KDHX was very supportive of LGBT programming and is a radio station with a commitment to being inclusive of the community it serves. We were often told by people (including one who became an announcer on the program) that *Coming Out of Hiding* was their first contact with the LGBT community; they could listen to us weekly and feel a safe connection with a community they hadn't even known existed. Our last program aired December 29, 1998.

Michelle King: KDHX made many changes within the programming of the whole station. *Coming Out of Hiding* was canceled, mostly [because] the rainbow community is out of hiding these days, but the biggest—there was not enough information being put out there for the community. With all this in mind, we came up with the *Rainbow Calendar,* a one and a half- to two-minute production of international, national, regional, and local news. Events such as benefits, pageants, shows, theater, film festivals, and anything that deals with the rainbow community. We also mention meetings going on in the St. Louis area. Of course, not all at once: There are anywhere from four to seven calendars at one time that get rotated throughout the daily logs that air during morning and evening drive times as well as other prime listening hours of the day.

Coming Out of Hiding ended six years after the death of its founder, Michael Ford.

Chapter Three

A Different Drum

The Queer Message in the Music

Within the last few years, there has been an explosion of artists and their music that no longer fit the stereotypical "gay" music. It blossomed into metal, folk, dance, punk and everything in between! Music is an entity of everyday life. Musicians that take that to heart are true musicians as well as artists.

—Michelle King, KDHX producer

Club Verboten[1] is a four-CD compilation of gay and lesbian musical influences, with ninety-six songs by and for the gay and lesbian community. The set is accompanied by a nearly 100-page booklet that claims to be the untold history of the lesbian and gay music community—from queer blues singers Bessie Smith, Ma Rainey, and Gladys Bentley to the pop artists of the 1970s like Lou Reed. The CD was produced by Marshall Blonstein and Richard Oliver. Blonstein is president of DCC Compact Classics and a former president of Island Records and Ode Records in the 1970s and 1980s. He founded DCC Compact in 1986. Blonstein hired Oliver to conduct the research for the project.

Songs not included in the compilation include "Lola" by the Kinks, Rod Stewart's "Killing of Georgie," and even the classic "YMCA." These songs—and those included in *Club Verboten*—are symbols of the American dichotomy over sexual identity and expression. Indeed, some of the most memorable trends or events in American history have been underscored, as well as defined, by the music of the moment. In 1979, America was captivated by the Village People and their songs "YMCA" and "In the Navy." At first, even some Navy recruiters liked the songs, until they listened a little more closely to the lyrics. Still, everyone seemed to know the words, and the Village People became part of popular culture and, indeed, American history.

The 1980s came in like a lion with artists like Prince, Madonna, Boy George, and others whose lyrics and MTV images reinvented American pop culture. "Like a Virgin" by Madonna woke up the nation to sexual expression, but her Erotica tour years later questioned traditional gender boundaries. Prince captivated the nation with the raw lyrics and sexual intensity of his music and videos. It was a sexual revolution on radio and television—one which prompted public calls for censorship, music labeling, and stronger Federal Communications Commission (FCC) policies and penalties as well as boycotts on stores and stations promoting such music. The conservative outcry against naughty lyrics seemed far worse than the reaction to Howard Stern's hate-filled racial and ethnic epithets and verbal gay bashing. Stern was becoming a national icon. But then so were Prince and Madonna. It was as if *Howl* had been set to music—and everybody was playing it on their radio station.

By the end of the decade, Melissa Etheridge, REM, and k.d. lang had broken through college radio and were becoming household words on mainstream radio. Etheridge had already become successful as a musician and songwriter when she publicly came out to the world. Since she is one of the top female musicians over the past two decades and host of Lifetime's *Beyond Chance*, most listeners see beyond her sexual identity and identify with her as a person. The Rock and Roll Hall of Fame in Cleveland, Ohio, acknowledged the gay and lesbian influence on American culture with its 1996 exhibit of some notable moments in queer music history, such as B-52's impact on the gay club scene, the dedication of Elton John's AIDS Foundation, David Bowie's cross-dressing, and the Etheridge and lang kiss.[2]

By the 1990s, the nation seemed ready for something different—and with the rise of alternative radio, a new breed of musician was arriving on the scene and its new young audience embraced the often mystic and mesmerizing video clips of life and love projected across the electronic screen. It didn't happen in one night, but the nation's religious right and conservative groups felt overwhelmed by what seemed the sudden loss of boundaries in sexual expression and definition, especially in the midst of AIDS, a rise in teen pregnancy and suicide, and gang violence in urban and rural communities. And music was to blame, at least according to some people, for the loss in America's morality. For some musicians, it was time for the next step—to out queer music. It was to this beat of a different drum that gays and lesbians would affirm their love for partners and passion for lovers, and these experiences would be validated by some passing refrain from a queer song that sank into their hearts.

Mark Weigle: We fall all over ourselves putting Cher on the covers of our gay mainstream magazines because she is famous, and the same thing for Melissa Etheridge or k.d. lang. I think a lot of it comes from our self-repression. I love that they came out obviously, but the fact is that they became successful by being in the closet. To me, that's insulting—it was then and it still is now. I compare it to congresspeople, like Barney Frank and others, who have come out since they have been elected. I love it that Tammy Baldwin, a congresswoman from Wisconsin, was just elected as an open lesbian from day one. That to me is the next step. Gay characters seem to be all over television and the movies. It seems this really hip thing that people are interested in and curious about, but even Melissa Etheridge and others are not singing about being gay—and if they are—it's encoded.

Michelle King: I have had the opportunity to interview or meet many musicians. I interviewed Rob Halford (ex-lead singer of Judas Priest) just after he came out in *The Advocate:* the first live interview about his coming out, his music with Priest, and being gay in the metal industry. From what many may perceive, he is a very gentle, soft-spoken individual, with great integrity and beliefs, considerate and intelligent with a heart for many issues that don't usually get much attention, like the suicide rate of gay teens. Wendy Bucklew is a singer-songwriter from California who lived in Atlanta for awhile, an amazing individual whose clarity comes from the center of her being, whose choice of poetry matches the greatness of her skills as a guitarist and vocalist. Transcend one's being with oneself. Loving with humor and criticism. Learning through one's emotions. Enjoying what life has taught. Wendy is also a great spiritual artist through drawings and paintings. Michelle Malone, also from Atlanta, is an artist that captivates through soulful passionate desires of loss, lust, strength, love, confusion, with deep southern gospel but bluesy influences. She is a very professional artist that has dealt with a lot in her life, challenging herself to become better with so many different issues at hand. She is serious but also a goof. Erin Hamilton is a dance diva who recovered Gary Wright's "Dreamweaver" and Cheap Trick's "The Flame" into dance tunes. Erin also just happens to be one of Carol Burnett's daughters. A beautiful energetic artist that is proud to be herself and work for what she has in her life. Strong and very independent. With artwork she designed herself, painting her skin with ink of her inner self. If that makes any sense? And finally Melissa Etheridge. What can be said about her? She is brilliant. And she is also an outstanding individual. She is full of emotion and passion that is 100 percent true. She believes in everything she sets forth to do. I have met Melissa on many occasions. She realizes that her fans are just as important as her music. Without her fans, she would not be where she is today. I have the ultimate respect for her because she keeps her life as private as possible but when something big does come along she does not hide it. She is as spiritual as anyone I have ever met, whether professionally or privately, in my own life. There are not enough words or expressions that could identify her as a whole.

Robert Drake: I have dedicated my own professional life to celebrating out musicians from around the globe. I think that barriers can be broken and those a little too narrow can broaden their horizons, just a little, hearing the passionate and powerful words and music that are performed by today's out musician . . . regardless of the genre of music.

Mark Weigle: The idea that all gay music can be reduced to a particular genre is absurd. There's this whole thing about what gay music is. . . . So yeah, I'm incredibly unhip. I'm not dance music. To me, most of that music is so completely soulless. It is supposed to be gay music, but it has nothing to do with our lives, if anything. Being a gay person in the world is not always an easy thing. And a lot of people just want to check out from that—and dance and party. There's a time and place for that. But I think it's also healthy and okay to look at some of the harder issues sometimes. I have had a real problem with not getting support from the gay media very much because I'm "not hip." I had submitted material to perform at Stonewall 30. That's a Labor Day weekend that I could be getting other gigs, but I'm waiting around to hear from them. That's my career. And finally a straight mainstream promoter in the Bay Area who knows my stuff (they brought him aboard at the last moment to kind of pull together the stages and performances) called me just appalled that they had four stages—and they were completely committed to house music, to deejays, and stuff. He kept on apologizing, saying "I can't believe with what you sing about and how good you are, that there's no room for you among your own community." It was a familiar story for me. On the other hand, some straight people in positions of power, like Lou Simon, head of Music Choice—the Primestar Direct TV, have been big supporters of my work and gay music in general, including the presentation of the GLAMAs [Gay and Lesbian American Music Awards].[3] It sounds contradictory. I definitely want to support gay people and validate our experiences and have them hear what I'm doing. Yet I don't accept being ghettoized and limited to just that. Larry Flick—an out gay man—is incredibly supportive of queer artists in his position as talent editor for *Billboard*, a mainstream magazine. Part of who I am is being from Minnesota, part of who I am is being a gay man, part of who I am is having a sense of humor, part of who I am is being my parents' son. I am an observer of the world so I can sing from other people's perspectives. So I don't sit down and say I'm a gay artist and that's the only thing that I'm interested in writing about. It's just whatever is up for me—emotionally or whatever my mind is chewing on—that's what comes out in my songs and that's going to be a really diverse bunch of songs.

John Frame: Music that speaks directly and positively to gay men will always receive preferential treatment with our show. A memorable personal milestone for me was in getting up the courage to proudly buy my first Pansy Division CD, *Undressed*. I felt like I was coming out to everyone in the store. They played live on-air at Triple Zed Radio when they toured in '95 and have given regular telephone interviews since. Pansy Division won one of our Kylie awards last year, for the band with the most songs played on our show. Conversely, an Australian band, The Mavis, whose album *Venus Returning* was written almost entirely from a gay male perspective, refused to be interviewed for *Queer Radio*—saying that they didn't want to be "labeled." They did not win a Kylie.

As host and producer of *Queer Radio,* his weekly program broadcast on Four Triple Zed Radio (4ZZZ 102.1 FM) in Brisbane, Australia, John Frame tries to play songs with a message, those particular lyrics that address the heart and soul of gay men. In the past two years, independent gay artists have contacted the station via the Internet and sent copies of their work to play over the airwaves, and it is this type of activity that has encouraged the station to work toward CD sales on the Web. Similarly, Robert Drake is working with Music Choice—Primester Direct to develop other gay music programs, which he intends to offer to the world marketplace in the near future. In the late 1990s, Drake launched *OUTsounds,* a daily national program created to celebrate the unity of the global gay and lesbian community by "exploring the diversity of the music that it produces."

Gay Cowboys on the Radio, on the Road

> *It's really offensive to me that some people in radio would equate singing about loving another man with dirty words. I don't accept that. I don't sing swear words. Hollywood still can't show two men kissing, but they can show two men blowing their heads off or beating the crap out of each other every five minutes . . . it's obviously insane.*

> —Mark Weigle, singer and songwriter

The formation of the Lesbian and Gay Country Music Association, founded in 1998, is just one example of the trend toward acceptance of queer country music in the United States.[4] Other signs pointing toward changing times include the acceptance of American queer country musicians across Europe. Mark Weigle and Doug Stevens are two independent singer-songwriters who have received regular airplay on Americana shows in Europe and Australia. Both men were featured in the *Journal of Country Music* in September 1999 in a feature article on gays in country music.

Mark Weigle: It took me ten years of adulthood to get the courage up to really put it out there for people. It's a vulnerable thing to put yourself out there. Getting my act together and believing I was worth being happy and worth being satisfied was part of it. Through working at the crisis center and a lot of my own stuff growing up, I learned a lot about myself through counseling youth. It was a twenty-four-hour crisis hotline where kids were going through a lot of abuse and really powerful issues. Kids would come in and live there so it kind of cut to the chase of what was real emotionally, which was what I hoped to do with my music, to not shy away from what is real even if it's difficult or uncomfortable or people may not want to deal with it. It's not all just dancing and being happy all the time, although certainly there is a place for that too.[5]

Weigle, thirty-one, grew up in Minnesota and moved to California as an adult. He spent seven years as a counselor at a crisis center for teenagers, a day job that would impact his music and willingness to reveal his most intimate thoughts. Weigle gave up the day job in 1998 and invested his money in the production of a professional-looking-and-sounding compact disc of his work.

Mark Weigle: I figured there was already going to be a tendency for people to dismiss me because they were uncomfortable with some lyrics . . . .or just ghettoize me. So I wanted to give as little cause for them to be able to do that as possible. I have had gay reviewers count how many out songs there were on my CD . . . and that's fascinating to me, that's ghettoizing ourselves, too. They're dividing it up—like there's nine out songs and there's four not out songs. How about there's one song about a woman finding out that her husband's gay and there's one song about being a kid growing up with your parents.

The CD *The Truth Is*[6] topped the *Outvoice* music chart for a record eighteen weeks, and one of its songs—"Oz"—was among the Top 10 songs of 1999 on GAYBC, an Internet Web station. Weigle was nominated (along with Ani Difranco, Rufus Wainwright, and the B-52's) for two 1999 Gay and Lesbian American Music Awards in the categories of Debut Artist and Out Song ("If It Wasn't Love") and has been praised by music critics in gay and mainstream music publications such as *Genre, Billboard,* and *Performing Songwriter* magazines. His ballads can be described as James Taylorish, and his Minnesota roots are evident in "If You Grew Up There"—the first song on the CD:

> And folks here just ain't that way
> It's blue and white and green
> But you know that
> If you grew up there like me.

Mark Weigle: My goal is for my CD to be able to stack against Dar Williams or John Gorka or David Wilcox or any singer-songwriter that is out there doing it on a national level. And absolutely it is a satisfactory thing to get feedback particularly from gay men. We never hear our stories really validated very often in music. And I know music is a huge part of so many

people's lives—mine included. Think back to a certain song that just defines
that one relationship which you were in when it was on the radio, or that one
summer you got in your car and drove across country. It's really great for me
now to have people tell me, "You know, 'I Confess' is my song—our song—
me and my lover. It was playing when we first dated, in my CD in the car"—
and that kind of stuff is great. I guess if I had a mission statement it would be
to educate straight folks and support and validate gay people's experiences.

> I been hearin' them tell me
> Right from the start
> All about what turns out to be
> My very own heart
>
> Sick by nature
> Against God's Law
> Perverted, sinful
> And just plain wrong
>
> And I'm takin' the hatred
> To my very core
> But I just don't believe it
> Anymore
>
> 'Cause it was my love
> That very kind
> That kept me right there
> By your side
> And I dare them to tell me
> What else it was
> If it wasn't love.

—an excerpt from "If It Wasn't Love"

Mark Weigle: To me, what else could be said about basic love songs; everything has been said a billion times before. I feel like the gay experience is
really fresh songwriting turf. "If It Wasn't Love" is about losing a partner in
the context of a world that fails to validate your feeling for someone's pain
because you love this person so much—but when you open up the newspaper, you read that your elected leadership says that your love isn't real. Or
what about a woman who realizes that her husband is gay, and all the stuff
like that we go through in our community—it's all really fresh stories and
fresh perspectives as far as songwriting material.

Four cowboy boots
Gliding on air
Turning and turning
While I stand and stare
At the two cowboy waltz

Grace, and dignity
So hard to come by
That I stand in rapture
As I watch them dance by
In the two cowboy waltz

With shiny pearl buttons
In faded blue jeans
He'll take my hand
Tonight in my dreams
We'll dance the two cowboy waltz

He'll take my hand
Look into my eyes
Then Stetson to Stetson
Together we'll fly
The two cowboy waltz.

—"Two Cowboy Waltz"

Mark Weigle: I go to the gay rodeos and sing and sell CDs and hang out and play for people who grew up in farms and small towns, and some of them still have ranches. They're not into house music. The perception that some straight mainstream promoters or managers have of the gay community is from seeing *Genre* or *The Advocate*. They see the stereotypes that we put on ourselves in movies and magazines. It's like none of those people ever look like me or any of my friends. They are always twenty-two years old, pretty, stylish, and I think that's a self-imposed stereotype.

In Europe, Weigle's music is considered Americana, and in the United States, he is a country musician. Weigle's songs are included on Americana playlists in Europe and Australia. He's mixed in with some established singer-songwriters like John Gorca, Steve Earle, John Pryne, Jonathan Brook, as well as a number of other independent artists. Several tracks from the CD have been aired on commercial, public, and college radio stations throughout North America, Europe, and Australia, and on Primestar DirectTV's Music Choice, as well as Web stations like PlanetOut and GAYBC.

Mark Weigle: In Europe, they don't make as much of a distinction as we do, like "Oh, that's our gay show and that's our gay artist." It's all just sort of integrated, and they really think of it as a style of music that fits their format. They don't get so quite wrapped up in labeling it gay music, as the gay community and mainstream media do in the United States. Gay artists need to be good artists. This has been a tentative topical discussion on *Outvoice*, an Internet music listserver. I think we undermine ourselves if we cry homophobia immediately. I think we all need to work really to be as good artists as we can and not just rely on the angle of being gay. Who knows what kind of stuff people go through in their own conscience about how they deal with me, that I'll never know. One of the good things that ripples out from what I'm doing, and I never really see it—is making people think about stuff, like if they go home and think, "I completely blew that guy off because it was gay stuff, and I'm afraid to put it on my radio station. I wouldn't think that's what I would do, but when it came down to it, that's what I did."

> I confess
> That I told a friend or two
> About this man I'd met
> The day that I met you
>
> I confess
> I remember what you wore
> That Tweety Bird T-shirt
> That you don't wear no more
>
> I confess I confess
> That when I'm next to you
> I never have my breath
> I confess I confess
> That bein' friends with you
> It's the worst 'cause it's the best
>
> I confess
> Every time you say my name
> It's not coincidence
> A smile comes to my face
>
> I confess
> When you hug me your goodbyes
> I listen to my heart beat
> and I close my eyes

I confess
That one time your sister watched me
When I was watchin' you
She caught my eye and smiled
She said, "I know 'cause I love him too"

—"I Confess"

Mark Weigle: I don't address straight people in my music. I just tell the story. If people make my stuff political, that's not my doing. "I Confess" is a good example. I use a male pronoun in there a couple of times and specifically it is about being in love with somebody that you can't have for whatever reason. And I specifically didn't get into "oh, he's straight, and I'm gay." People might immediately go there but if you notice that's your stuff— I didn't put it there. They may be both gay—the one guy's got a lover or he's just not interested, or they were boyfriends once and they just became friends, or the one guy is straight, who knows! But that's one that tells the story that a lot of people seem to be able to relate to. I recorded this song with a woman singing with me to pitch to other artists, and the consensus seems to be the most powerful rendition is from a man to another man. "Take Your Shoulder From The Wheel" doesn't have a pronoun in it, but it's to a gay man.

You work so hard for our good life
Thinking that's my dream come true
You ask me what more I need
Well there's one thing you can do

Please, for me, take your shoulder from
        the wheel
Long enough that I might have a place to
        lean
I know how strong your shoulder can be
If you'll take it from the wheel
And offer it to me

—an except from "Take Your Shoulder From The Wheel"

Mark Weigle: It is a song about how being gay and growing up in the society that we grow up in does a number on you. It's difficult especially as a kid to know that you are different and try to understand why people seem to feel the way they do about how you feel—gay people tend to be more inclined toward alcoholism, depression and suicide and gay youth suicide problems and all those issues—it is not about who you are as gay people; it's about what you have to go through in this survival context of knowing that people hate you for just who you are. And I think that causes us to have relationship issues with each other. Another song—a bit tongue-in-cheek—is "Oz," a popular tune among straight women because they can relate the song to their personal experiences with boyfriends.

> I think I've watched *The Wizard of Oz* too many times
> When I think about the lovers I've had along the way
>
> Steven was Scarecrow: I was grasping at straws
> By keepin' on hopin' he'd have a clever thought
>
> And Timothy Crim was my Man of Tin
> He had a great chest but nothin' beatin' within
>
> Then there was Larry-the-Lion come roarin' at my door
> Who when I told him I loved him wasn't roarin' anymore

—an excerpt from "Oz"

Mark Weigle: There's also a piece in that song about community—about what we go through as gay people—and there's a lot about wandering the Yellow Brick Road with fellow travelers who are also lost:

> Oh, how I can identify
> With Dorothy wanderin' through Oz
> Travelin' this Yellow Brick Road
>   with companions
> Who themselves are lost

Mark Weigle: I think really good-hearted people who don't have a problem with the gay stuff give way too much power to the bigot folks—and to even the potential. If a venue is going to book Tracy Chapman, they are not going to tell her, "Oh no, we're not going to book you in our club because there's a possibility that some racist, bigot redneck is going to be in the crowd and have a problem with it." That would be just ridiculous to imagine. But it's still okay to deny me a gig—as a gay artist—even though they're falling all over themselves, "No, we really like your stuff." I think that's a huge thing that comes up over and over again. And again, we don't give that kind of power to racist people. Some people have misinterpreted my powerful words and lyrics to be political statements. I am a storyteller who illustrates with words the experiences of the gay community. No matter however I do commercially, one really satisfying thing to me is that I'm out for the marginalized within the marginalized.

> We grew up learnin' to hate each other
> We grew up learnin' to hate ourselves
> We grew up knowin' that most of the world
> Would just as soon we were dead.

> —an excerpt from "Struggle of Love"

Mark Weigle: There's no reason why straight people can't get into my music. I can watch *The Color Purple* and get something out of it and understand it from some emotional level. I don't have to be black. And I don't feel there's any reason why straight people can't get something out of music and maybe even learn something along the way.

"Y'all Ready for Some Homosexual Country?"

> *It was a warm Dutch night. The dancers got sweaty fast! Rarely is a club air-conditioned in the Netherlands. Normally, it doesn't get very hot. More and more people arrived. I was surprised at how many different line dances they knew. In fact, every dance was a line dance, no two-stepping, no waltzing, all line dances. The members of the Eindhoven Stetsons were the best dancers. The men were something to see! All that masculine strength and energy! I had not seen American dancers this good or this sexy since I saw the D.C. Cowboys.*

> —Doug Stevens, singer-dancer

From Christopher to Castro, the 2000 CD project from Doug Stevens and the Outband, is an eclectic array of country music styles—ballads, waltzes, swing, and TexMex—that exemplifies the state of the queer country music scene. The album was the culmination of the life experiences of Stevens. He was raised in Mississippi and later studied and performed across Europe and eventually became part of its Americana movement in the 1990s. Stevens studied baroque singing at the Royal Conservatory at The Hague in the Netherlands in the late 1980s. In those early days, he toured Europe with The Ensemble for Early Music, not realizing that he would return one day to Amsterdam as a country music singer and dancer.

Doug Stevens: Each time I had stayed on to visit Amsterdam. I had made a couple of friends there and I loved just being in Amsterdam, feeling how different it was from Mississippi where I grew up. I guess I was trying to convince myself that I was not country. I did not want to be like the people I grew up with; those twangy southern accents, eating black-eyed peas and cornbread. I loved the canals, the seventeenth-century narrow houses and the museums. Even though I was trying to immerse myself in classical European culture, I remember being struck by all the American influences I saw. I heard American popular music in the restaurants and cafes and I saw advertisements for American movies on TV. Mostly, I found, the popular culture of Holland was the pop culture of the United States.

During the summer of 1999, Stevens found himself in Holland again for the first time in eleven years since he had studied there in 1988. He was hired to sing by the Eindhoven Stetsons, a gay country-western dance troupe that performed in the Royal Bar in Eindhoven in South Holland.

Doug Stevens: The first time I walked into the Royal Bar I felt that I had walked into an American gay, CW dance bar. The big exception to this was the two Confederate flags above the stage! There were American flags of different sizes hanging on the walls, some of American states and others of different European countries. Old cowboy boots and horseshoes hung from the ceiling. And there were some pictures of Elvis in different outfits and postures scattered around the room. Two mannequins dressed in country-western outfits were standing on the stage. When my hosts asked me what I thought about the decorations, I told them it looked very American.

Stevens was part of a European trend toward country music that has grown in popularity over the past few years, and especially in the Netherlands.

Doug Stevens: This time I was there to sing music that I had written. Country music! I spent most of my time in southern Holland in small towns like Eindhoven, Best, and Tilburg. Everywhere I went—in restaurants, on the radio, and in bars—American country-western music was playing. One night my hosts took me to a restaurant in a nearby town. I could tell from the hushed atmosphere, the linen tablecloth, and the silverware that this was a high-toned establishment. Imagine my surprise when I heard Conway Twitty's nasal serenade coming to us over the speakers! On Saturday night, the night of my performance, a tent was set up in the garden next to the bar. There were tables and chairs. Someone was selling hamburgers (they wanted it to feel authentically American) and, like many of the gay CW events I have played in the United States, there were people selling shirts, bolos, and country-western knickknacks. I saw a black shirt with a red yoke that had some really nice western swirling designs on it. I really wanted to buy it. In southern Holland, everywhere I went, I heard country music playing. There is a mainstream country music magazine and lots of Dutch country bands that play only American country music. Also, there are several openly gay Dutch recording artists who record gender-specific music (not country music yet, however). Their music has a lot of mainstream appeal and is distributed everywhere there. I am optimistic about getting some mainstream distribution for my recordings there. Well, I don't know what to say except, Whoo-doggie!! I felt like I was in Nashville. There are straight and gay country dance clubs popping up all over the place. On Friday I was interviewed by two radio stations. One of them was a local station in Eindhoven; the other was from Belgium. Yes, they drove up from a town near Brussels to interview me (a two-hour drive—and this was a mainstream radio program). And, boy, this interviewer had done his homework! I kept wondering, "How did he know that?"

And then there's the line dancing ...

Doug Stevens: The gay dancers in much of Europe pretty much line dance to everything. In the United States, if you don't tell them which line dance to do when you sing a song, nobody dances. But there, they are sooooooooo itching to dance that every song I sang packed the dance floor with line dancers! The Australian singer went onto the floor to sing, but, honey, you couldn't see her. My new friend who was housing me said he bumped into a woman, really hard, while he was dancing. He thought to himself, "Who is that person, just standing there?" Then he realized he had bumped into the singer! Oooops!! After I sang, she came on back to sing one more song, but she had learned, by then, to stand on the stage.

On this particular night, it was 11:30 P.M. when Stevens took to the stage dressed in a black cowboy hat and boots, black jeans with a big Mexican cowboy belt buckle (with the Aztec calendar on it), and a black shirt with a red satin yoke. It had a big D on one side and a big S on the other. And then he heard his name ...

Doug Stevens: I came up onto the stage, took the mike and shouted, in my best Mississippi country twang, "Y'all ready for some homosexual country music?"
    Then the pounding drum beats of "Out in the Country" began. I was twisting, wiggling, and shaking my butt in true Tupelo, Mississippi, form. Elvis would have been proud! When I sing, I go back to the accent I would have if I had stayed in Mississippi, the same accent that my daddy, mama, sister, and brother speak with today. I was worried that these Dutch people, even though

most of them spoke English, would not understand me. But I could tell from the laughter when I sang "White Trash" and the look in the eyes of some of the men when I sang "Pump-N-Go" that, yep, they understood! I sang "Mi Joven Amor Tejano," doing my Linda Ronstadt imitation, holding out those high notes as long as I could. I sang "Amor de Legos es Para Pendejos!" and people laughed. I knew where I wanted to take that crowd and I took them there. I fed off of them and they fed off me. It was better than sex. I caressed them and then shook them up with my melodies.

Also, during his stay in South Holland, the Eindhoven Stetson dance troupe performed to a crowd of 750,000 during the Cologne Pride parade.

Doug Stevens: I think most of the crowd had never seen gay people dancing to country music before (men dancing with men and women dancing with women). We received incredibly strong, positive reactions. Lots of cheering. In fact, the major TV station for the region filmed footage of the event, and the only group they showed (among the 120 marching in the parade) was us. They showed me dancing with Joop (one of my hosts) and several of the dancers—dressed in chaps, vests, and cowboy hats in the colors of the rainbow—who were leading our group. All I can say is Yeeeeeeehaaaaa!!—

Out for a Night of Glama

On June 26, 1994, the queer community celebrated the Stonewall Rebellion's twenty-fifth anniversary in New York, which attracted thousands of people across the world. Representatives from record companies were among the attendees, as a number of gay and lesbian artists performed during the anniversary celebration. The event acknowledged the need to press ahead for civil rights and the need for the record and broadcast industry to support queer artists who performed "gay" music. It seems that the message is central, not the particular genre of music. Gay music is "an expression of gay experience in all of its diversity, in all of its aspects," explained gay recording artist Tom McCormack, when interviewed by *Billboard* magazine in 1994:

> In the same way that "black music" expressed the experience of African Americans and comprises many styles of expression and content (e.g., R&B, rap, soul), so too does gay music encompass varied musical styles, content, and means of expression as it reaches out to gay and lesbian of all backgrounds.[7]

It is not so surprising that McCormack, one of the anniversary spokespersons, is one of the founders and executive producers for the Gay and Lesbian American Music Awards (GLAMA), the first and only national music awards program to celebrate and honor the music of queer musicians and songwriters. It also brings together radio and recording industry people, and producers and artists, who would have never known each other otherwise, as demonstrated by McCormack's relationship with "Audiofile" creator Chris Wilson and *Amazon Country's* Debra D'Alessandro. Both have judged for GLAMA in the past and each found GLAMA an integral resource in deciding what artists deserve exposure on their respective radio programs.

The idea for GLAMA was inspired in part by Outmusic, a New York–based national organization dedicated to "creating opportunities for and increasing awareness of lesbian and gay composers, lyricists, performers, and their supporters."[8] Outmusic workshops, led by industry professionals, instruct musicians on how to produce and publicize their own CDs and how to "come out" in their music. Outmusic has released two compilation CDs, featuring twenty gay and lesbian artists since 1995, and has regularly organized queer music festivals.

Tom McCormack: It was sort of my own coming-out process. Outmusic, which had been around for several years, was a place for queer musicians to come and try out their material. The range of experience was pretty broad from totally amateurs to people who had CDs out and what not. And I was very excited by the idea of queer songwriters and musicians expressing that part of themselves through their music and it was also a new idea to me. It had never even crossed my mind that I might express that through my music. It was sort of a self-censorship that was going on that I wasn't even aware of. I became involved in the Outmusic Festival of Lesbian and Gay Music one year, and in fact one of the directors, Michael Mitchell, asked if I would take charge of the event. It was very heartening from a personal standpoint and from a creative standpoint. The festival was expanded into a month-long event, so that concerts and performances were happening all around New York City in fifteen to twenty venues. Basically we were just creating an umbrella. We weren't producing all those events, but we were trying to encourage everybody to put together their own shows—band together with other performers to coordinate genre-based nights, so we had a cabaret and we had a rock thing and we had a punk thing and we had a theater thing and folk and what not. Just because someone is gay doesn't mean they are necessarily going to enjoy the same music because people have different tastes, so we really needed to be aware of the concept that genre and style of music were going to be probably more important to most people who were listening than the fact that it somehow was about gay life or gay experience. On another level, the festival was a mentoring experience, to sort of encourage a lot of these people to take control of their professional lives. Quite a few of them were already performing and this was nothing new, but a lot of them had never ventured outside of an open mike.

Chris Wilson: In the last five years, there's been an incredible explosion of wonderful musicians who are out—indeed music that is out. There was a real need for the community to know about musicians who are free and open to be who they are. In January of 1997, I created "Audiofile." It takes me between four to eight hours just to produce my six-minute segment. I review CDs from all over the world from gay and lesbian artists, and I choose the best from those musicians. Sometimes it is so difficult because there is so much good music out there, but I select three each month to be featured. I interview the artist and then, along with my coproducer, Pam Marshall, who is my on-air coproducer and my life partner, and our behind-the-scenes engineering coproducer, Christopher David Trentham, we put together a segment called "Audiofile," which airs once a month on *This Way Out* across more than a hundred stations around the world and on *IMRU,* which is L.A.'s local lesbian and gay radio show, the one I first became involved with.

Tom McCormack: Michael and I kicked around the idea of an annual music awards show. The idea was sort of Michael's. He just said, "I think we should do a music awards show, and I think it should be called GLAMA, the Gay and Lesbian American Music Awards." That was spring 1995. And I'm a sucker for a good name, and I just loved it. I've been roped into other projects just based on the name and this one was similar to that because we didn't have any clue outside of the name, what it was and what it was going to represent. But there was a certain amount of self-interest there because I thought that I could learn a lot in the process. We began to ask, "What should GLAMA be? How do the awards work? How should they be represented? How do we get the word out? Is this a gay thing? Is this a music thing? What is it we are trying to define?" We came in contact with a guy named Donald Eagen, who was very much involved with special events marketing, and also a gay man, and we started talking to him about it, and he said, "This is a great idea." He felt very strongly that it could be developed, so it was very encouraging and he kind of coached us in terms of finding a sponsor and things like that. We started with that. And then as Michael and I discussed it, I said what's really critical here is to get the involvement of the music industry and to define the music industry in its broadest terms—everyone from distribution to record labels to music press to radio to retail. We need to get all these people involved. We need to somehow get them invested in this process so it's not just about us, but it's about them sort of owning it. It's about getting the music out there.

One of the first steps was the establishment of a GLAMA advisory board, which would include the music industry people, the gay media, and the queer community. Some of the members included Bob Guccione Jr., editor and publisher of *Spin* magazine; Judy Weider, editor of *The Advocate;* Larry Flick, talent editor of *Billboard* magazine; and Janis Ian. The process, which was fairly informal, was used as a way to generate ideas and input into making GLAMA a successful event within the music industry.

Tom McCormack: The best piece of advice was from Larry Flick, then the singles review editor and the dance music editor for *Billboard*, who cautioned us against trying to take on too much too soon. It was April 1995, and the first annual GLAMA would have been held only a few months later in October. Instead, Flick suggested that we wait until the following October to debut the first annual awards ceremony and work instead on building national momentum toward the event with advance publicity and promotion.

And that's what happened. McCormack and Mitchell created a kickoff event, "A Night of GLAMA," along with what became known as GLAMA's National Concert Series, "Come Out and Play"—four concerts held in key locations (San Francisco, Chicago, New York, and Los Angeles). These events were designed to establish GLAMA as a national project, as opposed to just a New York event.

Tom McCormack: So we basically put together a package and we started to look for sponsors for the kickoff celebration, which was called "A Night of GLAMA," a concert to celebrate the creation of the Gay and Lesbian American Music Awards, set for October 1995. What we tried to do was create a sense of momentum and also exposure to these artists—setting the stage for "A Night of GLAMA."

"A Night of GLAMA" was held at Los Angeles's Luna Club in October 1995, and the performers included Disappear Fear, Joey Areas (a well-known female illusionist who does Billie Holiday), Tandy Division, Cris Williamson, and the Flirtations.

Tom McCormack: It was decided that we would give out two honorary awards. One is called the Michael Callen Medal of Achievement, which was given to Cris and presented by Bob Guccioni Jr. The Michael Callen Medal of Achievement is given to an individual, group, organization, or business committed to the great and important work of engendering, nurturing, and furthering gay and lesbian music. And we named it after Michael because we felt here was somebody who really did exemplify a spirit of commitment to being out, to being an artist, to marrying those two concepts, to being committed to his community as well because he was so active in queer issues and particularly HIV and AIDS.

ࣿ

Michael Callen helped organize the With AIDS Coalition and the Community Research Initiative. Before his death on December 27, 1993, he recorded the vocals for "A Love Worth Fighting For,"[9] along with more than fifty songs. In an interview with the Gay Wired Music Source, Callen shared his thoughts:

> Everyone's got a million reasons why one love is more acceptable than another. But those of us who love unconventionally—and I'm not only singing here about gay love, but interracial love, love between disabled people ... people of different cultures—know that this is love and it is worth fighting for.[10]

Tom McCormack: So we invited Bob Guccioni Jr. to present the Michael Callen award at "A Night of GLAMA." And you know, even though he wasn't responsible for choosing who would receive the award, he was supporting the concept of the award: "I would be honored to present an award with Michael's name on it." And we were unaware of the fact that Michael had, before he died, been writing commentaries for *Spin* magazine about AIDS issues. So Michael and Bob knew each other quite well, which was just one of those moments when we said, "There's something else at work here." We never in our wildest dreams would have thought that Michael and Bob Guccioni Jr. would have known each other, so that was encouraging. He was very supportive and his name was lending us some credibility. When it came time for the awards, Guccioni would represent a very contemporary view of what music today is—the cutting edge in the established music community. And Michael Callen's posthumously released album *Legacy* received nine nominations in six categories, including Male Artist, Album of the Year, and Original Out Song. The other honorary award given out that night was the Outmusic Award, which is given to a recording artist, group, or songwriter who proves a steadfast commitment to speak openly and specifically to the lesbian and gay experience in their music. The Outmusic Award represents an ideal to which the entire professional music community may aspire, and its recipient embodies the courage of truthful self-expression combined with the high level of music artistry toward which all in our industry should strive. That was obviously in honor of this organization—Outmusic—which helped to sort of generate the idea for GLAMA. The award was presented to Boy George, who had come out that year with his CD on cheapness and beauty, which was very out in its content, and we felt for a major artist such as that to be out in the recording itself was a major achievement. There had been some musicians who had come out who were big names, but for the most part there wasn't much in the way of content that expressed who they were as a queer person and here was Boy George doing that.

The first annual GLAMA ceremony happened at Webster Hall in New York City in October 1996, with about 700 people in attendance (see Appendix 3A). In the audience, there were music fans and members of the music press. The judges included music reviewers in the gay and mainstream media, leaders in radio distribution, major record labels and independent record labels, and people in performing rights, talent management, and retail.

Tom McCormack: The organizers wanted to make sure that someone who has a huge budget on a major label does not instantly win over an indie artist who was putting out a great release. We basically told the judges, if you feel really, really strongly about a song or album, the category "overall impression" was the place for these opinions. And people used that to express their negative opinion as well as their positive opinion. And what was very interesting to see was that depending on where people were coming from, some people had very, very strong opinions about GLAMA and what it should represent and what music should be honored. Some people felt that only music that was out, that expressed something explicitly about being gay and lesbian or bisexual or transgendered should be somehow honored. And other people didn't feel that should necessarily be the case. You know, when we started GLAMA, some people were saying that if this were an AIDS organization, or some sort of charity effort, our artists could be part of it. But because it is just about gay music, we don't feel comfortable about that. And basically that's what we were trying to say—the music is what we are honoring. It's not an award for being out. It's an award for offering music of merit that has been recorded in the past year. And the fact that people are queer is obviously integral, but it is sort of secondary—even though it is part of the name. What we did in this event is create a space where people were obviously being honored for their music. You were so aware of who was in that room; even though it wasn't exclusively gay, it was still a welcoming audience. So at times it became very moving because you saw artists who said I've never had this experience before where I could sing this song—and I've always known what it meant to me and I figured queer people would figure it out, even if it wasn't explicitly out. So what wound up happening was there was just a very strong bond and people walked away from that event saying, "I really didn't know what to expect. I thought it was going to be a boring awards show and there was something magical about it. There was something really powerful about what was going on." Subsequently we did the second and then the third awards, and k.d. lang and RuPaul received the two special honors. And each year GLAMA has kind of grown, and each year more people, particularly the bigger names, have heard about it and better understand what it is all about.

Chris Wilson: I'm one of the judges, but they have a lot of judges. The one great thing about GLAMA is it has a real broad cross section of judges. I think there is a mutually helpful relationship between "Audiofile" and GLAMA. I think that GLAMA gives exposure to artists who we might not know about otherwise. I know in my very first year, I had trouble identifying the gay and lesbian artists, and at that point I was having to ask for CDs. No one was just sending them to me. I had to introduce myself to them and say, we're a radio show that features gay and lesbian musicians. Please send me your CD. GLAMA told me who those people were and whose CD I should go after, because they had a lot of visibility and they drew a lot of artists who were interested in airplay. What is funny is the first artist who opened my eyes to the fact that there are wonderfully talented people out there who were not getting mainstream airplay was Jeff Krassner [ex-director of Outmusic]. Interestingly, he's never been featured on "Audiofile," namely because in 1996 I had already aired a full-length six-minute interview with just him. This is where the concept for "Audiofile" was created. I was moved by how great his music was, and I couldn't believe that I was not hearing him on the radio. It was Jeff who opened my eyes to the fact that there were so many wonderful, talented self-produced artists, and since then I've discovered others, one of which is Sonia. So many of these musicians are so appreciative when we feature them. I mean they are just genuine, down-to-earth wonderful people. They want to make themselves available for interviews, and they are generous about contributing their CDs to things like radio station fund drives. And I know that their out-of-pocket expenses have got to be greater than some radio companies.

Tom McCormack: We started to see more reviews of GLAMA submitted material in the gay media, and the same thing for radio. We actually had a good number of radio people who would basically take their compilation tapes that they got for judging or the CDs that they got for judging and put them on their shows.

Debra D'Alessandro: I appreciate the way that GLAMA and Tom McCormack have brought to my attention music I had not heard of previously, so I try to certainly let my [*Amazon Country*] listeners know about the events in Philadelphia or close to New York. I feel like GLAMA has an important music education aspect, allowing the public and radio broadcasters in particular to pay attention to some of the up-and-coming out artists.

Chris Wilson: Conversely, every year since the very first GLAMA, we, as radio producers, feel that it is important for our audience to know about

GLAMA and to know about some of these artists. It is an important event in the gay and lesbian community that we do our very best, budget permitting, to cover every year. Actually, we have no budget. When I say we need money, I've flown to New York at my own expense for GLAMA. *This Way Out* doesn't have the funds for that, so I just do it myself because I think it is an incredibly significant event, and I applaud what they are doing. It is always an incredible show, and each year there's more and more artists. I don't know if "Audiofile" would have built itself up to the level of recognition that it now has without GLAMA. GLAMA sets up events where the press can meet the artist. They make the artist very, very accessible to the press, so therefore I have an opportunity to introduce myself in person to the artist, get soundbites from the artist right then and there on the spot, then get a phone interview months later.

Tom McCormack: There is a certain perceptual shift and what we are saying is that this is a cultural thing. GLAMA is about that culture and the need to acknowledge the achievement of people within that culture and the importance of that culture. And if we can see that, then we can begin as a society, gay and nongay, to simply appreciate the contributions of these people. Whether you know it or not, they are standing on a soap box. It's really just about these cultural achievements. I think we've been quite successful at that, and one of the things that has been very heartening—and a major mission or goal for us from the beginning—is to get the music out there.

Chris Wilson: I love music and I admire the artists who are willing to put all of themselves out there. What we play on "Audiofile" is what you don't hear on the commercial mainstream Top 40 radio station. For example, with respect to music, Jay McLaren, who currently lives in the Netherlands, has a compilation CD *OutLoud*.[11] It is an incredible compilation of every single piece of music that in any way touched on the gay and lesbian community. Because of GLAMA I was able to meet this person from Amsterdam who put together this incredible encyclopedia of gay and lesbian music. Without GLAMA, we would never have met. So it has given me access to the artists and given us exposure. I am hopeful that all independent artists and lesser known artists, not just gay and lesbian independent artists, will have more of an opportunity in the mainstream. It will depend on the public, which is sometimes very trendy. I think we need to educate people that there is other good music out there, other than what they hear on Top 40. And that's good music too. I listen to it myself sometimes, but it is not all I listen to. I think that's a stereotype that is sometimes in and about the gay and lesbian community.

And that's the story of GLAMA. The Gay and Lesbian American Music Awards have been held every year since 1996.

The Movement Behind Women's Music

> *There was a phenomenon called "women's music," which was really lesbian music, cultivated for years and years at all-women music festivals, bucolic events resembling separatist summer camps with all the trimmings. . . . It may not have the purity of the Michigan Womyn's Music Festival (i.e., men are admitted and so are professional concert promoters), but how could any self-respecting gay girl on the prowl miss out on this meeting of minds and flesh? The real heavy-hitters of the Lilith tour are not the organizer, Sarah McLachlan, or the new stars like Jewel and Paula Cole, but the actual veterans of the lesbian music circuit, like the Indigo Girls, who are out of the closet on their latest album, or Tracy Chapman, who is so shy that she hardly says a word about herself in any direction, although she's made no effort to hide her relationships with women. The lesbo inspiration for the Lilith fest is overdue for an outing. Lesbians have been too isolated and paranoid to take credit for it, and straight music people have been too arrogant and indifferent to give it to them, but it took the combination of feminism and dyke attitude to give rock 'n' roll a female face.*

—Susie Bright (1997), columnist and author[12]

Before the days of Lilith Fair, there was a place where women gathered, socialized, and bonded with other women. Some brought their children. Some brought their lovers. Women would trek through the woods and erect tents. Some would sell and display crafts, while others would conduct workshops on empowerment, self-esteem, health, and performance. One of the longest running festivals is the Michigan Womyn's Festival, and it featured Jill Sobule of the Top 40 hit "I Kissed a Girl" during its twenty-fourth annual celebration.[13] Basically, 6,000 women take over 650 acres of Michigan's northern woods and listen to music about women by women.[14] Chris Wilson, producer of "Audiofile," says lesbian music today is not to be stereotyped, for it represents a diversity of styles and genres.

Chris Wilson: When I mention lesbian musicians, some have a mental picture of women with just an acoustic guitar singing folk songs, and that's not what the current state of gay and lesbian music is today, and I think people just need to be introduced to these artists. I have been amazed at the production values and quality. We've had rap, country, pop, show tunes, classical, and just about every genre. I hope to be as diverse as possible in the style that we feature on our show. I may not have a personal preference for all those categories, but I try very, very hard to make sure that the best of everything is represented, and I think I can usually find something to appreciate in just about every genre of music.

In 1971, the first lesbian-themed song about a woman who longed to hold another woman's hand—the hand of her female lover—in public was released and sung by Maxine Feldman, and it was called "Angry Athis."[15] Two years later, Alix Dobkin's groundbreaking album *Lavender Jane Loves Women* was released as a tribute to 1960s feminist activist Jane Alpert.[16] Lesbian / feminist activist—Representative Bella Abzug introduced gay civil rights legislation to Congress in 1974.[17] Two years later, in 1976, the Michigan Womyn's Music Festival debuted.

Susan Schulman's *My American History: Lesbian and Gay Life During the Reagan/Bush Years* begins where Stonewall ends, as she recounts how the '70s women's liberation movement brought lesbians and heterosexual women together.[18] Tension was already building between the two groups. A 1971 statement from the National Organization for Women (NOW) underscored the need to address lesbian oppression within the feminist movement and called for all women to come together to bring these issues to the forefront within the legislature, within society, and within the organization itself.

The significance of these women's festivals was overshadowed by sensationalized lesbian events through the years, like the palimony suit against Billie Jean King by her ex-lover, another woman.[19] New York's WBAI-FM aired a special show dedicated to women's music about the time that the Michigan Womyn's Music Festival debuted, and it seemed to segue nicely with all the festivals held annually throughout the United States. These festivals were, and in many instances still are, an integral part of the feminist movement—although straight and lesbian women have differed in their definition of this movement on more than one occasion. The festivals delivered a message of empowerment in the music, and it was this sense of mission and purpose that drove these events.

Nancy Kirton: There was a show at WBAI that focused on women's music festivals. In one room, we had never brought together so many hot shots from the Michigan Womyn's Festival and the New England Women's Festival.

The music brought these woman together for three days a year, so it seemed only natural that radio would become an extension of lesbian and feminist expression the other 362 days of the year. *Lesbian Sisters, Amazon Country, Amazon Radio,* and *Face the Music* and other lesbian shows were created on the premise of broadcasting to women, by women, and about women.

Sisterhood of Lesbian Radio

Historically, noncommercial radio has provided an outlet for lesbian-oriented programs in the United States, dating back to the 1970s and 1980s in many cases. Through the years, programs have included *Feminist News* in Columbia, Ohio, *Everywoman* in Cincinnati, Ohio, *Women's Music* in Eugene, Oregon, *Women Soul Collective* in Portland, Oregon, *The Purple Rabbit Show* in Altoona, University Park, and Hollidaysburg in Pennsylvania, *Wimmin's Music Program* in Cupertino, California, and *Woman's Hour* in Houston, Texas. The power of community radio in training and organizing lesbian voices began to emerge over the airwaves in the mid-'70s.

Two of the longest running programs are ones with a strong lesbian music emphasis—*Amazon Country* and *Face the Music*. *Face the Music* is promoted today by WCUW 91.3 FM as the second longest continuously running lesbian/feminist music program on community radio in the United States, and it still airs Thursday nights in Worcester, Massachusetts.[20] The first women's show targeted to primarily lesbian listeners is speculative. As early as 1923, the British Broadcasting Corporation aired a show called *Woman's Hour*, but it was not until the early '70s that lesbian-themed shows really began to surface in the United States and Europe. *Sophie's Parlor* was among the first lesbian/feminist programs in the United States. It began on Georgetown University's campus station in the early 1970s and found a new home on Pacifica's WPFW in Washington, D.C., in 1976 when management at WTGB-FM dropped the program after it decided not to support homosexual content on the air.[21]

In 1972, Gloria Steinem, in a speech to Hollywood High School, told students that "lesbians are on the cutting edge of change ... they have much to teach us."[22] One year later, *Lesbian Sisters* aired on Los Angeles' KPFK, and it was also in 1973 that a national lesbian kiss-in was held on the front steps of the L.A. County Museum of Art.[23] Radio became an outlet for community and national activism in the 1970s by women like KPFK's Helene Rosenbluth (producer of *Lesbian Sisters* and *Feminist Magazine*) and Frieda Werden (producer of *What's Normal?*). Other women like Josy Catoggio and Cindy Friedman were introduced to radio through their street activism and began to volunteer at KPFK.

Josy Catoggio: I was involved in a couple of different projects—the first happened in Vermont in '75, but it died after several years. Several women from California went there and then tried to start something called Califia. We were the teachers and we would do workshops on all the sort of basic 'isms that kept women apart from each other—racism, classism, ageism, homophobia, that kind of stuff. Basically my presentations were based on getting people to understand that it wasn't so much homosexuality that people hated as it was the perception that we were a threat to the so-called natural order of things, of gender roles. I was also, as a working-class feminist, doing workshops on class in relationships, what happened when middle-class women and working-class women got into relationships and would clash over things like money and loyalty and words versus action and all those things.

Frieda Werden: Probably the first nationally syndicated radio series on lesbian/gay issues was *What's Normal? An Exploration of Homosexuality and the Gay Subculture in Our Society*—thirteen half-hour programs on homosexual lifestyles [see Appendix 3C], distributed by Longhorn Radio Network in 1975–76. It was carried by only thirteen radio stations, but it received more mail than any series the network had ever distributed. People wrote in to get a bibliography on gay issues. I think the bibliography came from the Gay Academic Union, as I was on the GAU Texas board of directors and had wanted it to be a GAU project. I proposed the series, chose two or three guests per show, and was the volunteer producer. Stewart Wilber was Longhorn's staff producer for the series. He is now a priest. Beulah Hodge, a straight woman from public TV, hosted. Among the guests and topics were Robin Birdfeather on lesbian separatism, Marc Sanders on "genderfuck" (I can't remember how we handled that word on the radio; basically it meant wearing a dress and a beard), Art Addington on the GAU, gay men discussing radical sissies, and lesbians discussing child custody and employment issues. I appeared with others on a program titled "The Gay Bar." The series is archived in the Longhorn Radio Network collection at the Center for American History, University of Texas at Austin.

Josy Catoggio: I was approached by KPFK's Helene Rosenbluth, radio producer of both *Lesbian Sisters* and *Feminist Magazine,* to discuss my involvement in feminist education. I can't remember which one she asked me to be a guest on, but probably *Feminist Magazine.* I talked about the workshops I was doing in those days, and I was doing workshops all the time. I worked at the Gay and Lesbian Community Services Center and I would go out and do these antihomophobia workshops for mental health centers and high school and college classes and making the connections between sexism and homophobia, the fact that I thought that homophobia was based on gender role stuff so that gay men were hated because they were perceived as acting like women. I mean that's kind of a long, complicated theoretical discussion. They had something called the "Alternative Lifestyle Conference," and they'd have this smorgasbord of workshops for lesbians. I was doing this one about class, so she had me come in and talk. I realized, thinking about all the years that I'd been involved in this work, I was reaching rooms full of people, but theoretically with the radio you could reach way, way more people for a lot less money and time expended and that it was a way to reach people who couldn't afford to take time off from work and come to a workshop or a retreat or a camp or a school or anything like that. And so I got really passionate about the idea of doing radio as a way of sort of spreading the political work I was already doing—antihomophobia workshops and antisexism stuff. Cindy used to tease me because I'd say that the "tidal wave of my feminist politics could not be captured in the thimble of gay and lesbian radio."

Frieda Werden: The late cofounder of WINGS: Women's International News Gathering Service, Katherine Davenport, also did broadcasting on lesbian and gay issues. Some of her interviews from the '70s and '80s, including tapes on controversial topics like National American Man-Boy Love Association and what happened to the money from the first lesbian-gay march on Washington, are in the WINGS collection at the Center for American History at the University of Texas at Austin. Others are still uncatalogued in the Pacifica Radio Archives in Los Angeles. Katherine was media co-coordinator for that first ('79) gay march. She did much of her radio work at WBAI-FM in New York, where she coproduced both the lesbian series *The Velvet Sledgehammer* and a program called *51%—The Women's News* with Judie Pasternak. After leaving New York, Katherine produced in Boulder, Colorado, and then at KPFA and KALX in Berkeley, California. One of her favorite shows from KPFA in the '80s was called "Lesbian Non-Mothers."

By the mid-80s, Reaganism, corporate politics, and right-wing conservatism had pulled the two women's groups apart—lesbian and straight. The increased insistence among lesbians, not willing to tolerate homophobia, and the failure of others to recognize the significance of these issues, divided the movement. The '80s was an era of apathy or passivity, and eventually direct action gave way to the rise of women's studies, bookstores, and women's music festivals more concerned with self and social expression than with challenging the system.[24]

By 1987, the AIDS Coalition to Unleash Power (ACT UP), described by Schulman as the "largest grassroots, democratic, and most effective organizing in the history of both the gay and feminist movements,"[25] called for direct action and street activism and became the spark that reunited lesbians and feminists, alongside drag queens, people with AIDS, and gay professionals. "Singing for Our Lives" by Holly Near,[26] lesbian songwriter-activist, became symbolic of the decade, as gays and lesbians struggled for their identity—individually and collectively—against the American bastion of conservatism.

Meg Christian, raised in the South, also became a leading songwriter and performer during the early feminist movement. She was one of the founders of Olivia Records and the first artist to be recorded on the label, dedicated solely to the promotion of women's music. "Ode to a Gym Teacher" is per-

haps the most memorable of Christian's early songs on that first Olivia album *I Know You Know.*

Ode to a Gym Teacher

Chorus:
She was a big tough woman. The first to come along
that showed me being female meant you still could be strong.
And though graduation meant that we had to part.
She'll always be a player on the ballfield of my heart.
I wrote her name on my notepad and inked it on my dress.
And I etched it on my locker and I carved it on my desk.
And I painted big red hearts with her initials on my books.
And I never knew till later why I got those funny looks.
In gym class while the others talked of boys that they loved
I'd be thinking of new aches and pains the teacher had to rub.
And while other girls went to the prom I languished by the phone.
Calling up and hanging up if I found out she was home.
I sang her songs by Johnny Mathis. I gave her everything.
A new chain for her whistle, and some daisies in the spring.
Some suggestive poems for Christmas by Miss Edna Millay.
And a lacy lacy lacy card for Valentine's Day
(Unsigned of course).
(Here comes the moral of the song. . .)
So you just go to any gym class. And you'll be sure to see.
One girl who sticks to Teacher like a leaf sticks to a tree.
One girl who runs the errands and who chases all the balls.
One girl who may grow up to be the *gayest* of all.[27]

—Meg Christian, singer and songwriter

Many of her songs became lesbian folk anthems during the women's music
festivals and marches of the late '70s and early '80s. Another significant
song recorded by Christian was "Face the Music." It was composed by Annie
Dinerman.

Meg Christian: One of my guiding principles as a feminist performer was
to sing and acknowledge the great songs that other women were composing.
And when Annie sent us her "Face the Music" song, we were thrilled to be
able to offer her the support and validation of my recording her song and
telling audiences about her.

Debra D'Alessandro: It is one of those great musical testimonials about the power of music, and I use that song on a lot of fund drives.

D'Alessandro is host of *Amazon Country,* which celebrated its twenty-sixth anniversary in 2000. Its first show debuted only one year after the founding of Olivia Records. Other *Amazon Country* hosts have included founders Rose Weber and Jesse Ford, Roberta Hacker, author Victoria Brownworth, Laney Goodman (host-producer of *Women in Music,* an Internet women's music show produced in Boston), writer Sue Pierce, and photographer Elena Bouvier. Through the years, lesbian programs have impacted the lives of a number of female listeners, many of whom eventually decided to get involved in feminist/lesbian broadcasting at the community level. Indeed, *Amazon Country* was the recipient of the 1999 Lambda Award for Outstanding Overall Performance by an organization/social-cultural group. The program continues its run every Sunday night 9 to 10 P.M. on the University of Pennsylvania's public radio station WXPN-FM, and features a lesbian/feminist perspective in its music and interviews with artists, authors, and leaders throughout the nation.[28] *Amazon Country* is followed at 11 P.M. by *Q'zine* (formerly *Gaydreams*)— the queer arts and culture radio magazine hosted by Robert Drake. *Q'zine* also first aired in 1974 on WXPN.

D'Alessandro has more than ten years of experience as an activist, educator, and performer in Philadelphia's feminist and gay communities. She has performed her original poetry, comedy, and music in Philadelphia, Harrisburg, New York, and on the "festival circuit" including the Michigan Womyn's Music Festival's August Night Stage, the Campfest Butch Café, and as M.C. of various events including the Sisterspace Pocono Weekend and the Philadelphia Diversity of Pride Parade. She also sings with the Anna Crusis Women's Choir.

Another show—*Amazon Radio*—was founded by Pamela Smith in 1989 on WPKN 89.5 FM in Bridgeport, Connecticut. Smith grew up listening to early lesbian/feminist shows as a teenager and became active in the women's movement in New Haven during the early 1970s. Her show was modeled after *Amazon Country,* but it is programmed from a black lesbian feminist perspective. Along with her life partner Susan, Smith hosts the program—now in its eleventh year—on the first and third Tuesday night of every month on WPKN from 6:35 to 10 P.M. (see Appendix 3B).

Debra D'Alessandro: I was impacted by lesbian broadcasting as a fourteen-year-old when I was growing up in a suburb of Pittsburgh and I discovered college radio. The radio station WRCT that broadcast at the time from Carnegie-Mellon University had two shows that I couldn't tear myself away from. I made sure I heard them every week. They played very similar music. One was Feltman Feminist Radio's *Women Held Up Half the Sky* and the other one was called *Woman to Woman,* a lesbian radio program. They played, this was like 1977–1978, Ferron, Margie Adams, Cris Williamson, Meg Christian, and Holly Near. It was so powerful for me as this young, not out but struggling with my sexuality, teenager to hear love songs by, for, and about women. That was so incredibly powerful for me—I did have a relationship at sixteen with my seventeen-year-old best friend, and I was able to call in a dedication to her on the radio. I mean it was just earth-shattering and kind of mind-expanding to realize that there was a culture of women who loved women.

Pamela Smith: I never did radio before *Amazon Radio,* but I always liked music. Actually I've been involved in the women's movement since the early '70s. And I've always been a fan of women's music. I mean I used to hang out with the New Haven and the Women's Liberation Rock Band. In the '70s, everyone thought the revolution would start in the center of New Haven, and it was a fun time. I think then the music was sort of what held us together and I think music is in itself a very big political tool, much like the slave days when they used to sing songs like "Follow the Drinking Gourd," which is actually about going north, or like the labor unions and their songs and the women's movement and how their songs did the same thing for us early feminists.

Debra D'Alessandro: When I came to Philadelphia in 1982 and I found *Amazon Country*, it felt like wow! They've been my network for lesbian radio, and that was so wonderful. I came to volunteer with one of the previous hosts in the early '90s, Elena Bouvier, and then kind of lost touch with listening to the show. When I tuned into it in late '92, I found that Elena wasn't the host of *Amazon Country.* There was someone saying she was a temporary host and the job was open.

Pamela Smith: The radio station that I listened to, well, that would be my college radio. The university stopped funding them, and so they needed people to come in and answer the phones. While their general manager was figuring out what to do about me, I happened to be in the recording studio, and on the other side of this thick piece of glass was the program director on air. I kept looking at it and kept looking at it, and then, then finally I realized that what was in front of him was exactly in front of me, and so I sort of told Harry I was interested in doing radio—and I told him I'd like to do a woman show, and so it came to be. That was around 1989.

Welcome to Amazon Radio!
Women's Music for all who color outside the lines!

WPKN 89.5 FM—Bridgeport, CT

Debra D'Alessandro: I had not done radio before. I have a background in entertainment, as a poet and a performer of my original music and comedy. I had familiarity with video production, but audio was a whole new ball of wax, and I learned it on the job. I've been doing it for three years now, and I really feel like it's my way of giving back to the community of lesbian broadcasters that were there when I came out, and to be there for the women who are coming up now.

Pamela Smith: There's not really any other show like *Amazon Radio* in this area. As for other shows, there's *Amazon Country* in Philadelphia and it's really ancient. And that's where my name came from, because I had been in Philadelphia a couple of times and listened to the show. Amazon signifies for me strong women. Primarily I look for music that I like and that has something to say. Occasionally I play stuff that I don't like, but that is because they have something to say and I thought it was important to get out the message. It's different all the time. Basically a lot of what I can say is that primarily my artists sing about women and their lives, their hopes, their dreams, independent of men. If you talk to any producer of a women's music program, you'll find out that most of the callers are men, which is quite interesting, and the only way I can judge who is out there is through our fund-raising twice a year. Otherwise, we don't have any ratings of anything.

Debra D'Alessandro: I have stayed true to the original *Amazon Country*. I have pretty much maintained a similar format because the show has been around for a long time—music, public affairs, and a calendar of events, and I still have that as kind of a breakdown of programming. I think that I've brought more live musicians into the studio to perform for *Amazon Country* than past hosts have, so that's probably one change but that's kind of just a variation on the theme. I mean we still interview artists, authors, and activists who are relevant to the lesbian community.

Pamela Smith: *Amazon Radio* has gone through several shuttles in communication. At first, it was just all lesbians, and then I added a straight woman to the mix, and then I started adding gay guys to the mix, and that's about where we are right now. But proportionately, it's still mostly lesbians and straight women, but I had a gay guy in there for a short time. The mission of the show is just my mission, and my mission is to get voices out there where they are really heard. So, you know, I'm not going to play a lot of Sarah McLachlan. You might say, I play a lot of people who have never been heard of. It's amazing to me the number of lesbian and gay men who are coming out with music, particularly the gay men's music. I actually count on the GLAMA nomination list to get me in contact with a lot of artists. And during March and April, I play a lot of nominees. I try to play all of the nominees, except for comedies, I'm always listening to music—it's something I'm sort of always doing. And so as I listen to music, I might just take out one and say, I'll play that this week. And I find a lot of it lately on the Internet and a lot of artists contact me because of my Web page. My favorites always change. I play what I have and what I can get a hold of. For example, a woman in Japan sent me recently four or five CDs (all in Japanese so I can't read the titles of the songs) of Japanese artists, Japanese lesbians in particular. Anyway, I sent her three CDs of American artists. And then, I receive e-mails all the time from people in England who've also sent me their music.

Debra D'Alessandro: The Internet has been incredible for me to connect with listeners because we got a Web site up within the first year that I was doing the show. A listener and volunteer offered to create the Web site, and she still maintains it. And we got an e-mail address which the show had never had, and the immediacy of listeners being able to zap me an e-mail, right after something they heard touched them, has been really, really wonderful. I've heard from teenagers who say "You can't write back to me at this address but I just needed to tell you how much your show means to me."

Pamela Smith: I've gotten a couple pieces of mail from people on the Internet, who haven't even heard the show. Actually I was sick most of the summer with pneumonia, and a couple of people wrote me and wanted to know when I was going to be back on the air because now they can hear me on the Internet. Most places I go, I am fairly low-key, and people don't even know who I am. Although people have come up to me and said "thanks," it's because they recognize my voice. When I was at Folk Alliance in February out in New Mexico, a lot of artists came up to me and thanked me for playing their stuff.

Debra D'Alessandro: I've heard from fifty- and sixty-year-old women who tell me they get in their car and drive around to listen. They're struggling with coming out and they're married and this is like the one way that they can connect with a lesbian culture, and I think that radio is incredibly powerful. The Internet has done this too but radio's been there long before there was an Internet. Radio is a powerful way for people to access queer culture in a nonthreatening way. When I was fourteen, I wouldn't have been allowed in a bar. I would have been too scared to even pick up, if I could find, a lesbian or gay newspaper. I didn't have the courage to go to a meeting or a bookstore. Radio came into my bedroom, and I think it's the intimacy of radio and it's the access that anyone can find you on the dial that makes it such a powerful medium, particularly for lesbians.

Chapter Four

Beyond Wayne's World

Queer TV on the Public Airwaves

Welcome to community television—Electric City Network—
(affectionately known as "Cheap TV")! Electric City has
surpassed the pressures of HIV and AIDS through the power of
the community and the control of our true image. It is with
pride we remember countless talents who built Electric City;
and who will never be portrayed as victims!

—*Electric City* web page[1]

San Francisco's longest running cable access Queer TV program is *Electric City*. It airs on San Francisco's public access channel City Visions and is managed by the San Francisco Cable Television Company (SFCTC.) Since 1984, its mission has been to confront dramatic and controversial issues and to embrace events in the queer community:

> Our unique style presents history as it happens, rather than interpret views, reinvent ideas, or censor images. Electric City's format keeps a margin for free thought within each show. . . . We've sent footage world-wide to the BBC in England, Australia, Germany, Mexico, and Brazil. Writers, performers, activists, musicians, singers, Drag and Leather from all genders and colors appear frequently on Electric City. Street fairs, parties, and marches of all kinds are covered weekly. We are irreverent, funny, poignant, sexy, and always truthful.[2]

Electric City is part of a larger trend toward independent Queer TV collectives on cable access stations throughout the nation, from the West Coast to Denver to New York. To its credit, Queer TV's *Electric City* has been dubbed "Best Queer Cable Show" by the *San Francisco Bay Guardian* and it won the 1996 Cable Access "Special Programming" Award. Cheap TV, San Francisco, is a member of the National Academy of Television Arts & Sciences, the Lesbian & Gay Press Association, and the Actors' Equity Association.[3] One of the founders of the local Queer TV program has been there from the start:

Sande Mack: In San Francisco, I've gone from the satirical, live comedy group The Committee to my favorite activist group, the Food Conspiracy. Summed up, the Food Conspiracy had everyone put up five bucks to go towards food items like peanut butter, rice, and beans in bulk. Everyone eats. In 1968, I went from the Gay Liberation Front to the antiwar movement in 1969 to the Society for Individual Rights. I danced, acted, and sang in *Oh, Calcutta* in San Francisco (until 1970) and volunteered time for the Community United Against Violence (CUAV) Street Patrol in the early '80s (a very violent time), and then worked with Gay Cable Network and out of that was born *Electric City.** In the late '80s, the queer community found itself in the middle of police riots, demonstrations, and homophobic behavior by city officials. *Electric City* was there. We joined the AIDS Action Pledge in the mid '80s to combat HIV, which later became ACT UP. *Electric City* later became ACT UP media. In our kitchen, we conducted interviews fed over the world, which included CNN and Japanese television. Limited resources were available, and it was all done with mirrors and smoke, but it all worked. A lot of truly dedicated people—over 400 people at one point joined in ACT UP meetings. ACT UP stood up to the San Francisco Police Department. We began getting subpoenas from the courts for videotape. We would not give up face shots of activists participating in civil disobedience. They sent us the subpoena in the mail. We began to fight back, and all of a sudden we found that everyone around us was dying. Those fighters were dying off: Mark Wang, Augie, José, John, you can go on with thirty or forty more, Bryce Brandon, Jerome Caja (world-renowned artist). They were all part of ACT UP and *Electric City.* Jerome created something called Bozo Nation. It was a group that dressed up as clowns and did political actions around town. You're only as good as your last hit! We got a commendation from city hall for doing AIDS benefits for the community. We've been doing benefits since 1985. We started with Rita Rockett in Ward 5–A at S.F. General doing brunch with Richard "Daddy" Locke, feeding people with AIDS every Sunday. We found ourselves helping Richard Locke pirating HIV drugs across the Mexican border because our government would not release them. Looking back, we were on dangerous ground, and always have been. Now we have a whole new group of artists, such as Arnel Valle (Rice Patte), David, and Gina. After so many years on cable access, we received an award in 1996, and a second award in 1997 for "Best Comedy Variety Show" on cable access. In the early '80s, we were called "video garbage" by the same people giving us this

---

*Queer TV is similar to a network—it is defined locally. There is no such thing as a Queer TV national network, but many stations use *Queer TV* as an official umbrella to house all their LGBT shows.

award. In 1990, we did a show at the Strand Theater called *Nightmare on Market Street* where we did our first Cheap TV Awards. Recipients of the Cheap TV Awards include Rita Rockett, Al Parker, Jerome Caja, Dennis Perone, activist group Dykes from Hell, and many others. So we work with porn stars, hookers, city hall officials, leather, drag, ducal, imperials, nonimperials, nontitle holders. We work with political activists, we work with everyone and anyone who is pushing the movement forward. Anyone who is in the way, we point to them, especially those who ride the AIDS gravy train. We've been blacked out, nominated for an Emmy; we have had police call every cable system we played on and demand footage. What they want is our footage of police actions through the '80s and '90s which shows police raising their batons over their heads and hitting fags on the head, which is totally illegal. They're basically afraid of the footage we have because we are the only ones with footage of those actions.

Mary Kennedy: One of the goals of public access is to be inclusive of minorities and to give community groups a voice when they were underrepresented in broadcast television. Fairly even progression, rather than immediate change, has come since Clinton has been in office and thereafter on broadcast TV. In cities like San Francisco, Chicago, Boston, New York, and Philadelphia, there are a lot of public access shows that sprung up during the time that cable came into that area. Much of the time that's part of the contract with cable companies—to provide public access. In order to obtain these areas and market shares, they agree to set up a public access system and then gays and lesbians are able to get on public access television. Yet, as far as cable access is concerned, it's all over the place in terms of quality.

Mary Kennedy is the producer of a cable access program called *Pridetime* in the Boston area. She decided to abandon commercial cable aspirations after several months of struggling for sponsorship. Instead her program continues, since 1985, to air primarily on cable access.

Mary Kennedy: I had a friend who was working in cable and she knew I had been in the gay press since 1976. She said why don't we do a show since I had the inroads into the gay community and knew who to hook up with and she had the technical know-how. So that's how I became involved in *Pridetime*—the cable access show. . . . I've been doing it off and on since 1985. Originally we covered the Gay Pride events, the Gay Pride March and so forth, and now with a cable caster in Boston named Joyce (she basically started with me), we're doing what essentially is an entertainment movie review show. Prior to that, we had leased some broadcast time on

Channel 27, a Spanish station, and attempted to sell more advertising and that wasn't very successful so we discontinued that after a year. We had done some shows for *Dateline NBC* when they were doing some gay pieces about violence and so forth and we had some footage for them. Right now, we're doing a weekly movie review, and have produced a number of pieces in Provincetown.

Quite a few gay and lesbian programs have appeared on cable access over the past ten years. *The Fresca Vinyl Show*[4] began in 1992 on Los Angeles cable television and was the winner of the Best Gay and Lesbian Programming in the 1995 Hometown Video Festival. Segments included topics such as gay parents, politics, gay benefits, special events, and a variety of lesbian/gay issues, and the program airs on several cable access channels in Los Angeles and on New York's Cable 69. The host, Douglas Lee Long, is HIV-positive and an outspoken community advocate, but the real star of the show is his cohost, Miss Vinyl, a fifteen-inch plastic glamour doll.

Then there's Los Angeles's Nicholas Snow, who has been called the "queer version of Larry King," and his show, *Tinseltown's Queer,* has been described as "Lifestyles of the Queer and Fabulous."[5] *Tinseltown* aired throughout Los Angeles cable television on The L.A. Channel, Century Cable, and Media One through the late 1990s. Snow has recently introduced a self-titled show on Los Angeles television, and the original *Tinseltown* is archived on Gay Wired's Webcast Channel. He is Wired's primary public relations spokesperson and media personality and has been instrumental in the company's content development in cyberspace.

Other shows across the country include *Gay USA,* a gay news magazine show that includes a regular segment on gay legal issues on DCTV Channel 25 on Friday nights.[6] All over California and in Nashville, cable access stations air *Outlook Video,* a news and entertainment show.[7] Also in Tennessee, *GAY Cable Nashville* has aired over Viacom's Channel 19 on Saturday nights. Until recently, lesbian and gay viewers tuned into Seattle's Channel 29 for *The Homo Home Show,* which earned rave reviews from the local press. On Tuesday nights through the 1990s, a number of gay and lesbian cable access programs aired across the nation: *Forward & Out* on TCI Cable 14 in White Plains, New York: *The Queer Program* on Milwaukee's Warner Cable Channel 46; Pittsburgh's *The Gay Nineties* on PCTV Channel 31; and San Franciscans grooved to the sights and sounds of the *Lavender Lounge Dance Party* on TCI Cable 14.[8]

Pursuit of Human Rights

Just As I Am debuted in 1996 as a religious information and music show that challenged the religious right's views on Christianity.[9] In addition to airing on cable access stations in Los Angeles and Southern California, it became one of the first shows of its kind to regularly air on commercial television, in particular Fox TV in Sacramento. Reverend Freda Smith, the former vice moderator of Metropolitan Community Church Worldwide, as the spiritual leader challenged homophobic religious right rhetoric and discussed issues impacting the gay community, many involving the protection of civil rights and liberties. Today, a number of access stations broadcast religious programming specifically targeted toward gay and lesbian audiences throughout the United States.

Equally important, international community television is on the rise and has been similarly concerned with gay and lesbian civil rights and inclusivity in its programming. Rogers Television in southern Ontario airs a weekly TV magazine show called *10%–Qtv* that targets gay, lesbian, bisexual, transgender, and queer audiences. The program won an award at the 2000 Hometown Video Festival (Gay/Lesbian Category, Professional Division) for the fifth episode of its 1999–2000 season.[10] Diversity is the underlying goal of the show—to give voice to the many diverse perspectives, including feminist and youth, within the queer community in Canada and the United States (see Appendix 4A).

Pursuit of Dyke Rights

By the 1990s, virtually no TV shows had targeted lesbians until *Dyke TV* aired on June 8, 1993 in Manhattan.[11] *Dyke TV* still operates exclusively on donations, sponsorships, and some limited institutional support and through the volunteer efforts of 350 women, with many lesbian groups nationwide producing segments. It is a thirty-minute monthly program that is syndicated over cable access on sixty-six stations in the United States, and each show features news, political commentary, arts, health, sports, and comedy:

> typical broadcast begins with the News—from a dyke perspective, of course. Next is our trademark Eyewitness—an in-depth look at an issue of particular interest to the lesbian community. Eyewitness segments have covered such topics as domestic violence, the murder of Brandon Teena in Nebraska, lesbians in Mexico, and the first Dyke March at the March on Washington. In addition, each show contains segments that change from week to week. A favorite among viewers is "I Was a Lesbian Child": a lesbian narrates a montage of childhood photos, retelling her past in her own words. Other segments include Workplace—where we track lesbians on the job, Street Squad—quirky "dyke-on-the-street" interviews, and Lesbian Health.[12]

Dyke TV airs in at least one city in seventeen states in the United States: Arizona, Colorado, Connecticut, Hawaii, Illinois, Indiana, Louisiana, Maryland, Massachusetts, Michigan, Minnesota, Vermont, Washington, D.C., Wisconsin, and several cities in California, New York, and New Jersey. Another cable access television program is *Sister Paula*, which airs in Portland, Oregon, and Hollywood, California. Otherwise, very few TV shows targeted solely to lesbian audiences broadcast on public access stations, and virtually no lesbian programs air on commercial and public broadcasting stations; for this reason, Terry Schleder and others created *Dyke TV*:

Lesbian visibility is left out of both the gay and straight mainstream, so it's up to us to provide another point of view.... There's still a lot of hatred out there towards lesbians and even our show.... We get plenty of hate mail ... and for that reason alone 'Dyke TV' needs to be on to educate those who don't understand and to support those who do.[13]

On occasion, stations unwilling to provide air time to lesbian concerns exclusively have instead aired cable access shows with a much broader Queer TV format.[14]

Give Me My Queer TV

I am going to Nevada in a couple of days. I'm going to a really small town there, and I know there's a lot of history there. I was talking to Cece Pinheiro, and I said I don't know much about the gay element there. I'm going to be interviewing, hopefully, these two scientists suing the government about medical marijuana. But, as I said, I don't know if I can bring back any gay stuff, and Cece said, "But you're the gay element." Whatever we do, we're the gay element; we're the gay voice. I think that was a really good point that she made because I have to deal with how society views me as a lesbian, and as far as I see the world, I think this is important because hopefully something I say may help some kid. You just hope that what you are doing will benefit our whole community. I don't know if I'm role model material, but you want to put your best out there so other people can be inspired.

—Hilary Hamm, *Queer TV* Producer

Tom Kwai Lam's vision to create a queer program on cable access television began even before such a station existed in the Santa Cruz community. *Queer TV* represents the collective effort of a handful of volunteers committed to producing programs reflective of the diversity within Santa Cruz, and it airs every Saturday night at 11 P.M. on AT&T Cable Channel 27. Tom Kwai Lam, Cecilia (Cece) Pinheiro, Eileen Halvey, and Hilary Hamm are some of the volunteer producers associated with *Queer TV*—often giving freely of their money and time to cover issues and events within their community.[15]

Tom Kwai Lam: The idea for *Qtv* began in 1991. I had been doing fine art photography, which was sort of fantasy images of satyrs and fairies. Multiple exposure, that kind of stuff. I got to the point where I wanted to do storytelling. I'd take words and sounds and sequence them to still images, but it is also very expensive, or it was then, to reproduce and distribute color images. I thought, "Gee, you know, I could do a lot of this on tape." So that was the two things that came together for me personally. I also started working with a local performing arts group here. And I started working with them videotaping their productions, partly because I have a strong oral history bent and also just because I like doing it. At one of their productions, I met this other woman Jennifer, who was also there to tape, and she was doing a show on a community UHS station based in Salinas. I don't know if you know much about the geography here. Salinas is about an hour away. And you can't get the station in Santa Cruz because we're a little coastal town with the mountains between us, and basically everything else. Her show was called *Straight Talk,* and she had produced a couple of episodes. It was a very low-budget community station. And it was sort of a magazine format show. Half an hour. Different stuff. She had people approach her and they would be interested in working on the show—and I joined her. I had people who wanted to do stuff as well, but the problem was that the station was almost impossible to get in Santa Cruz. So I approached a local cable company—we both did—in August '91. We met with the general manager and had a very nice meeting. I gave him a tape. After that, things became very surreal, and it was clear that the tape had made him nervous, and we were supposed to meet with him, and he kept delaying, and finally we met again. He basically said, "I'm sorry, it is not going to work" without giving us any reason. We kept pressuring him, and the one thing that he finally said was that "it wasn't balanced." And we said, "Balanced? What do you mean balanced?" And he hesitated, and one of us finally said something to the effect that "You mean, we don't have a preacher saying we're sick," because the tape was very positive. And if you think back—when historically ACT UP and stuff was going on and, yeah, there he was looking at our literature where we mentioned ACT UP and Queer Nation—it was definitely out there in your face stuff. And this was eight years ago. It had some performance stuff, some interviews, a little bit of newsy stuff. We've mostly not done news. We've done short segments about various topics. And the guy did say our show would be perfect on public access. The only catch was that public access did not exist here, yet. But he gave me the name of the local governmental committee that was involved in working toward getting it to exist.

Cece Pinheiro: I worked in a school as a school community coordinator. I help kids get jobs and go to school. I created Safe Queer Space at South California High School when I worked there. I made sure that I put myself out there—and everywhere—as an advocate for queer youth. That's just what I'm interested in, being a lesbian mom. I've just been interested in youth. And now my kid is eighteen so I'll probably move on to something different or maybe not. I felt that my part—what I wanted to do—was queer youth: those were the voices that weren't being heard.

&

Tom Kwai Lam: Fast forward two years: once the organization actually gets formed, they have an initial board of directors of seven. And basically, they looked around at each other and said, "Gee, we're all white." And this was a community with a significant minority population in most places. So they put out a call for additional board members, and I think they had fifty to sixty applications to fill four seats, and I was one of them, and they chose me. This is a local public access organization, which was set up by the cable commission. The organization's name is Community Television of Santa Cruz County. I joined the board and was actually chair for a few years. I think I'm the only one from that period who still is on the board. So it led me to get involved in community broadcasting as a whole. Fast forward another couple of years, it was around May 1996, before our annual Gay Pride thing. I put out a call in our local community newsletter, looking for volunteers, got about twelve to fifteen volunteers, brought them and trained them. And our first shoot was the Gay Pride celebration. We did some stuff on the stage and did a lot of little interviews with people, and of that group, there are two to three people who are still actively involved—one of whom also put together *Queer Youth TV* (in 1997)—and that's Cece Pinheiro.

Cece Pinheiro: We did a lot of interviews and got a lot of rock and roll bands, Feron and the lesbian musicians who came to town. We did a few things in San Francisco, but mostly locally. I actually went there for a couple of my projects and there is an organization called the Gay Lesbian Straight Network, from which I started a local chapter in Santa Cruz. I have gone to two or three of their yearly meetings where they have people from everywhere working on the issues of gay youth in schools—safety of gay youth in schools. I interviewed a lot of people—political people who are working on the political end of that. I videotaped a lot of that—and also any of the other videos that pertain to that organization. They have given us permission so we've aired other people's work besides ourselves.

Tom Kwai Lam: *Queer Youth TV* was a summer program for queer teens. Cece Pinheiro got some foundation funding from the Community Foundation of Santa Cruz County and paid people. She was the key person behind that project. And Cece actually works for the school system and is also the union steward and is very involved on the various queer youth task forces. She is very connected. Anyway, going back three years, I brought in a bunch of people, trained them in editing.

Students Speak Out: Excerpt from *Queer Youth TV*[16]

> YOUTH 1: I've been out since I've been fifteen. . . . I haven't been gay bashed, but some of my friends have. I haven't had trouble talking to teachers. But I've been having problems with people calling me names.
>
> YOUTH 2: [The students at the school were] not the most gay-friendly. The teachers and the administration were . . . a lot of support . . . like when I came out in the second half of my eleventh grade to myself.

Cece Pinheiro: In one of our neighboring school systems, a young man who had a gay dad got harassed in school. The school has a "news in school" program—and there was an article about a camp for kids who had gay parents. His teacher asked him if he could talk about this in class. He said sure. They got into the article and talked about the camp. What it is like. He was very happy. And some of the parents found out, and one of the parents took their kid out of the classroom. And the newspaper found out about it. These parents who were prejudiced, to say the least, went to the newspaper and ran articles saying how bad the teacher was, how bad the school was, and how bad it was for doing this and they shouldn't be promoting this. They totally blew the whole thing out of proportion. They said it was about gay lifestyle, and I interviewed the kid.

?&

> MARCUS: We were reading the *Mercury News* like we do. . . . My teacher asked me to read an article about Camp Tolerance [a camp for the children of gay parents]. . . . I felt terrible. I thought it was my fault because I recommended the article. The father and his wife wrote a letter . . . and it had many lies in it—that it was a sex lesson and about how a child brought up [in class] how do two women have sex. . . . They call me these names like queer and faggot . . . it makes it a lot harder to learn.
>
> —an excerpt from *Queer Youth TV*[17]

?&

Cece Pinheiro: I think the important point is that this kid lost one of his schoolmates—his friend at school was pulled out of class because of who his friend's dad was. I think that it is important that we honor the kid's process. And if I could have, I would have talked with the kid who had been taken out of the class because we had no way of finding out if he was getting his emotional needs met. He was being a victim of his parents as well and their beliefs—in that he had to get out of his class and go to a different school, just like that. The show also included an interview with the youngest drag queen in Santa Cruz, who was actually attending an alternative high school. And we talked with him. We also talked with Chastity Bono and others. This is the program that we showed to the Community Foundation that gave us the grant afterwards. People were really excited—it was the best show that we did and it made a difference in the life of that kid who had to go through this whole thing. And he got to build a better relationship with his dad. His dad is also a musician, who wrote a song specifically about this, and we featured it on our show . . .

> Right here in our own hometown
> Lives a man who's filled with fear.
> He's thrown a fit in our 4th grade class
> 'Cause one kid's dad's a queer.
> I'm here.
>
> He's crucified the teacher,
> The raging insults swirl
> But just like Adolph Hitler
> The sucker'd love to rule the world.
>
> Refrain
> Homophobe, homophobe
> Go get a life, you homophobe.
> Repeat.
>
> You rant and rave at school boards
> And you queer bash in the press
> While your uptight wife's mouth
> Is tersely lost in your self-righteousness.
> The size of your agenda
> Is about three inches long.
> But unlike your attention span
> It's bigger than your dong.
>
> —Christian Left[18]

Cece Pinheiro: I wanted queer youth voices to be heard and we were in the middle of doing *Qtv.* It was my idea, and Tom wrote the grant. And really without his expertise, I don't know if we would have gotten it. We wrote it for a community foundation and we used it to train youth and do video production. There was a young man [Brendon Constans] who was doing video down the hall at Community Television. I'm down there once a week doing our thing, plugging away, editing stuff, looking at stuff, getting it together for *Queer TV*, an hour once a week. This kid asked me to help him on some of his shows.

Tom Kwai Lam: *Qtv* is the name of the original show. And *Queer Youth TV* was the program that Cece put together with Eileen Halvey. But basically they did it all. So they did a bunch of stuff with kids. *Pulp Non-Fiction* is a slightly different story. This kid who is quite amazing—I think he is about eighteen now—Brendon Constans was actually doing a weekly studio show on Community Television. And then he came out and started doing more stuff along that line, and decided to make it into a queer show.

Brendon Constans: I was doing work at the community TV station, volunteering on some shows. I had wanted my own show, so in January '97 I just started it with some friends from school and it basically was just a show for youth in general. It really didn't have much of a subject either. It was just random things and I just talked about whatever. I had friends from school come on and stuff, but then they stopped doing it, so I had to go and grab people from the street because they just weren't showing up. Altogether, it ran two years. A little before the original host stopped and decided not to do it anymore, we changed the name of the show to *Pulp Non-Fiction*. I needed a host, and it was right before a show so I walked into the editing booth here and asked if anyone would be willing to help me out. Cece said she would and she did a really good job.

Cece Pinheiro: Brendon was fifteen at the time—and basically anyone who wanted help, I'd be there. He ended up coming out as a young gay man. I was so privileged that he told me. Part of our network is just be who you are—be out, be gay, and see what happens. So I suggested to him that he change his show to a gay show—and he thought it was a great idea. As part of the queer youth grant, we could supply all his tapes. I could be an interviewer with him because he was the behind-the-scenes guy. So I was in front of the camera until I could recruit some queer youth to be in front of the camera. It is that kind of support like I'm not going to ask you to do anything I haven't done myself. I'm sitting here doing it, interviewing people, and I'll totally teach you by doing. And then we finally let the kids take over and that's been really successful. The show was called *Pulp Non-Fiction* and Brendon Constans was the young man who did the whole thing—and we just supported him. Brendon came up with the title. Before it turned into a gay youth show, it was already called *Pulp Non-Fiction*. It was just a youth show. He was doing youth interviews on the street. And I helped him actually do that. And when he came out, he changed the format to a show of interest to queer youth.

Brendon Constans: Cece said she would host the show until we found someone to replace her, so she kept doing it for awhile, and then she decided to switch the show's format toward gay youth—with the focus more on gay and lesbian youth. Cece suggested that we have a mature focus or a popular topic because the show was really lacking focus. That is one of the reasons we did it, and it just started being a much better show and then Cece got some younger people to do the show with her—I was the producer and the director. I decided the material and got the crew and basically ran the show. We did some shows that I think really might have helped people. One was on homophobia in the workplace, which was about a friend we knew who had just recently been fired from his job and he was fairly sure and had some good reasons to think it was because they found out he was gay. He was thinking about taking it to court and we were talking about that. He was telling what he knew, like why or why not it is a good idea to come out there. We talked about all this on that same show that we talked about the whole Christian right campaign. They had been putting ads in newspapers, trying to convert people, saying people can change and be straight. We did an episode on "homophobia in school." The Queer Club from Cabrillo College and the Rainbow Alliance from Santa Cruz High School, and all sorts of people and groups were willing to talk about these school issues, and what it is like being gay at different schools, and the things that some are doing to help with that.

Cece Pinheiro: In the community—one in ten—we will find a gay youth kid. And we also have straight kids. Everybody wants to do TV. There was this one boy who ended up working on Brendon's gay show. He has a great family, and he's open-minded. He was eight years old and Jewish, and he wanted to work on queer TV. He wanted to actually be part of queer youth television. And we educated our audience through him. We made a difference in that kid's life because we got involved on a show about the history of the Holocaust. You see, not only were the Jewish people persecuted but the gay people were too. We were all in this together so we combined his history with a piece of history that he never learned about—the pink triangle and the Nazis and the discrimination against gay people as well. That was a really good show and his dad agreed to do camera for us for awhile. His father helps with some other stuff at the community television station. That boy was the youngest person in our *Queer Youth TV* show.

Brendon Constans: I think it is good for gay youth in particular to see other gay youth, and they also relate to them. I dropped out of my high school sort of early so I didn't really have that kind of setting to get feedback from. I got my high school diploma though, and I did it so I could go to the local community college. I've learned to relate to people who are more in the community college age range than I do with people my own age. We stopped doing *Pulp Non-Fiction* after a hundred shows. I would like to eventually start a new show, but not necessarily gay youth–oriented, yet definitely with gay content in an entertainment format or sketch comedy thing.

Cece Pinheiro: I am always fighting for the rights of the disenfranchised groups, but that is not exclusive to the gay kids. I also work a lot with disabled students, the special education students—that's been the main priority of my work at school. I have taken this role at work and brought it to television. It is more than a gay thing for me in television. This year, I have worked for integrating the disabled community into community television as part of my role on the board of directors, and so my efforts encompass a larger spectrum than just the gay stuff. We have three gay people on our board, so we have a lot of people doing a lot of stuff in that regard, and we've been really successful. And as a board, we must also look at what's lacking. Brendon, for example, is not going to do just queer programming. He is also going to help with producing disabled issues. His work as an editor sort of overlaps everywhere. And that's been the project on this year's board agenda—to get the disabled kids down here and taking classes and getting experience. My plan is do more. I want to do more networking with the Gay, Lesbian and Straight Education Network (GLSEN) because they have a lot of resources and videos that need to get out to the public and I also do some work with a program called Work with Pride, which is the gay union organization in Washington, D.C. And I sent them a show, one of my most recent endeavors, on union and gay issues so maybe that's my next project. The video was actually part of one of Brendon's *Pulp Non-Fiction* shows that we did on homophobia in the workplace.

Tom Kwai Lam: In the future, we are going to chronicle less events and create more of them in the studio. This sort of coincides with the fact that the public access organization of community television just recently opened a big studio space which we haven't had before. Now we have a nice place to do events.

Hilary Hamm: The new studio has really opened up a lot of opportunities for the community. It has a really great light grid and it really has good sound now. It has a fairly up-to-date control room allowing us to now do some live or live to tape shows. So it seems that the studio that we used before at our station was just a little room, like an office. And now that we're in a big studio, you can actually do a lot in terms of production. We are at the next step—we are beyond [the movie] *Wayne's World* now, definitely, and just the availability of the equipment is amazing. The prices have gone down quite a bit, so it is definitely making it a lot more affordable for the "prosumers." Personally, I really enjoyed learning digital editing, the nonlinear editing. We've had a Media 100 [non-linear video editor] in the station for a few years. It's funny, I'm one of the only people that uses it because it is kind of complex. The technology is a couple of steps behind what's out there now, but they've put enough money into the machine so that it works fairly well.

Tom Kwai Lam: We thought about doing some typically focused community forums that we could do in the studio—and we'd be very clear that these forums would be recorded and played back later, possibly done in a panel format and with a lot of audience participation. We've also made jokes about trying to find a local Geraldo in our community. Things that we talked about doing include a take-off of a dating game and a show called *The Ex Files,* which would be a show about people's exes. In a small town, there's a lot of exes who intersect and lots of stories. It could be interesting to have these people talk and figure out who really is someone's ex and who isn't because it might be one of them or all of them or maybe none of them. Until now, almost all our *Qtv* shows were field produced. We did almost no studio stuff. I help with multicamera field shoots on *Qtv.* I've been around a little bit, but I basically dropped out from day-to-day participation in the show for a variety of reasons, mostly just personal. Also, it had been my intention to set *Qtv* up as an umbrella and an incubator. And that's what we did. We also do some multicamera remote shoots. For the past couple of years, we've taped a "Gay Evening" in May, which is this big community-fund raiser—a musical variety show that happens in the civic auditorium to an audience of 1,000 to 2,000 people. There's probably a hundred performers on the stage, so it is this huge thing. And they pay us to videotape them. We partly do it because we love to do it, we partly do it as a little fund-raiser to help make money to buy tape for ourselves, and we partly do it because it is great programming.

Hilary Hamm: Sometimes we try to videotape local dance and music cabaret kind of stuff. The performers always like it when we're there because they like to be able to see their dancing or whatever. So the community likes that we're here. I just wish we had more feedback on how many people actually watch it. But people have come up to us, and said like "Yeah, I saw the show. It was great."

Tom Kwai Lam: Fairly typical, in terms of public access, is that sometimes there is a lot of audience reaction, but often there is none. And I've talked with people who do queer radio shows—there's about three of them in town here, and they say sometimes you don't know if anyone is listening. Other times, you bump into people on the street, and they say, "Oh, I heard this and I really loved it." We always get reaction from those people we featured on our shows and from their friends. You literally sometimes wonder whether anyone is listening and at other times you meet people who say, "I really liked that; it changed my life." I also was vice president-cochair of our local lesbian, gay, bisexual, transgender community center for a couple of years. We did a newsletter, and sometimes you literally didn't know whether anyone was reading them at all; other times you'd get more response—usually I'd get a general appreciative response and I think that is true for Qtv. But actually, it does bring up creative things we've done that have received the most response. For awhile, we did this little miniseries in two- to five-minute pieces called "Barbie Goes Butch," using sort of an animated thing with Barbie dolls. Barbie comes out and Ken comes out. He says, "Barbie, does it match?" Then, there's dolls having sex. Pretty funny and very short pieces. And that was one of the things that got the strongest reaction. We also did a series called "Helen," which was basically a take-off of *Ellen*—only she was out, and we did this before she came out. And I think Eileen Halvey actually went to L.A. and gave Ellen a copy of that tape. And I don't remember what Ellen's reaction was. But those were the two things that probably, in some ways, got the strongest reaction—when people would ask, "What's going to happen next?" or say, "That makes me want to tune back in again. I can't wait to see what happens next."

Cece Pinheiro: Tom wants to do an elder's project, and we have done some of that. We did a couple of interviews and we've put on an elders show that was done with footage from what we shot in the past. And that's one of his projects. And I will probably now support him in doing that—do whatever, run some camera, actively coordinate the people.

Tom Kwai Lam: I'm into oral history. And I'd like to do some discussions with some people of different ages and do some oral history. But instead of using a peer model, we might try to find a couple of people from the '50s— two or three—and have them sit around and talk. The problem is that everyone has been doing Qtv for awhile. There are basically two to three core people. And some of them are getting a little burned out, and we are trying to figure out, "What do we really want to be doing?" Because you may have guessed, we didn't really have a strong direction for the show. For awhile, we were literally trying to cam any queer event that happened, since we would be there shooting anyway. So we're sort of looking around trying to see more of where we are trying to go.

Pursuit of Queer Life, Liberty, and PBS

> In the Life *is on PBS. I know Jon Scagliotti down in New York City has been doing a lot of entertainment type material and the quality of his program is fairly good. When you think about it,* In the Life *is actually on PBS. They finally came around, about six or seven years ago, and put on a gay show. In terms of cable, I think it's all over the place. I know HBO has had some specials—"The Funny Gay Males" and "Suzanne Westenhoefer." They've had a lot of gay comics on and entertainment type programs. HBO and others have gone places prior to anyone else, specifically broadcast.*

> —Mary Kennedy, independent producer

Some Public Broadcasting System (PBS) stations and cable networks like Home Box Office (HBO) and Showtime have seen opportunity where the traditional three networks have feared controversy. Suzanne Westenhoefer is the first lesbian to have her own HBO Comedy Special, and her show was nominated for the Annual Cable Awards (ACE). She has also appeared on HBO's *Comic Relief VII*.

Chuck Hoy: It must be mentioned that both the noncommercial broadcast network PBS and cable channels have broken barriers in their portrayals of gays and lesbians that commercial networks have yet to accomplish. Of particular note are *In The Life* and *Tales of the City* on PBS, *More Tales of the City* on Showtime, and even the dramatic series *Oz* on HBO.

In The Life was created by John Scagliotti and further developed by a team of dedicated volunteer producers who pursued his dream of a nationally distributed PBS gay series. The show now airs on more than 120 stations in the United States, and it is requested by schools and libraries throughout the nation. *In the Life* is the only ongoing PBS television series dedicated to those living the queer life.[19]

Nancy Kirton: There is comparatively very little radio programming and a lot of TV programming that's lesbian- and gay-centered. I wonder how much of it reflects the incredible number of lesbian and gay people who are involved in mainstream TV. Certainly one show that I think has perhaps reached a level that's notable is *In the Life*, created by John Scagliotti. And interestingly, he was the program director at WBAI many years ago. Then he decided to do cable. And he really worked himself into creating a very professional show.

John Scagliotti: Everybody thought I was crazy when we started *In the Life* in my kitchen. Finally I raised enough money to get a pilot going and we actually started doing our series. It was touch and go all the time in the beginning—really hard work, not enough money, but really a creative staff of people who wouldn't give up and it kept going and now it is much better financed and greater. I'm no longer with it, except in the creative and sometimes as an adviser to the board every once in awhile. It went from six or seven stations each program to 125 and that worked out well. When I left, it was around a hundred stations, so in five years we really built it up.

Charles Ignacio: I had been working in television at the PBS station in New York, WNET, and was very interested in getting involved in the gay community, doing something that would combine my interests in television production and doing something for the community. Then I read, in one of those magazines that no longer exist here in New York, a small article saying that John Scagliotti was planning to do a series for public television on gay issues and culture. So I somehow tracked him down in New York and started meeting with him and a few other volunteers on a regular basis to do fund-raising. And one of the first events that we worked on was a benefit auction at Limelight to raise money to do the pilot. I know at the same time John was busy trying to establish a membership database for people who wanted to contribute money to the concept. And when I decided to leave WNET 13, I called John up and said I was available and free and I was willing to do anything from being an assistant or a gopher or whatever, and John asked if I wanted to produce the pilot. So I actually coproduced the pilot with another person. Her name is Pamela Jennings, but that was the only episode that she had worked on. So after that it was just myself who ended up producing the episodes.

John Catania: I met someone involved with the project. I had never heard of *In the Life* and I could not believe there was a gay TV show that was on public television, and I found the project so interesting that I just started to volunteer my time. I got involved about one year after it started—the summer of 1993. I came to *In the Life* like many people come to the program, in that it needs an enormous amount of help. At the time, it needed a lot of volunteer help because in the beginning there was much less funds available. I just began volunteering on the production side, being a production assistant. I was actually stage manager for a number of the studio shoots. My whole background is actually in theater. I was an actor and mostly a theater director for about a decade so the transition into television as a producer was pretty easy. The theater is really all about storytelling. You know, you're telling a story in about two or three hours and with television I was just telling a story now in five or four, six or seven minutes, because we are a television news magazine. I would say by the end of that first year, which would have been the spring of '94, I actually had my first producing assignment for *In the Life*. By the second year I was actually coproducer of the series. I have since become the director of communications, in charge of all contacts with the press and media, but I continue to produce for every show, as a contributing producer.

Charles Ignacio: *In the Life* was born out of John Scagliotti's experience on radio. I talked to John Catania about this a lot and I tell our producers this too, that for storytelling on television, really the foundation is the voice, and you almost have to tell a story to the audio and what we've been calling a radio cut, and then the pictures will follow the visuals. People listen to television more than they actually watch it 'cause they are busy in their living room, so if you can catch their attention by what is said, the visuals are just that other icing on the cake, at least from my point of view. That's the kind of television that I respond to when I'm watching. What are people saying? What's the content? I'm not really into the flashing visuals, and maybe that's why *In the Life* may not be considered really hip with certain audiences in that we're into the story.

John Scagliotti: In the early days of organizing it, we developed this membership thing and the membership was not only to raise money, which it did—people would send in aid to support the program, but membership was more important in places where they couldn't get the program. We started with six or seven stations in New York and L.A. and maybe Seattle. But when we started, most stations in the country wouldn't do it. A lady called me from Maryland and said, "I don't know what's going on, but I just got 500 postcards here saying we should air this series. We're giving up, send us the programs—we can't keep it off." For those kinds of things, the membership really helped. Part of the public television experience has been creating programming, but a political system and organizational system to change how program directors will perceive the programs is just as important. That was the whole idea behind *In the Life* in its early days when there were one or two programs on public television.

Charles Ignacio: I remember when there were writers who came to visit our office. They likened it to a very, very busy college newspaper office, and that was really what it felt like. A lot of different people walked through the doors who were very excited and wanted to contribute or volunteer in any way they could from helping to write the script to mailing envelopes or putting stamps on newsletters. It was a very exciting time back in '92 and '93 and a lot of things happened in the gay world then. I believe *Out* magazine was being launched and a lot of new media things were happening. People were starting to come out publicly like Melissa Etheridge and Elton John, and so there was a lot of excitement at that time. It was a bit chaotic. None of us were full-time staff people. We were all really volunteers and freelancers, so it was rather touch and go in terms of working and a lot of us had other jobs too. So it was a very different animal back then.

John Scagliotti: When we were trying to get stations to broadcast *In the Life,* every phone call had to go through to a program director. We had a full-time staff person and we would go to every station and say, "Do you want to take it?—it's free on the satellite." They would say "No," except for the six or seven back then or maybe ten stations a year. We just kept talking to TV stations as well as to our members.

Joe Liberatore: I did an interview a year and a half ago on *Gay Radio* or *Rainbow Radio* here in Washington and somebody asked me about *In the Life.* I said what they do is incredible but it's a different ballpark, and they're on PBS stations across the nation. We're on cable access and a few PBS stations. I don't look at them as competing. We do different stories. We have completely different approaches. They're very documentary style, sort of long format story, and our show is very fast—beginning to end. We sort of hook you in, sort of like CNN does, and pull you in with factoids and tease you with something else and keep it moving all the time.

Charles Ignacio: If we were on commercial television from the very start, *In the Life* would not be around right now. There is no way that, given the skips and starts and the format changes that we've had in the first three years, we'd still be on because commercial television is so competitive, if you don't find your rating or your audience at first go-round, you're canceled. So we've had the luxury of kind of experimenting or finding our path into what we are now, which I don't think a commercial network would allow any series to do.

John Catania: I think that what is really important to *In the Life* is right now we are a bimonthly series, and we are a not-for-profit member-supported organization. We receive no money from PBS or the Corporation for Public Broadcasting. We are not a PBS program. We are an independently pro-duced series that then gives rights to public television stations, and we have relationships with like 125 public TV stations. *In the Life* is given to these stations free of charge, so that there is really no reason for them not to air it except for their own concerns about their viewers. *In the Life* is not shown in twenty states because of those concerns. It is still a very controversial series, simply because it talks about gay life and gay issues in America. So what we need is more programming. There is a plan right now, a year from fall 1999, to go monthly, which would double our programming. We've also talked to big gay Web sites and things like that because it is important now to get some of our archival material on the Internet so that people around the world can see it. *In the Life* is now in its eighth year. It is a very long-running public television series. It has a very good reputation by TV critics across the country, as well as public TV, so what is important now is that we keep getting more and more images on the airwaves because we have only a fraction of the amount of representation that we need about gay people on the air, and *In the Life* is the only really serious program in that regard.

Charles Ignacio: Now we are an established not-for-profit organization. At the time that we were working towards getting that status, we were a sponsor project for a larger media organization here in New York. We were also trying to establish a board of directors at that time. We made a lot of wonderful shows, we had some great successes, and we made many mistakes. It was a lot of hit-or-miss. And it was exciting and frustrating and crazy and all those things that any start-up company goes through, I'm sure. There were many steps as part of that process. I don't think it was one thing. One event that a lot of us who were on staff thought, "Just now, this is the product that we really want to work on and want to do" is when we planned for the "Stonewall 25" episode, and we planned it as a sort of in-the-field news magazine show, where we did different segments on different subjects in the field and we had correspondents out in the field. Before that we had already switched from a variety show format to six correspondents in a studio environment, and I don't think that really worked well with our audiences or was what we wanted to do, and I think going outside really liberated us. And at that time, we also expanded our thirty-minute program into an hour-long format. So that really was the beginning of the way *In the Life* is now, in terms of the structure and the format of the show. I think that it came into fruition a year or two later. We put together a really solid board of directors who had worked on other boards of gay not-for-profits or who had come from the television industry. With that kind of structure in place, that really liberated us and created a momentum to move forward to look at the long view. And there's so many stories. One story that comes to mind, I guess, because it just won recognition from the American Legion Auxiliary, was a story we did a couple of years ago on two men who were named Foster Parents of the Year for the whole state of Iowa, and these two men had raised fifteen boys. They were nominated by one of their foster kids. So we flew a producer to Iowa to meet with them and interview them and tell their story. It was a very powerful, heartwarming one where the story is really told by their kids. There's a lot of love in that family. We did a story last year on the gay deaf community, where we visited with one gay male couple, one who has hearing challenges and one who was born deaf, and a lesbian couple—both who were deaf—who were raising a deaf daughter. I think she was only three years old. But I really like stories like that because they kind of intersect being gay or lesbian with a different aspect about life, like overcoming some other obstacle in your life. That kind of thing contributes to American culture.

John Catania: I have produced personally several dozen pieces, but one that stands out is the interview with George C. Wolf and all about his play about gay Asian men, and that piece actually won an award from the National Lesbian and Gay Journalists' Association. I felt very strongly about that piece. Another piece I produced was on Lady Chablis from *Midnight in the Garden of Good and Evil.* I went down to Savannah and spent a weekend with her and followed her around. That was also a very fun segment to work on. One of the segments I'm probably most proud of is when I went to Hong Kong to take a look—and what I believe was the first look on American television—at the gay community in Hong Kong and China. I spent a week interviewing gay people there on their very new gay rights movement and gay visibility in Hong Kong. I also gained footage of gay life in Beijing, so I folded all of that together into a story about Hong Kong and China and that was really quite an ambitious story, but it was one I enjoyed very much. I've also done several stories back in my home state of Wisconsin. I did a nice story on two gay pig farmers, and that folded right into the mission of *In the Life,* which is to show gay people in urban settings and rural settings and all across the country.

Charles Ignacio: John Scagliotti came from the world of public radio and public television and really believed strongly in the mission of public television and PBS and how it is supposed to really serve voices that aren't normally heard on commercial networks. I don't really think the kind of show that we do would work commercially because we cover so many different aspects of the gay community that aren't necessarily things that would get high ratings. We're very conscious of the diversity within the gay and lesbian community and we go out of our way to find those stories. What has been wonderful about working on public television is that we have not had to worry about the commercial potential or how much advertising revenue we were raising or what the rating is. We're just free to go and tell people's stories and not worry about that sort of thing, but obviously we're interested in getting more and more public television stations around the country and getting better airtime and getting feedback from those program directors who have the decision-making power to put us on or not.

John Catania: Stations know that putting *In the Life* on is a risky decision if they are in the deep south or in the mountain west. And I would say that other TV shows you may have heard of, like *Tales of the City*, are in some ways easier for a station because they come and then they are gone. But with *In the Life*, a station is saying we're making a commitment to air gay programming year round—and even if this show has offended you, there is another one coming in a month or two, so it makes it problematic at times, but we've had extreme progress. We started on six stations and now we're on about 125 stations. We're reaching about 80 percent of the U.S. population through broadcasts in major metropolitan areas, and we reach almost all of the Canadian population. They watch us across the border because they get public television there. Public station WNET, Channel 13, in New York City is our presenting station. And there is no financial relationship, but they have put their stamp of approval, their moniker, whatever, on the *In the Life* series. They are the largest public television station. They are presenting it to the family of public television stations across the country. Those stations then know that WNET stands behind this series. The other important entity is—and this is important for viewers to understand, or gay viewers when they want to know who to support—a distribution company called American Public Television. They distribute *In the Life* and they do not charge us any fees because of our mission with minority populations. So without American Public Television, without WNET Channel 13, *In the Life* would have a hard time getting on public television in America. It is a very complicated system, but it is very important that the gay community understands it because public television is where the best gay programming is happening, with regards to *In the Life* and with a lot of documentary work. It is where gay and lesbian communities should really be looking first for programming about their lives—rather than to characters on sitcoms and dramas and prime-time network programming. When it comes to really good, intelligent, and honest issues-oriented programming, it is already happening on public television.

Charles Ignacio: We've done so many wonderful entertainment-based stories where we've spoken to people like Tony Kushner when he was doing *Angels in America* and we got into his head on how he created that work;

we've spent the whole day down in Savannah with the Lady Chablis and really saw what it was like to be an entertainer who lives her life as a woman but was born a man; and there's so many stories from people who live in the rural areas to the interviews of celebrities like Patrick Stewart when he was in *Geoffrey.*

John Catania: One of my more interesting credits might be that I was a drama director at a Catholic high school in a very conservative city in Wisconsin, and they knew I was gay. But there was no problem with that. It is very interesting what happens below the rhetoric: that is why I felt *In the Life* was so important. I come from a small town of 30,000 people in Wisconsin, and what happens below the politicizing of the movement and the politicizing of the debates on both sides is people are for the most part getting along. There are rather horrific situations and there is still a lot of prejudice and uncomfortableness about gay people, yet it is amazing when you get down to people just working together and being neighbors because, for the most part, people are really getting along and that needs to filter through. This is not a movement or debate that needs to filter from the top down. This is not a trickle-down theory. To me, the gay movement is about a trickle-up process, which is people finding out that they have gay relatives, they have gay friends, that they have gay coworkers, and getting that message filtered up to the hierarchy in politics or the church or the school systems so that the people with power are not afraid to make the right decisions. That is what *In the Life* is about—educating people to what it is to be gay in this country, taking away the sensationalism. In my home state of Wisconsin, *In the Life* was attacked by a state senator, and I debated him on a very popular radio show there, and the station stood behind *In the Life.* He had called for the show to be blacked out because of my story about the Wisconsin gay pig farmers who happened to be in his district, and he was a little bit offended that this image of Wisconsin was going out to the nation. So he called for the show to be blacked out. I really think he was just looking for political points and he stumbled onto something because he didn't know what our show was about, and the newspapers made him look very stupid. But we get those things all the time. But generally there has been a slow steady rise in the stations that carry us, and public television has come to accept *In the Life* as a very important series.

Stonewall, the Benchmark

John Scagliotti's broadcast career began in the early '70s, and he soon became one of the first producers to create gay programming for national distribution across the Public Broadcasting Service. In 1973, Scagliotti and his partner, Andrew

Kopkind, debuted *The Lavender Hour* on Boston's rock station WBCN. It was one of the first—if not the first—gay and lesbian radio programs on commercial radio. Experienced as a radio news and documentary producer, Scagliotti debuted his first PBS documentary in 1986: "Before Stonewall." In the years that followed, he created the PBS series *In the Life*, became the program director for WBAI in New York (and the driving force behind a number of LGBT shows that aired on the station), and most recently finished the production of "After Stonewall"—a look at the twentieth century after 1969. As part of the media, he has witnessed many changes in attitudes toward the acceptance of queer programming over the years— that is, before and after the production of his Stonewall documentaries, both of which document and preserve the most significant events within the LGBT community in its quest for civil rights.

John Scagliotti: My partner, Andy Kopkind, and I met in 1971 and after hanging out in Europe for awhile we came back and joined a radio collective called Unicorn News, which was a gay collective basically. There was a straight woman in it, but she kind of identified with everything going on. Well, it was pretty gay. Our job (as far as the collective) was to make radio news stories that we would send to the newly emerging sort of progressive FM radio stations in and around Washington, D.C. These reports had covered aspects of what was going in Congress, things going on that affected the war, and the counterculture in Washington. The reports were designed with music and sound effects and things like that—and that was the early concept of what National Public Radio and other people would use many years later.

From there I moved with Andy to become news director in Boston at a radio station. We were there for about a year and that's where we started *The Lavender Hour* in 1973. Anyone on Sunday night who worked at the station aired what was called "potluck," one hour of anything they wanted to do. I did one called the "Lavender Hour" and we continued doing them. It was the first time a gay radio show that was mostly cultural—as in poetry and things like that—aired on commercial radio. The station at that time was becoming a pretty big rock-'n'-roll station and had a very large listenership so a lot of people heard this program. I stayed doing news at the station and became news director, staying for about ten years. I also did photography for the *Gay Community News*. I did a lot of gay coverage on our regular news too by bringing people like Neil Miller on the program. We did some programs with him, just some regular coverage of the Gay Pride marches. Things like that started being incorporated into our regular news too.

We did documentaries too and every once in awhile a documentary would report on something in the gay community, so we were very conscious of incorporating gay and lesbian issues within our regular coverage. Andy, being a journalist, was also doing it within his editorials on our news. He wrote for local newspapers in Boston as well as nationally and he would incorporate the gay and lesbian experience in those pieces. I then decided I would like to get into films after about ten years at the station. So we moved to New York, and I went to NYU and started doing films, documentaries. One of the first documentaries I did of course was "Before Stonewall."

My partner, Andy, died in '94 and that was one of the reasons why I left. I wanted to take some time off to come back to my farm here in Vermont and I opened up my production office a couple of years later and started "After Stonewall." I knew in order to get funding aid for "After Stonewall" from the Corporation for Public Broadcasting, which we did, we had to go through PBS (there are only a few programs they're going to say yes to and I knew they felt comfortable with "Before Stonewall" because it had done well and stations liked it). There was not only a need for the program, but PBS and CPB and the powers to be would at least look at it as a proposal and take it seriously, which they did, and we were able to get the financing and support needed to do a very large documentary. With technology much faster this time around, the whole project was done in two and a half years.

"After Stonewall" was on PBS nationally and has been seen by about 3 million people. When I started in the '80s, public television was the only world that you could sort of speak into, and now you can get into other places. I knew at the end of the century that people would want to see something that captured part of this momentum. The whole point was to build a documentary based on the end of the millennium so that's what "After Stonewall" did—from after '69. "Before Stonewall" and "After Stonewall" have probably been seen by more people than any other gay and lesbian documentary in the world. They have international distribution, too. "Before Stonewall" is probably the number one seen documentary. "After Stonewall" in a couple of years will also be in that category. They're both history films. "Before Stonewall" was produced at a much more difficult time, beginning in 1983. It was the height of the AIDS crisis so it was very difficult to get people to concentrate, to give money, and support it because of the time. It went on to become a very important film seen in 1986, still during the height of AIDS crisis. Over the years at PBS, it still continues to have renewals and had another national air date in 1994.

So millions of people have seen this film, and each date comes with five repeats for each station so it's shown by public television stations again and again and again, and probably "Before Stonewall" has been shown on major public television eight or nine times. The first national air date for "After Stonewall" was June 23rd [1999] and it got very good ratings across the country. It was shown in New York, San Francisco, Los Angeles, and the whole evening was dedicated to "Before and After Stonewall." Some people actually pledged around it. For example, one Denver station reported that evening was the best of their nine pledge nights. Mitchell Anderson of *Party of Five* was the pledge person. KCET in Los Angeles did the best night they had ever done and raised $80,000 during "Before and After Stonewall." Public television itself is beginning to see these as not only good programming but ways to bring in the gay community.

If you put down how many hours were dedicated to gay and lesbian programming, it was outrageously small and still is for PBS. A lot of local stations like WNET in New York bring in other programs—they buy them, rent them, or have access to them, and so for Gay Pride Month now you watch Channel 13 in New York. You'd think on PBS that they would really have a lot of gay programming, but they don't. That month they put on one "After Stonewall" and that was it in 1999. Last year, they put on "Out in the Past"— just one program. So that's PBS, a system of which 300 stations. PBS itself does very little gay and lesbian programming nationally—so a lot of what we've done isn't just programming. We've had to go to PBS meetings and talk to program directors.

South Dakota, North Dakota, Chicago, Cincinnati, St. Louis—all these places aired "After Stonewall." Alabama put it on at one o'clock in the morning, but they put it on. Many that wouldn't put on "Before Stonewall" many years ago put both on beginning at one in the morning. That was a big step for Alabama, a big step for a lot of these southern stations. We finally made it to Orlando, after years and years of never being able to be on in Orlando, and "Before Stonewall" aired in Orlando at eleven o'clock instead of 9 P.M., which was the national airdate time. So we opened up a lot of stations to change. "After Stonewall" finally aired on a New Hampshire station. It had been on in Vermont, Maine, and Boston, but it wasn't on in New Hampshire. So while I was at a state legislation party, I said to one of the state legislators, "Too bad you couldn't see 'After Stonewall' in New Hampshire." You know he's gay and also now so are six state legislators in New Hampshire. So what do they do? They write a letter to the program director, cc: to the governor, to all these people about how awful it is that New Hampshire Public Television decided not to put it on. An Atlanta station manager of Georgia Public Television said, "No, we're not going to air 'After Stonewall' in Atlanta." It was outrageous but luckily the *Atlanta Constitution* thought it was a big enough story to put in their newspaper and they did a piece on it. They published the story in their style section on how the station had censored "After Stonewall." Three days later, the station manager was fired, of course for a lot other things besides this, but this was the straw that broke the camel's back and "After Stonewall" finally aired. A lot of what we've done is not only create programming that people can watch—and this major change has taken place in the media—but it is the way that programs should be seen that is equally important and so that was a really big step.

Because of the programming time, it was hard to organize a gay and lesbian program for national television on PBS when they have only aired five within their whole life out of twenty years, which is .0000001 percent of prime time programming about gays and lesbians. On public television, we're talking about a very small percentage and that is what people don't realize. You'll see a lot of big stories about it and every once in a while you see "Tongues Untied"[20] and you think they must show gay stuff all the time on public television. The percentage is increasing and that's very exciting but we're not talking about a huge amount of programming here.

Get Your Vision Out There

Cece Pinheiro: If I had a vision for the distant future, ten years from now, I would hope to do more work like Michael Moore is doing—which is saving lives with television. He did a segment called the "Sodom Mobile" on his show *The Awful Truth* on the Bravo Network. I wrote to him and he gave me permission to put it on our Qtv. And that's one of my latest favorites. And he's like, "Keep up the good work." He and a bunch of gay men went to every state in the United States that had sodomy laws and broke every law. That was sort of the gist of it, and they confronted Reverend [Fred] Phelps and the other known Christian rights people who are very opposed to gay rights. He confronted them, by going to every state and shooting video, and put something together that's on the Bravo Channel—that is something to be admired.

Tom Kwai Lam: We are thinking of trying to do more program exchange. I know there's people all over the country doing stuff. This takes me to my next tangent. In October '91, we put together this one-day session at the Creating Change West Conference in L.A. for gay and lesbian media people. And we had about thirty people there, and we talked about what people's problems were, what they want to do, about doing some organized program exchange, setting up an informal network, and things like that. Anyway, there was a lot of stuff that came out of that and most of it didn't go anywhere, for a variety of reasons, I think. There was a lot of interest. One of the common threads that connect us to what I was talking about is that the people said they could get a one-time audience for things, but the real trick was to get people to want to tune in every week. And the soap opera type idea was one of the techniques some people had used with some success, and that was one of the things we all talked about—maybe doing something through syndication. That was part of the discussion. We talked about doing a West Coast satellite network for sharing programming. There were some good proposals. Again, nothing directly came out of our discussions. And that was '91.

Mary Kennedy: I think the ball has been started and there's no going back. When Clinton came into office, that's when things opened up for television and were no longer taboo. With AIDS impacting in a way that there was no more being closeted, people were forced out—celebrities like Rock Hudson and other high-profile people, but also on just a personal level. Many people have been forced out of the closet, especially because they've contracted AIDS. As a result, more people knew somebody with AIDS. What happened from there was people became more visible. A lot of people rallied under the AIDS banner, so to speak, and obviously impacted the dialogue and forced people to become more active than previously. I think the times have changed immensely, and it's not just with TV, but every aspect of people's life.

Charles Ignacio: I think what we do is very unique at *In the Life,* not only in terms of the program that we put out but in the way that it is produced and the way the organization is formed. I don't know of any not-for-profit lesbian or gay organization that produces a product on a regular basis which has been viewed by a lot of people and is relatively inexpensive. We've been able to do it on a very shoestring budget, and I don't know of any other not-for-profit television producing programs for public television, whether it is the Children's Television Workshop or other companies associated with other PBS stations, that deal with lesbian/gay subject matter, so we're an interesting hybrid in the fact that we've done this for eight years now with a very tiny staff. I think it never ceases to amaze me. I really take my hat off to the rest of the staff here as well as to our volunteer board of directors, who work very hard to keep us on the air.

Hilary Hamm: Just get your vision out there—and find out if your community has a public access station. They are always willing to train you. That's what they are there for—they are there for us.

Chapter Five

The Rainbow's Gold

Prophets of Profit in Queer Broadcasting

Radio is consolidating, imploding, with most stations in the hands of a few big players. Licenses have traded hands at stratospheric prices, meaning that cash flow and profit returns on stations are exorbitant. As any of the broadcasters in this book can tell you, gay broadcasting is not a highly profitable format. A quick analysis of gay-owned and gay-targeted business tells you why. In Chicago, for instance, almost all the gay businesses transact under $10 million per year. Most are under $5 million per year. We are still an emerging economy of small businesses. Marketing to this audience is a delight and a challenge. The people who most quickly respond and become devoted listeners are often isolated. Fifty percent of our listeners are suburban. To reach them requires aggressive public relations and advertising through mainstream, expensive venues.

—Alan Amberg, president of LesBiGay Radio

After the peak of the AIDS crisis in the late '80s, many companies began to reconsider the marketing power of the gay consumers. Some are quick to assign a value to the queer market—anywhere from $35 billion to $450 billion. Alamo, Johnson & Johnson, Subaru, and United Airlines were some of the sponsors to jump on the queer bandwagon.[1] Only recently, the broadcasting industry has joined in the fanfare. The reaction from the American public, once mixed, has become increasingly supportive of these efforts.

In the early to mid-1990s, antigay legislation spurred a number of pro and con commercials in Ohio, Colorado, Idaho, and Maine.[2] Then, in 1995, KSFO's initial decision not to air AIDS public service announcements targeted toward the gay community caused a media frenzy and public outrage. Two years later, the Southern Baptists' boycott of Walt Disney Company because of its gay-friendly policies made the evening news, and ultimately the protest lacked strong public support. In late 1998, all the major network affiliates in Orlando refused to air an antigay media blitz, created by the Center for Reclaiming America and the Coral Ridge Ministries,[3] that claimed gays and lesbians could be helped through prayer and willpower.[4] The campaign theme was "It's not about hate. It's about hope." In one commercial, several couples and their children are presented on the screen, and then one partner in each couple is identified as formerly gay. In another commercial, a mother says, "My son found out the truth—he could walk away from homosexuality. But he found out too late. He has AIDS."[5]

In response to antigay messages inspired by conservative religious leaders, the Cathedral of Hope, the largest gay and lesbian church in America, produced a thirty-minute infomercial called "Holy Homosexual." It begins with a montage of antigay demonstrations and speeches by televangelists, but most of the commercial speaks to the inclusive nature of the church, with images of its members, gay and straight, worshiping and singing together. A number of cable companies refused to air the infomercial. The church filed suit against WGN-TV for rejecting to air its infomercial campaign.[6]

Fewer and fewer advertisers are willing to alienate gay and lesbian audiences and supporters. For instance, Procter & Gamble withdrew its sponsorship of Dr. Laura Schlessinger's TV show before it even made its national debut. In March 2000, A Coalition Against Hate, which represented the collective efforts of several gay and lesbian organizations and their supporters, launched StopDrLaura.com on the Internet in an effort to keep Schlessinger's TV show off the air. To no avail, the coalition pursued Schlessinger for some sort of dialogue and posted transcripts of her show on its Web site[7] for public reaction.

In May 2000, another campaign was launched against Schlessinger. Gay & Lesbian Alliance Against Defamation (GLAAD), the National Organization for Women, the National Mental Health Association, the National Conference for Community & Justice, and People for the American Way conducted a $2 million print campaign against the antigay comments made on her radio show.[8] The campaign was designed to pull away other sponsors of her show:

> Laura Schlessinger has angry and hurtful things to say about all kinds of Americans. Many advertisers don't realize how alienating her program has become. Consumers judge brands by the company they keep. Aren't there better ways to reach women 18–49, or anyone else? ... Dr. Laura, we don't buy it.[9]

Equity in Electronic Ads

To provide gender equity in its long-running team of anthropomorphic candies, M&M/Mars added its first and only female candy character about three years ago—the star of its current lesbian-theme commercial. In it, the green female M&M is walking down a sidewalk to many catcalls from men. With a furled brow she harumphs,"Men!"Then a pudgy woman turns to say "I'd like to get my hands on some of that." The M&M rolls her eyes and says with equal contempt, "Women!" Her closing contemptuous line is, "Go buy a bag!" The commercial ran in the United States and Canada for a few weeks in January and return[ed] to air March 20 through June 5 [2000].[10]

In the past, those companies proactive in their desire to reach gay and lesbian audiences had no alternative but to advertise in the print media—first gay and then straight newspapers and magazines. For many years, the IBM Corporation placed its diversity recruitment ads in gay print media. In 1996, R.J. Reynolds Tobacco Company tested an alternative Kamel brand of cigarettes in gay magazines, and Bristol-Myers targeted gays with its Clairol Men's Choice hair coloring product with an ad in *Out* magazine. Other companies that have advertised in the gay print media have included Sprint, Alamo Rent A Car, Hartford Financial Services Group, and Seagram's Tropicana orange juice.[11]

Conversely, the broadcast industry's inability to accurately estimate how many gays and lesbians actually tune in to watch a show simply because one or two characters are gay has limited advertising dollars from corporate sponsors. Likewise, there is little known about the listening habits of queer radio audiences. Would queer listeners relate more to an openly gay deejay or news reporter, than to someone who is straight? Paul D. Poux, a reporter for *Advertising Age*, put it this way:

> What portion of the people who watch TV's *Ellen* are gay? Advertisers have no idea. . . . No organization—not Nielsen Media Research, which counts TV audiences; not Arbitron Co. or Scarborough Research, which count radio audiences; not any general-interest magazine or newspaper—measures the number of people watching, listening or reading who are gay or lesbian.[12]

Truly, little is known about the gay and lesbian market. Many of the large corporations have conducted their own research, and an increasing number of commercials have appeared on television regardless of the unavailability of accurate gay audience counts. In 1997, Olivia Cruises aired a TV commercial during the "coming out" episode of *Ellen* that showed two women on a cruise. The spot only aired in a few markets because ABC network refused to air it nationally. During that same show, two men featured in a Volkswagen commercial were perceived as a gay couple by many in the gay community.[13] The men drive down the road. No words—just their animated expressions, in sync to the beat of "Da, da, da." They they see an abandoned chair, pull over to put it into their hatchback, and then dump it off a few blocks down the road when it starts smelling up the car.

That same year, British-owned Virgin Cola aired a series of commercials that included a real gay couple being married on the Santa Monica beach.[14] Other companies that have led the way include the Swedish furniture retailer IKEA, which made history in early 1994 when it aired the first prime-time television commercial featuring a gay couple shopping for furniture. In 1996, an MTV commercial featured two male surfers who fall in love and run off with each other—holding hands—into the sunset. More recently, Levi ran a series of "lifestyle" commercials on MTV in which teenagers talk openly about their lives—one of whom recounts how he accidentally told his father that he was gay.[15] In 1999, an Abercrombie & Fitch TV commercial showed male college students playfully wrestling, purportedly playing on gay innuendo. The commercial was also televised inside Abercrombie & Fitch retail stories nationally.[16] Another MTV commercial showed a young teen listening to music in his bedroom and obviously distressed about his recent breakup with his boyfriend. On the wall behind him, the viewer can see a photo of the boy and his friend embracing as a couple. The commercial was named "First Love" and debuted during the 1999 MTV Awards Show.[17] In another MTV commercial promoting Mistic fruit drinks, a young woman addresses the camera and says, "Mom, Dad, if you're watching, I wanted to let you know I've finally found the person I want to spend the rest of my life with. Mom and Dad, this is Jenn." Then the girlfriend pops her head into the shot and says "Hi" into the camera.[18] MTV was honored during the Fourth Annual Fairness Awards on October 27, 1999, by GLADD for its inclusion of gay people and themes in programs like *Real World, The Blame Game,* and *Undressed* and in commercials like the one Mistic aired on its network.[19] As the presence of gay characters has increased on American television, so has the willingness of advertisers to support these efforts—and that means that the networks will likely view gay inclusiveness as a significant ingredient within their programming mix.

Selling Radio or Selling Out

> One of my pet peeves is that there are so many well-funded
> religious wackos on the air. I don't have to tell you how many
> religious, Christian radio stations and networks there are in the
> United States, and you would think that the national political
> queer leadership would recognize the value of at least having
> some counterprogramming on the air, but they just don't get it.
>
> —Greg Gordon, executive producer, *This Way Out*

In the United States, the majority of queer radio programs are aired on noncommercial outlets, and many of these shows have few or no underwriters. Moreover, the handful of mainstream radio stations that broadcast queer programming continually struggle to maintain sponsorship. And those stations not already airing gay programming have been reluctant to air commercials with gay themes. Nevertheless, commercial radio has made some significant inroads in airing queer programming, especially in the '90s.

Several commercial radio stations produced local gay- and lesbian-oriented shows in the early to mid-'90s, only to discover that their efforts were short-lived. Beginning in fall 1992, commercial AM outlets WFTL and WVCG debuted two of the first commercial gay and lesbian shows in Miami. Hosted by Charlie "Super Queer" Bado, WFTL-AM aired *Queer Talk*, a three-hour listener call-in show that was intended to spark controversy among both gay and heterosexual audiences. Sixty percent of its commercials were for gay-oriented businesses, while the rest were for mainstream clients.[20] WVCG-AM's *Alternet*, on the other hand, was a news magazine show that programmed music, news, and information to gay and lesbian listeners, with commercial sponsorship by gay-oriented businesses.[21] Both shows went off the air in August 1993, nearly nine months after they began. Another commercial station, WWRC-AM, in Washington, D.C., canceled its three-hour Sunday night talk show, *Ten Percent Radio*, in 1993. Only months earlier, WWRC had expanded the program by one hour. Advertisers included both gay-oriented and mainstream business, but there were not enough sponsors.[22]

College students in Boston, a city where one of the nation's first gay civil rights laws had passed, were extremely receptive to Modern Rock WFNX-FM's *One in Ten*. The magazine show was more than three hours long, and provided a variety of music, news, features, and call-in discussions about gay and lesbian issues. Predominantly record stores and restaurants sponsored the weekly Monday night program.[23]

In 1992, Adult-Alternative WNUA-FM debuted *Aware: HIV Talk Radio*. The show became the highest rated in the Chicago market on Sunday mornings, attracting over 111,000 gay and straight listeners.[24] Chris DeChant, creator and cohost, stated that it was important for his show to air on commercial radio, as opposed to public radio: "That way you can reach more people and you can't be categorized as just another public-affairs program."[25] Walgreen, Clairol, Kemper Financial Services, Playboy Foundation, American Airlines, and pharmaceutical companies were some of the sponsors.[26]

In March 1993, another commercial outlet began to experiment with gay talk. Cleveland's Talk Radio WHK-FM initially aired *The Gay '90s* on Friday nights, 9 P.M. to 11 P.M., but soon moved it to Monday nights to reach more young people. Despite the show's success with listeners and advertisers, program director Paul Cox believed that syndication was not in its near future. Cox didn't think America was ready for a gay talk show, adding that "it would take a lot of GMs [general managers] and PDs [program directors] with a hell of a lot of courage" to syndicate a gay talk show in the United States.[27]

All Gay, All Day

Nearly one half of the shows mentioned lasted only several months. One of the most ambitious commercial enterprises of the early 1990s was KGAY Radio Network. It failed within its first year, yet KGAY's vision of an all-gay radio network became a reality—even if only for awhile. On November 28, 1992, the KGAY Radio Network was born in Denver in the midst of the controversy surrounding Amendment Two, a Colorado statewide referendum that prohibited laws protecting gay and lesbian civil rights. The publicity initially generated by the amendment's passage drew attention to KGAY. Its programming, namely lots of music, and some news and information, radiated across the United States, Canada, and the Caribbean. KGAY was the inspiration of Clay Henderson and Will Gunthrie. The KGAY founders planned to move from a local Denver operation to cable FM on markets across the United States. Their previous efforts had included a short-lived thirty-minute, weekly, gay commercial radio show and a weekly gay and lesbian news show called the *Lambda Report*, which first aired on public access cable television in 1989. Three years later, KGAY's decision to air its programming over satellite in Denver, then known as the cable hub to the world, seemed easier and least expensive than purchasing a commercial radio station in a large or medium market.[28] KGAY would broadcast a five-minute newscast targeted to gay audiences every other hour throughout the day. Talk shows like *Ground Zero, This Way Out,*"and the network's own *Speak Out America* filled the weekend. Nightly public affairs shows focused on issues relevant to the gay community, with artists, authors, educators, ACT UP spokespersons, and drag queens. But the production quality of many of the shows was marginal. KGAY—with all its big ideas and plans—had the sound and budget of a small-market radio station. The base format was alternative music, and it aimed for an urban niche. What made KGAY different from any other commercial station was its same-sex dedications, a special commitment to play gay and lesbian artists (such as Melissa Etheridge, Meg Christian, Flirtations, Cris Williamson, and Army of Lovers), and a bit of personal activism (often against the wishes of management). Here's a little of what you might have heard on KGAY if you listened in the late afternoon to Vicki Dee, the program director and the only full-time woman deejay:

> We're going to start off our next set with Erasure's "Over the Rainbow." I'm doing that because I take a lot of personal pride in being a lesbian ... and being part of the gay community. Personally, I love it. I would not trade my life and love for Marie for anything. So I want to honor gay pride a little bit here this afternoon. We're also going to hear from one of the courageous lesbians of our time. We should call this the k.d. lang Radio Network ... and we're going to end the three-song set with "Enough Is Enough" because enough is enough, people. We have had it with the far right. Enough *is* enough.[29]

Overestimating the number of homes with personal satellite dishes and underestimating the number of commercially owned satellite companies, many of which were operated by cable companies that refused to air KGAY programming, were only two of the obstacles that KGAY would never overcome before the operating expenses took their toll. Near the end, KGAY had secured a partnership with Austin Cablevision to expand its programming, and other cable companies were beginning to take note of KGAY's potential. The biggest misconception among cable executives was that gay radio meant sex radio, according to KGAY's general manager, Dan Radcliff:

> The leaders in the gay community pressured city hall, and city hall in return pressured the cable company. Once we were on the air, and [Austin Cablevision] realized that we weren't doing live sex radio, we weren't doing sleazy radio, that we were so nauseating squeaky clean ... they really went out of their way for us.[30]

But opportunity came too late in the game for KGAY. It could no longer afford to operate with sparse sponsorship and a financially burdensome barter arrangement with the only KGAY affiliate, a 500 AM Colorado Springs station that provided free access to its satellite uplink in return for gay programming. KGAY faded to black only a year after it had begun. Radcliff never regretted his involvement nor investment in KGAY:

> What made it worthwhile on a day-to-day basis were the phone calls coming into the studio. Some 17-year-old kid calling from his dad's car phone, hiding in the garage, from the middle of nowhere U.S.A, who was crying and glad to know that he was not the only one in the world. That's what made it worthwhile.[31]

In the final analysis, KGAY programming consisted primarily of music. In an interview on *This Way Out*, Radcliff said that he realized early on the need for quality news and information:

> We didn't have enough news and information. And the news and information we had was sporadic, not necessarily the best quality. Because we were undercapitalized, we were understaffed. Because we were understaffed, we couldn't do a whole lot of things we needed to do to get expansion. And without expansion, we didn't have a big enough listener base to get the advertising we needed, to get the money, to hire the people, to do the work. It's just a circle.[32]

The Fragile Bubble

> *It's a fragile bubble we've created with America's only drive-time gay radio show. Or perhaps not so fragile as we've survived three radio stations, six studios, 1,200 editions and 3,000-plus hours of programming and brought in about $1.4 million. What a ride. Disney World never envisioned anything like this!*
>
> —Alan Amberg, founder and president of Lesbigay Radio

KGAY Radio was the first attempt to program gay and lesbian issues and music around the clock on a national basis. Prior to that, *This Way Out* was created to reach an international audience, airing on primarily noncommercial stations in the United States and a few commercial outlets (including KGAY) since its inception in 1988. In 1990, Thomas Davis bought into the western Massachusetts market that includes Springfield and nearby Northampton, a renowned gay and lesbian community. Davis is president and general manager of WTTT-AM and WRNX-FM in Amherst (the home of the University of Massachusetts). Davis's company purchased WTTT in 1990 and later built WRNX-FM. One of his largest areas for listeners and advertisers is Northampton, and as a result his programming is sponsored by many gay- and lesbian-owned businesses. The station also belongs to the Gay and Lesbian Business Coalition.

Another major commercial effort at broadcasting into a gay and lesbian community began in June 1994 when Alan Amberg launched *Lesbigay Radio* on WCBR-FM as a four-hour Sunday morning show. Its weak signal reached into the gay neighborhoods of Arlington Heights, North Chicago.[33] Eighteen months later, in November 1995, the show moved to WNDZ 750 AM. The stronger signal carried the daily format in morning drive time, targeting weekday commuters. In June 1998, nearly four years after its inception, *Lesbigay Radio* moved to the evening rush hours with an even stronger signal and was simulcast on WSBC 1240 AM in Chicago and WCFJ 1470 AM in Chicago Heights. As of June 1, 2000, the show also can be heard across the Internet at www.lesbigay.com. Amberg—president of Lesbigay Radio and Amberg Communications, Ltd., has been praised by other gay broadcasters for his tireless efforts and commitment to his audience and sponsors.

Marle Becker: Someone like Alan Amberg, who I absolutely adore, has to really go out and hit the streets and get advertisers. I can't imagine how difficult it must have been for Alan in the beginning. I know that when we've talked to each other, he would say I want this sponsor and that as a sponsor, and obviously his perseverance has paid off because he has some of the really great sponsors.

Alan Amberg: It's been several years of doing nothing but *Lesbigay Radio* and only now am I getting a life again. People can't quite imagine how sitting and chatting insightfully with guests for two hours, every weekday, parlays into thirty or forty hours off air for each on-air hour. Mainstream radio stations have a staff our size just for a show. We sell our time, promote our station, do all the things a radio station must do. We show up at or create hundreds of events. *And* we do 520 hours of programming a year.

Thomas Davis: Our programming philosophy has been to target lifestyles—inclusive lifestyles—rather than target specific groups of individuals. The WRNX midday host and host of our jazz show on Sunday mornings is an out lesbian, and another bright spot was the discovery of "Officer Mike," a Springfield police officer who is gay and out, and came on the show as a guest one morning. He was conducting an AIDS fund-raiser and was receiving much publicity. He knew WRNX well and had supported our programming philosophy of being accessible and open by his steady listenership. He has since become a regular guest on the program, via telephone, and is a welcome representative from the Springfield portion of the market. The key is to be inclusive, not make a big deal about it, and enjoy putting the programming on the air every day for such a fun, intelligent, and diverse audience.

Alan Amberg: Gay/lesbian/bisexual/transgender (GLBT) people are trying to figure out how to live, socialize, pray, date, and fight for their lives.

More than half of them *never* see a gay newspaper. *Out* magazine may have a national circulation of 120,000, but where's anything like *Ebony* (1.5 million)? No local newspaper prints more than 50,000 copies and most are closer to 20,000. The fraction that do see papers often get weekly or monthly male-bar-going social publications. Radio is cheap compared to print and the distribution is much superior. In most cities, the gay population may be substantial—but only a small percent of GLBT people live in concentrated neighborhoods. In my research and calculations, no more than 15 to 25 percent of the total live in the Halsted Streets and Dupont Circles of America.

Thomas Davis: The key, in our opinion, to marketing the gay and lesbian population is not to market them at all. They are woven into our society in this market and bring that added richness that makes this the remarkable place that it is to live and raise a family.

Alan Amberg: The desire to be all things to all queer audiences is another compelling issue when deciding what song to play or what issue to discuss, which is further complicated by listener demands for something new and fresh. What do you say to an audience that comes from everywhere? Many of our listeners ask for more music. Seems easy, right? But do they mean dance? Melissa Etheridge? Opera? Folk music? Show tunes? Aaaargh!!! Other stations by contrast have it easy. They program the same hundred country (or rock or classical) songs, perfectly researched and niched. Finally, what do you say to an audience that's exploding and changing in its self-perception daily?

Thomas Davis: Our stations do not carry any programming that is for gay and lesbian ears only. The entire philosophy of our programming is to be as openly inclusive as any public media outlet can. We feature news stories involving gays or lesbians in our programming, tracking stories such as the Tinky Winky story—making clear our viewpoint on those types of stories. We have also helped in fund-raising for a number of gay and lesbian concerns, such as AIDS research and hospice funding. WRNX recently ran a promotion called the Commitment Game, where three couples vied for an expensive diamond ring following the same format as the old *Newlywed Game.* We tried hard to recruit a gay or lesbian couple to participate and received an entry for a lesbian couple who squared off against two heterosexual couples, ultimately winning the contest. It was *not* fixed.

Alan Amberg: Five years ago a gay radio show struck people with awe. People in outlying areas would hold the antenna just so for hours to listen. In those first years, everything we did was history. Radio car commercials with gay characters. The first billboards proudly announcing gay business hours! TV commercials on *Oprah*. Our daily coverage of the Republican and Democratic National Conventions. The first on-air congressional candidate debate for a gay audience. Our audience heard it first when protease inhibitors were approved, when Colorado's Amendment Two was struck down, when New Jersey overturned the ban on the Boy Scouts. Today, oddly enough, the news is just "another new AIDS drug," "yet another major company with domestic partner benefits," another court win or loss. How do we stay that fresh and exciting post-*Ellen* and with the "acceptance" of *Will and Grace*?

Thomas Davis: One of our previous news directors was openly gay on the air. It was an important part of our morning show. This gentleman cohosted the morning show on WRNX for about six years and was quite involved in the gay-lesbian community. He made a point of reporting stories that directly affected gays and lesbians and would not hesitate to make them part of his cast when other stations would not touch them. He did this without political fanfare, and his good-natured and professional demeanor on the air was the source of affection for gay and straight listeners alike. He had a keen wit and was extremely well read, and had a theatrical background that made him extremely well rounded. He could bring humor to any topic, yet still make his point clear about the seriousness of many of the G/L issues before society. Over the years, he built up a great deal of credibility as a media personality and newsperson. His occasional letter to the local paper's editorial section regarding G/L issues and the paper's mistreatment of them was always printed. Later, he brainstormed a daily feature called "Stump the Gay Man" and "Stump the Straight Man." In this feature, the morning show host would ask him stereotypical "gay" questions, usually on the topics of show tunes, fashion and design, and cuisine. The news director would ask equally stereotypical questions to the "straight man," usually about sports, cars, tools, and other "macho" categories. It was only fitting that our news director was so well rounded that he knew the answers to all of the questions. The feature sent an excellent message. It was all done tongue-in-cheek to show how absurd many of these stereotypes were, especially given that our straight host is a gentle man with a love of old show tunes and really can't stand sports, and our gay news host was very handy with tools and quite knowledgeable about many "manly" topics.

Alan Amberg: Why do we fight and innovate and try everything to keep *Lesbigay Radio* on the air? Ask the other broadcasters in this book and I bet you'll find a common vision: to tell our stories where most of America gets its information. We want to be at the table of a medium loaded with shock jocks, preachers, and conservatives. We want to give our people a safe place filled with our voices. And each day on *Lesbigay Radio,* as I get to meet and talk with the people who are creating our world, I am certain of the value of doing this. Our enemies certainly know the value of it. How many Christian full-time stations are there? Thousands. How many full-time gay stations? Zero. I decided that I didn't need security, money in the bank, or decent hours. And that's certainly true. Yet because my staff are some of the very few people in the world who make living wages and benefits from this line of work, I count myself the luckiest guy in the world. I work with them and do this and make my living from it.

Greg Gordon: I don't know where to find the substantial funding that *This Way Out* needs to really take that next step to be able to hire an executive director or something equivalent. I don't know if and where that money is going to come from. I don't know whether corporate funding is the answer. I know that some of the people involved with *This Way Out* would fight that tooth and nail because of their own political perspectives. That is Pacifica Radio's philosophy, in which you want to avoid the appearance of compromise by taking a corporate foundation grant, for example. So I don't know, because we've never been able to get major funding from any of the more mainstream foundations, and we've had to patch together funding from some of the gay-specific foundations. Our actual operating budget is more like $30,000, and you know, it's difficult to raise that kind of money.

Thomas Davis: The purpose of our programming is to make the station accessible to everyone while at the same time educating the masses to the idea that gays and lesbians function so much like any other member of society on a daily basis and that there really is no need for breaking them into groups.

Alan Amberg: Historically, we are only just emerging from the days when gay businesses had to exist in secrecy to survive. If you knew where to go to get a gay newspaper, you probably weren't a risk to everyone's safety and confidentiality. We are also newly emerging into the world of gay-identified consumers who are willing to identify themselves to the sponsor. Most people would no sooner fly to the moon than identify themselves to an unknown clerk. This becomes a problem for tracking results or for Arbitron surveys. We are, after all, the only station in the market that requires listeners to identify themselves as queer. That brings us to the whole problem of getting and building audience. Radio, like retail, is all about location, location, location —as defined by time of day, dial position, and signal strength. Getting on a known station with a decent signal at a regular time when people listen is quite difficult without at least a quarter to a half million dollars.

Greg Gordon: People always ask how many people listen, and it's a catch-22. Because first of all we have no idea really what our audience is. We can only guesstimate based on the letters we do get. I do know that nongay people listen to us because they tell us. I think we're interestingly produced and entertaining and informative. I mean clearly Pat Robertson is not going to listen, but somebody who has gay friends or gay family members, someone who is gay-supportive or is potentially gay-supportive, will listen. All we can do is extrapolate from ratings of local stations that carry us. That's always been a frustrating point, but I don't know any way to deal with it. There have been obviously low points and high points along the road and every time there's a low point, I would joke with a guy who produced a local program in Philadelphia and every time I feel like throwing in the towel, then you get a letter from one of those damned sixteen-year-old kids who tells you that you helped save his life. It's difficult to walk away from the project when you get feedback like that.

Honey, We *Are* the Gay Topic!

Charles "Karel" Bouley II and Andrew Howard are an openly gay couple whose show, *Karel and Andrew Live,* became the number one afternoon drive radio show, 4 to 7 P.M., in Los Angeles after only several months at KFI-AM 640, the number one talk station of Southern California. In 1999, Clear Channel bought KFI, and soon afterward they were moved to 7 to 9 P.M.—still considered part of the drive time in the city of Los Angeles. To Karel and Howard, it is not about being gay, the point of the show is about being relevant to the listener.

Karel: If I'm Margaret with my kids in the back of my minivan and it's 4:30 in the afternoon and I'm driving home, how is what you're saying on the radio relevant to me? You know, if I'm Ernie and I'm driving home from L.A. to the valley, to my wife and my two kids, how is what you're saying relevant to me? If I'm Rick and I'm driving through West Hollywood on my way to see Steve, how is what you're saying relevant to me? It has to be relative to the listener, it has to be.

Karel is a singer, songwriter, journalist, and comedian. Howard is a writer for the screen and stage. Previously the duo worked as a team in Seattle, Tacoma, and San Francisco. The show *Karel and Andrew Live* has exposed millions of listeners to gay and straight scholars, media personalities, politicians, and community leaders, including Martin Landau, Natalie Imbruglia, Kenny G., Donny Osmond, Cyndi Lauper, Bill Condon, Bryan Singer, Eartha Kitt, Michaelangelo Signorille, Morris Kight, Martha Wash, Sandy B., Stacey Q., Joi Cardwell, Arye Gross, Albert Hague, Renee Orin, Patricia Nell-Warren, Tommy Tang, Jason Stewart,

Lacey Harmon, Robyn Greenspan, Senator John McCain, Pat Buchanan, and even white supremacist Tom Metzger (see Appendix 5A).They reported live from the 1999 shooting at the Jewish Community Center in Northridge. Their afternoon show was on the scene for the shootings at the West Anaheim Medical Center that same year and followed the fires in Big Bear from a helicopter.

Karel: There was a shooting at a hospital, a hospital that me and Andrew had both been to—we went to the hospital to broadcast live. In another instance we were at the Jewish Community Service Center when the idiot hate-crime guy just walked in and started shooting the kids. We were there, broadcasting live all day long from the scene. Then there's when Andrew was flying in a helicopter over the Willow fire here in Big Bear in September 1999, and he was talking about the devastation; I was concerned about his safety, telling the pilot to fly higher. "I don't want him in the smoke," that sort of thing. People e-mailed and said, "You know, I'm not gay, but the amount of love that you showed for Andrew when he was in that helicopter really touched me." That's what we do each day. We celebrate that from the foundation of us being two gay men that have been together for ten years as a couple, and we grew this wonderful exchange between us which we could then bring to radio.

Karel and Howard were also on scene in Norco, California, when Betty Topper was removed from her home after being chained to her bed for five of her six years of life. The duo interviewed neighbors, and the women who finally reported the tragedy to the police talked to them before any other news outlet.

Karel: We needed to know why they didn't get involved and we had to ask firsthand the ex-neighbors who finally turned in the abuse, and they talked to Andrew and me first, before any news outlet. We went around and interviewed the neighbors that very day and said, how could you not know she was tied to her bed a hundred feet away from you? How is that possible? You know, is that what you expect two gay men on the radio to be doing? No. But that's what we do. You know yesterday we did a story about how 17 million women are at risk of HIV or STDs because their spouses have been unfaithful and have not told them. And we've got so many calls from women who've gotten STDs from their husbands. Is that something you'd expect us to do? No. We never want to do what they expect us to do. Never. The minute you do, they stereotype you and tune you out.

It all started when Karel was promoting a dance record under the Jellybean Benitez label (a tune which topped at No. 10 on the *Billboard* Dance Chart). He was asked to host the morning show of Groove 103.1 FM in Los Angeles. He had been a print journalist for twenty years, basically interviewing people for a living, when the radio offer dropped into his lap.

Karel: Someone was putting together a gay and lesbian show for a small station. And they went to the music director there and asked do you know of anyone who'd be a good host?

And as the story goes, Karel was not only recommended, but hired as the morning host. After two shows, he asked Howard to fill in as cohost while the station searched for a cohost, "but he worked out so well that he just got drafted into doing it." They stayed there for a year, and then the station was sold. Then they were hired by Triangle Broadcasting to host *Good Morning Gay America,* broadcast over a 5,000–watt AM station in the Seattle and Tacoma markets. Although they worked for Triangle Broadcasting for only a year, they secured top-name guests, from superstars to the cast of *Ally McBeal* during that time.

Karel: Because of my years as a journalist and a publicist, I'd be writing a story for *Billboard* interviewing Kenny G. or whoever, I'd just tape the interview and play it on *Good Morning Gay America.* We didn't treat it like it was only on a 5,000-watt station in Seattle or Tacoma. We treated it like it was a nationally broadcast show, and so the good memory was that there was not the intense pressure that there is at KFI in terms of every single day being your very best show, every single day being something new and unique and innovative, and it's tiring being innovative every single day. But by the same token, it wasn't the same amount of challenge that this is. We are so much better now than we were when we were on Triangle.

Actually, halfway through their stay with Triangle Broadcasting, they switched to afternoons and the show became *Karel and Company*—a move that would prepare them for their next radio gig on the most listened to talk station in the United States.

Karel: We sent a tape to KFI. They arranged a meeting and in September of last year they let us try out on a Sunday night, and then they started having us fill in, and that was the birth of *Karel and Andrew Live* because they didn't want the *Karel and Company* thing, since Howard was the cohost. On March 22, they gave us afternoon drive. KFI management—David Hall in particular—took a chance on us. And it is a chance. Believe me. Every book that comes out, we're sweating. It's, you know, a business and our station's been bought and sold twice in two weeks, and now Clear Channel owns us. Are they going to be receptive to this, you know, this idea, this grand experiment? We are building an audience. . . . Our summer book will be higher than our spring book, and we're in the middle of the fall book now. You see, you have to go after your target audience. *Good Morning Gay America* was specifically designed for the gay community, so we had to cater to their likes and dislikes. Our market at KFI is the non-gay community—90 percent of our listeners are not gay, so we have to do a show that is equally as entertaining as the other one, but relevant to the listener. You always have to be relevant to the listener. *Good Morning Gay America* was relevant to the gay listeners. With *Karel and Andrew Live* on KFI we have to be relevant to all listeners, gay and straight. So it presents more of a challenge. It's been the most intensive eight-month learning curve I've ever had in my entire life because we took a job that people had waited ten, fifteen, twenty years in radio to get. I mean you don't just get given afternoon drive at the number one AM talk signal after not being in radio for five years. But we did.

It's not just another radio show—sometimes it's the typical radio stunts, but done from a gay perspective.

Karel: We went to a female strip club because some community members wanted to make it illegal to tip the dancers. So me and Andrew went and sat there and watched a woman get totally naked on stage 'cause we'd never been and we thought, well, we'd better go and check it out. We taped the whole thing and it was just hysterical. I mean only we would comment on her shoes, you know. She's stark naked and we go, oh look at her shoes, you know, and we played it on the air.

And there's the time that—

Karel: Andrew gave me a polygraph test one time on the air because the government was going to insist that everyone that starts getting government jobs take a polygraph test, so we thought, well, let's have one. So we did it, and you know right there in drive time, 5:15 on Tuesday afternoon, he says, "Have you ever cheated on me?" and I'm like, "Well no, I've never cheated on you." And you know, that is innovative because it's not being done any-where else where a nongay crowd can hear it. There were people in their cars that moment that—if they were homophobic or whatever—they had to hear one man ask another, "Have you ever cheated on me?" Now I realize that when you cross over into the mainstream you actually make a bigger differ-ence for the gay community. We were trying to make a difference in the gay community at *Good Morning Gay America*. At KFI, we're trying to make a difference for the gay community.

Karel has been criticized, particularly by the gay press, for his outspoken views regarding his desire to reach beyond the gay community into mainstream America.

Karel: The shows that cater for gays, about gays, with gays, they do a good service in the community but they don't do a good service for the community because you're preaching to the converted. It's when you go out and you change the minds of those that would oppress or hate you, and through example—through showing them that you are what you have been professing all of these years. We are more than sex. We are not deviants. We are interested in what's going on in the real world. When you go out and you prove that you are more than your sexuality to them, that's where you win, and these shows don't do anything to progress that agenda. All they do is cater to themselves, to their own community, and that doesn't do any good. A straight person's not going to listen to an all-gay network. It's not going to happen. So incorporation into the mainstream media is the only way that we will get what we want from all of this, and we seem to be fighting that tooth and nail because we go in very militant—you must accept me as I am. No, they don't have to. It's a business. Show them you can make money as you are and they'll accept you, but just stand there and scream at them and they'll be like, "Bye." We get flak every day—"do more gay topics," "do more gay topics," "do more gay topics." If I have to tell people one more time, "Honey, we *are* the gay topic," I'll just explode. Every queen on the road says, "Do more gay topics." When they're relevant, we will do them. When they're relevant to everyone across the board. When marriage is on the ballot here in California, we will do that topic. October 12, Matthew Shepard's death—we will do that topic. It's when it's relevant, but every day there's some new gay this or gay that on the Internet. I'm on all these news groups and there's an attack on some front every day, from the religious right or from government or from this or from that, and each day we could go on and say, and today, blah, blah, blah, and no one's going to care. No one is going to care. No one cares except gay people and that's 11 percent, 20 percent at most of the population. And how are you going to make that into a commercially successful viable entity that's going to progress your movement? You're not.

Karel, longtime journalist, vented his frustrations toward those who criticize his success at top-rated KFI by posting an editorial on his Web site—"Opening the Vent: Thoughts on Frontiers, Al Rantel and Such"[34] (see Appendix 5B.)

Karel: I don't condemn the *IMRUs* and other shows like that. They're great shows. I've done them. You know, they're marvelous shows, and the *Advocate* and all the other publications and all the gay and lesbian media outlets and radio, they're great. They're wonderful, we need them. We need someone who's just coming out to be able to find one of those shows and feel a sense of community. Yet we should not put all of our eggs in that basket 'cause that's not where the success will come from. It is through commercialization, going beyond the gay community into the mainstream, that these issues will be advanced. There's nothing wrong (a) with commercialization, and (b) there's nothing wrong with furthering your agenda by stopping and not screaming it all the time. Just further your agenda by example. Show them you're a competent broadcaster. If you're in gay radio, show them you're an excellent talk show host and that you can do a show on any station up against anybody.

KFI's talk lineup includes Dr. Laura Schlessinger, Rush Limbaugh, Art Belly, and a slew of other conservative talk hosts. In between all of them is *Karel and Andrew Live* in afternoon drive. From the onset, KFI has been supportive of the duo, and what Karel calls the "grand experiment" seems to defy its critics.

Karel: We're going to invite Dr. Laura on our show, and we're not going to talk about why she always bashes gays. That's a moot point—why bother? We're going to talk to her about why men cheat on their wives. . . . This woman who condemns homos every day says she finds us hysterical. If that's not an inroad, what is? How can you start changing a closed mind if you can't get into it? Your yellow brick wall, it's not going to crumble. You start tapping at the loose bricks, they might fall. So we find a loose brick and we enter that way. Her loose brick is she finds us hysterical. Okay, you find us hysterical. Maybe a year down the line she might go, you know, they're not deviants. That's how you make the inroad. Flowering her house, condemning her in the media, all of that, that doesn't do crap. She doesn't care. It's great publicity.

In another editorial, "Must There Be a Great Divide?" Karel underscored the importance of his presence as a gay man on KFI and the need for recognition of the larger issues confronting the gay community (see Appendix 5C).[35] More important, their sincerity, honesty, and commitment to relevance have won over their straight audience. Karel explained that he and Howard "celebrate the fact each and every day on air" as a couple; "We fight like a couple; we call each other couple names." Karel's conversion of his Los Angeles audience—one listener at a time—becomes evident in the following excerpt from one of his editorials posted on his Web site:

> It was just two weeks ago and she was like, when I first heard you guys were on, we immediately turned you off. My husband and I were furious. We couldn't believe it. Then out of necessity because your station was the only one that came in, you know, to and from Vegas, we listened to you and kind of liked you, and then listened again, and listened again, and now you're our old friends, and you know, that sort of thing.
>   I mean we get emails all the time from people who say I never thought I'd have anything in common, I never thought I would understand, I never wanted to know anybody gay, and now, my husband, me, my kids, we all listen to you.

We find you informative and entertaining, and you've really opened up our minds about everything. And we can't do that by sitting there and doing gay topics every day. It's not possible. They'll tune out. They don't care.[36]

Karel and Howard have a larger vision than drive time at the number one talk station. For the duo, it is more about making a difference within their community, but on a much grander scale than they might have done by continuing their work in exclusively gay media. Karel and Howard are the founders of Equality Through Pride, an organization whose mission is to instill a sense of pride in the gay and lesbian community through positive representation in the arts and media. As part of this effort, Karel will star in the feature-length film *The Second Story* as David Trufell, the owner of a fictional gay bar. Other projects include *The Karel & Andrew Hour,* a one-hour television talk show that will not only highlight the best of the duo's radio show, but feature special guests, performances, interviews, and topic discussion. Among his many projects, Howard is writing a book, *Guarded Optimism,* that documents his life with Karel.

Karel: It's about Andrew's journeys before me, during me, and now at KFI. Andrew has full-blown AIDS, and he's had HIV for 13 years. We've gone through some really hectic times with that and also this whole thing—we're two openly gay men. We're on the number one talk station in the country. He's got full-blown AIDS . . . it's just been one enormous roller-coaster ride, one on top of the other of really extraordinarily bizarre things that have happened to us, from me signing with Jelly Bean Binetez, producing my own dance record that became No. 10 on the *Billboard* dance chart for the year end, and finally just on down the line, and all the while living with HIV and AIDS.

Hangin' With the Big Boys

> *As commercial network television moves into the next decade, it seems it too will eventually break more barriers as they pertain to gay and lesbian issues. Part of these barriers will be broken in order to compete with cable program channels in an effort to stem the eroding network television audiences. Secondly, these barriers will break down as society breaks its barriers on accepting gays, lesbians, and other minority sexual groups and begins viewing gays and lesbians less and less as demoralizing, sick individuals and more and more as productive, moral members of society.*

> —Chuck Hoy, assistant professor, Grambling State University

Off the Straight and Narrow: Lesbians, Gays, Bisexuals, and Television, a video documentary produced by the Media Education Foundation, provides a comprehensive examination of gay and lesbian characters on television, as well as network documentaries and news reports, from Stonewall to the "gay chic" of the 1990s; from ABC's *That Certain Summer* aired in 1972 to CBS's exposé on *Gay Power, Gay Politics* in 1980; from Mariel Hemingway's kiss on *Rosanne* in 1994 to the outing of Ellen.[37]

Fred Fejes and Kevin Petrich also conducted an exhaustive study of gay and lesbian presence and characterization in television, film, and the news media published as "Invisibility, Homophobia and Heterosexism: Lesbians, Gays, and the Media."[38] It was comedians like Edward Everett Horton and Milton Berle in the early days of broadcasting who were perhaps the first to introduce gay characters and images into the American living room. Cross-dressing and a limp wrist were sight gags that did little to advance the gay and lesbian movement on the little screen—images that still provoke laughter among straight and queer audiences (often for different reasons) and reinforce the white, wealthy, and well-educated gay stereotype.

Chuck Hoy: Unless you consider Milton Berle's drag character in the 1950s, which he states he wanted to do as a gay throwaway,[39] it was not until 1967 that television had its first gay character in a prime-time entertainment program. The program was *NYPD* and the gay character presented was something to be pitied because he was homosexual.[40] Other than some homosexuals appearing on *The David Susskind Show* with bags over their heads to prevent themselves from being identified, the American public was not subjected to any other gay images during television's first couple of decades.[41] This was probably beneficial for gays and lesbians in America, who were perceived by creators of television programs as people who should be pitied, dressed in clothes of the opposite gender, or wearing bags over their heads when in public. Several years passed before television aired another prime-time program with a gay character. This time the program was a made-for-television movie which aired on the American Broadcasting Network. The movie, starring Hal Holbrook and Martin Sheen, was about a father who reveals his homosexuality to his son.[42] To avoid problems, the program used a vast array of consultants and was given many screenings. *That Certain Summer* was praised by many and even today stands as a landmark for gay characterizations on television.[43] Gay activists objected to two things in the program that still persist today when television deals with gay images. The first of these objections concerned the lack of any affection shown between the two gay characters in the program.[44] The second objection centered on a line spoken by one of the gay characters which network psychiatrists insisted be inserted in the program to present prevailing public opinion at the time.[45] For gay activists, this was the equivalent of adding comments by racist hate groups in programs about racial and ethnic minorities. These television images of gay men were created primarily by heterosexuals for a primarily heterosexual audience.

Network television continued to experiment with broadcast images of gay characters—and portrayed them as comedic and sometimes sexually confused. The 1970s and 1980s represented two decades of transition on network television and premium cable.

Chuck Hoy: *That Certain Summer* set up an explosion of gay male characters on prime-time television as well as setting the tone for how they were portrayed. During the 1970s and 1980s, a variety of different television programs would present a gay character in one or more episodes. While some of these characters were negative, such as a child molester on *Marcus Welby, M.D.,* most were positive in their portrayal of gay males. Many of these television program episodes were so similar in their plot lines that the scripts could have been passed from one to the other with only minor changes. The plot always seemed to center around someone, who tended not to represent the effeminate stereotypical gay male, telling one of the regular gay characters that they were gay. At this point, the balance of the program would deal with the main character coming to terms with their friend or acquaintance's homosexuality. It was as if television program creators were attempting to instruct the American public in Homosexuality 101. While many of the stories were similar in their plots, they also share similarities to *That Certain Summer.* These programs' plots not only had the same tired coming-out stories, but the story line usually contained some type of statement reflecting homosexuality's negative aspects. Further, gay characters on prime-time network programs did not have any type of love, sex lives, or demonstration of affection so prevalent among heterosexual characters, who seemed to fall in and out of beds like guests at a hotel. Television seemed to say it was all right to be gay, just don't be too gay and show it openly. It was as if television creators and programmers wanted to give the American public a peek inside the gay closet, but not open the door wide enough for a good look. It created among straight television viewers an atmosphere of faggot freak show voyeurism. For gay men and women, it became a matter of any character is better than none at all. It was in the 1970s that television also gave us the first recurring character in a series. The program was *Soap,* and the character was Jodie, played by Billy Crystal. This is the first prime-television program to ever have a recurring gay character. Any expressions of same-sex affection was limited to dialogue. At one point, Jodie even becomes involved with a woman, as if he could switch off his homosexuality.

Joshua Gamson: There's this sort of nostalgia within the talk show genre at least when I talk to gay people about it, or when I first studied talk TV. It is a kind of nostalgia for the days of *Donohue,* when you would have these shows that were sort of either for or against homosexuality, and the people who would represent the gay and lesbian sides of things would be very presentable. There would be the standard pro and con discussion of the controversy, and I think some nostalgia is partly for the middle classes of that forum, as opposed to the more street and working-class, less white version of the genre that has happened since *Ricki Lake.*

Chuck Hoy: In the 1980s, the number of gay characters continued to grow and there was even another recurring gay character. This time it was the continuing drama *Dynasty,* and the character was Steven Carrington. This character seems to go from straight to gay with each new television season. It was only Steven's straight years that he had a love life. For many gay media activist groups, this was a problem in the portrayal of gays and lesbians on television. It was a problem that would continue until today.

The American public were fed contradictory images and messages through an electronic stream of consciousness, a sensory overload without retrospection. In the 1980s, the sexual revolution of the 1960s was redefined by George Michael and Madonna in the electronic media, as both challenged and toyed with gender boundaries in their music and videos. MTV was criticized for its willingness to challenge society's traditional values. The practice of "outing" the famous became "in" among young queers who wanted to end the hypocrisy in the media. A number of radio stations aired promotional announcements that assured their audiences of "safe" lyrics, and the FCC began to wrestle with "safe harbor" policies designed to protect children from undesirable broadcast content. The resistance among many mainstream broadcasters mounted during this acceleration of social change. Media mogul Rupert Murdoch, CEO of 20th Century Fox, the Fox Broadcasting Network, *TV Guide,* the *New York Post,* the *Chicago Sun-Times,* and several other entities, proclaimed in 1980, "I don't believe in the gay movement....I think they should stay to themselves, just climb back into the cupboards. . . . I don't believe they are gay at all, they are very unhappy."[46]

Beginning in the 1980s, the American public became accustomed to gay characters appearing on television dramas and sitcoms. Some programs began to include gay and lesbian couples—but no affection would be displayed between the lovers. *Rosanne* and *Northern Exposure* broke down another barrier in the broadcast of a same-sex commitment ceremony or wedding. On the May 9, 1994, episode of *Northern Exposure,* two gay characters, both ex-marines, who ran a bed-and-breakfast in fictional Cicely, Alaska, got married. Andrew Schneider, one of the producers, was quoted in *The Advocate:* "It's just another wedding. The point of the episode is that this is not about gay people getting married; it's about how two people relate."[47]

Chuck Hoy: Gay and lesbian media activists denounced the way the kiss culminating the wedding ceremony was handled on *Northern Exposure*. When it came time for the men to kiss, the camera panned away from the couple. Although the *Simpsons* would be the program that would break the same-sex kiss barrier for men and animation, it was *Rosanne* who accomplished it for women. The kiss itself was between the star of the program, Rosanne, and Mariel Hemingway, who played a lesbian attracted to Rosanne. These were but brief moments in television history, but shining ones in the portrayal of gays and lesbians.

After several seasons on the air, the *Ellen* program began to experience declining ratings. In a mirroring of reality, Ellen DeGeneres came out publicly as a lesbian along with her partner Anne Heche, while the character of Ellen came out as a lesbian on the program of the same name. The show received a great deal of both good and bad publicity. Stations in some cities, including Birmingham, Alabama, refused to air the program. In these cases, local gay and lesbian groups held their own showing of Ellen's coming out. *Ellen* becomes the first television program to have a gay or lesbian character as its title character. Although the coming-out episode gave this program a temporary ratings boost, it was not enough for ABC network program executives, who canceled the program that season.

The cancellation of *Ellen* in 1997 by network executives appeared to affirm the "Don't ask; don't tell" motto of the Clinton administration. Burger King, General Motors, Domino's Pizza, Wendy's, Johnson & Johnson, Bristol-Myers Squibb, and Mazda Motors were some of the sponsors who pulled their advertisements when Ellen came out on network television.[48] Would Ellen have been more acceptable if a *straight* actress had played the part of a lesbian? Lesbian kisses on *Rosanne, Party of Five,* and *Ally McBeal* made network history in the '90s. Then, in May 2000, Jack and Ethan became the first male characters to romantically kiss on the season finale of *Dawson's Creek*—a sort of teen soap opera on prime-time network television. This time around, Dunkin' Donuts, Visa International, the Gillette Company, Dentyne, and soft drink companies sponsored the kiss, so to speak, while the program quietly made history in millions of American homes that night.[49] It was a television kiss that had been in the making for many years.

John Scagliotti: There have been a couple of commercial successes like the networks had with *Ellen* and now *Will and Grace*. These things are all a part of the major changes that have taken place in the '90s. In terms of soft gay and lesbian issues, it started mostly in theater, then a little bit on public television, but then it really took off in the '90s as a commercial thing. Everyone knows the purpose of commercial is to make money, so no matter what that programming is, it is not going to be that deep. However it's very important.

I can't tell you how many kids got excited about *Ellen*—you know, the whole Ellen coming out thing. This is important in their lives and being a part of the whole world where you see it day after day, you know these straight people making love, having families, and all these other things, and there are no images of you and it's really important, no matter if they're great or bad programs, to have these images. I happen to think that Ellen's program was okay. I didn't like it too much but I was very excited that it was happening. Commercial TV has been a very important field to change because for many years we couldn't get in the commercial world.

Joshua Gamson: There has been a huge explosion on prime-time TV in the last couple of years of openly lesbian and gay characters. On some level that is something to be excited about and to celebrate, but these characters represent very cleaned-up images. I think you see this kind of dynamic, and the portrayal of a lot of marginalized groups and minority groups, where the response to complaints about stereotypes is to stereotype in a different way. It used to be that all you saw of gay people on TV and film was limp-wristed men, butch women and flamboyant and hypersexuality and suicide and unhappiness and all that. So there was a period where people were really resisting that, trying to get that changed. Then, you have a period where characters are homogenized, you know, where the characters who are on TV are almost exclusively white, all middle-class, just like the rest of TV. The gay characters are as palatable as can be. They might be a little bit more humorous than some of the straight characters but there's nothing to distinguish them. It is just a replacement of one stereotype with another, I think. And, you know, I think the goal of diversity, of diverse images and diverse representation culture-wide, is a good one. I'm not sure that is something we are going to get from commercial TV—at least not network TV.

Chuck Hoy: On television of the late 1990s, there are several programs with recurring gay and lesbian characters and one successful program with a gay man as one of the title characters. Even though *Ellen* was canceled, it served as an example that overall the American television audience was ready for gay and lesbian characters in leading roles. The problem of showing affection in same-sex couples is a barrier that on commercial network television has been problematic. The gay male title character on the program *Will and Grace* is a roommate of a straight woman. While this straight female character has had a love life, the gay male character has not.

Marvin Schwam: There was a show with a woman and an openly gay man. It was a hit show a few years ago. . . . I can't remember the name of it.

Anyway, I asked a dozen gay people if they watched that show, and nobody even watched it. The network purpose of the program was to show how gay people assimilate in this world and live in a straight world, which we are forced to because nine out of ten people are straight, etc., and show how it's accepted, how they get along and the comical situations they get into. Nobody watched it—which is an indication again that nobody cares that it's a gay show on television or whether it is broadcast on a gay network. The gay community is not interested in a gay network. For what reason? There's enough gay characters on television that gay people don't watch anyway. They're going to watch the programs they like and it makes no difference whether it is a gay/ lesbian network or if it's NBC: if the program is good, they're going to watch it.

John Catania: I was not one to get excited about *The Birdcage* or *In and Out* and I know there was some uproar about those things, but I think that is simply a different battle. There are battles that are happening on many fronts, and here I am sensationalizing it by calling it a war, but what I mean is, there are efforts that are happening on several fronts. It is very important in entertainment media, like films and television and magazines or whatever, that we also become part of the humor of this country, that we become part of the fabric of just basic storytelling of universal theme stories. You know, gay people can fit into any universal theme story whether it is about jealousy, or loss, or ambition. You know they say there are seven stories that are told, and we keep on telling them to the generations. Well, a gay person or a lesbian person can fall into any one of those stories, and entertainment media are starting to get that, and they are putting people in those situations. That is a very important effort. But the other effort is like our new magazine series *In The Life* on PBS. We must take that frank, intelligent look at society, and as far as television goes, there is not much of that happening. There is *In the Life,* and there are good documentaries, and of course a *20/20* or whatever will visit the gay experience when it is sensational, when someone is murdered, or to focus on the whole gay marriage issue, or gays in the military, but it sensationalizes the issues because the debate is so heated. But a show like *In the Life,* which is the only one, is just about so many other issues. So this is another effort. This is another kind of battle front where it has to happen. But I don't have any trouble with, for the most part, gay characterizations because, you know, they are again adding to the mix.

Queerer Than Fiction

So what happens, in the case of the show *Ellen,* when fiction becomes reality? Or when fiction is not enough to sustain an audience? In the year 2000, the networks began to cash in on "real-life" drama in prime time, perhaps following the lead of daytime tabloid TV. One month after the *Dawson's Creek* kiss, one of the fourteen castaways on CBS Network's slice-of-life drama series *Survivor* revealed that Richard Hatch, the corporate executive from Rhode Island, was gay, and the network capitalized on the reaction of the other islanders.

When coming out goes beyond the simplistic plots of fictitious television characters in prime time, and moves into real life and issues—such as gays and lesbians living and loving in the straight world—many station managers (commercial and noncommercial) refrain from broadcasting what they believe to be controversial programming. In 1991, 127 of 320 public broadcast stations refused to air "Tongues Untied"—Marlon Riggs's autobiographical account of life as a black gay man.[50] For years, the gay and lesbian media were the primary vehicle for communicating the gay and lesbian perspective to their community and, increasingly, to a straight audience.

Moreover, the traditional networks have been criticized for their exploitation of the gay community, especially in regards to their representation of LGBT guests on the tabloid TV talk shows of the 1990s—although shows like *Ellen, Will and Grace,* and *Dawson's Creek* are signs of the changing times.

Joshua Gamson: We're not all lily-white, middle-class, highly educated. I think that gets lost sometimes in the discussion. The other thing that I think might be useful to think about is just what lays the groundwork in media culture for the kinds of things, the efforts of other people in broadcasting, that are specifically gay and lesbian. And I think that talk shows were a pretty big part of just getting audiences used to images of gay people. Just for the fact that on the cultural landscape, gay people exist. There were so few places for such a long time on television where you would ever see an openly gay person, or try even to see a bisexual person or transgender person, who you would almost never see anywhere but on a talk show. And I think that is the groundwork that was not intentional on the part of the talk shows particularly, but that just happened because of the way they made their money, but it was actually ultimately pretty important for just laying tracks that other people could then follow in more self-determined ways later.

Joshua Gamson is the author of *Freaks Talk Back,* a book about the cultural implications of tabloid talk in American television.[51] He has found both positive and negative effects from the networks' selective emphasis on one segment of the gay community. Gamson, a sociology professor at Yale University, is on the research advisory board of the Gay and Lesbian Alliance Against Defamation (GLAAD).

Joshua Gamson: The networks feel that they must try to reach for a broad audience unless they discover some segment of the market that they want to sell to advertisers; you know, if they stumble onto something that is working, they copy it. I was just watching TV, and it was in a period of time when daytime TV talk shows were being attacked. I turned on *Ricki Lake* or one of those shows about "no gays around my kids" or something like that. And there were several antigay bigots brought on the show, and the audience and the host more or less demolished them. Then, there was a presentable but kind of shrill gay male couple that came on at the end and kind of got the last word, and I thought I'm not sure that this type of programming is the worst thing in the world or the worst kind of publicity in the world for gay people. The attempt to shut the shows down, which was going on at the time, seemed to me more like a sort of attempt to shut down the little tiny corner of publicity that various kinds of marginalized populations were left with. I started to think about how not just gay people but other groups were kind of funneled into this subliminal spot in our TV culture. Clearly to some degree, people are being fed up with tabloid shows. Even on the nontabloid shows, certain populations, especially people who don't conform to traditional sex and gender norms, are being set up as freaks—as well as those who are from different class backgrounds than middle-class. A common perception of this type of program is that they are freak shows, and I think one of the important complications of the genre is that they are shows on a stage, shows in which the people who are treated as freaks get to contest that perception. They do talk on the show and they actually get a lot more time and a lot more unedited time than they get elsewhere in the culture, which is not impressive. They don't get a whole lot elsewhere, or at least not a lot of time where they are writing their own story.

Alan Ross: When I founded Gay Fathers, I was living in Philadelphia and really feeling great about my leadership. There were talk shows going on and Maury Povich, back before he met Connie Chung, hosted *AM/PM,* and he wanted to do a show on gay fathers and lesbian mothers. So he asked me to go on the show, along with Dr. Mary Cochrane, a well-known lesbian mother and psychologist in Philadelphia. Maury's producer told us that it was going to be a program supportive of gay parenting, but what he didn't tell us was that he had stacked the audience with homophobes, and this one guy from Save the Children (or whatever its name) was awful. This group had a front-row seat and kept popping up to condemn us and say "God condemns you. It's against the Bible." He had a German accent and sounded like a Nazi to me. It was the most horrendous thing, but Mary and I really overcame this beautifully. There was a very beautiful turning point in the show when I talked to one of the people who had apparently ridden the bus in with him—a woman. I forgot the question that she asked to prompt me to respond, but I said to her, "May I assume that you are heterosexual?" She said, "Yes." I said, "Let me ask you this: what would you do if tomorrow society were completely turned around and everybody was gay and you were married to this great guy whom you love, but all your friends, your church, and your religion, and everybody else is telling you that you have to leave your husband and become a lesbian. Would you leave your husband, and send him packing, so you could be right with your church and friends, or would you stay with your husband?" And she looked at me, and she looked into the camera, and you could just see the change in her face as she said "I get it. No, I'd keep my husband. And God bless you boys." It was just the most amazing thing to see her change like that.

Joshua Gamson: I think, as a genre, tabloid TV talk shows will stick around for a while because they are relatively inexpensive to produce and it is not that hard to make them profitable. The stories that get told are the kinds that you can tell over and over and they're fairly compelling. A lot of them, especially with the newer types of shows, really get into personal conflict almost exclusively. Those stories are old, archetypal stories about betrayal, which is the mainstay, I would say. Betrayal and change, the way people handle change, what you do when people suddenly change, those kinds of things, those sort of gender and sexuality themes that remain very much unresolved for people. When I first started writing the book, there were twenty-something shows because of so many shows copying *Ricki Lake* and other shows at the time. They cannibalized each other's ratings, so the number of shows decreased pretty quickly.

Chuck Hoy: The *Jerry Springer* show, which is in first-run syndication, deserves special mention. While the program is sensationalistic, it often includes as a matter of fact gay and lesbian couples with straight couples as part of many programs dealing with problem relationships. As commercial network television moves into the next decade, it too will eventually break more barriers as they pertain to gay and lesbian characters. Part of these barriers will be broken in order to compete with cable program channels in an effort to stem the constant erosion of the network television audience.

Joshua Gamson: Well, Jerry Springer is still doing pretty well, and I think talk shows are likely to come and go. And, according to the internal dynamics of the market, I think where you get somebody who is playing really nice for a while and then some one like Jerry Springer who steps in to be not so nice, then that makes room for others to be nice. We're not a celebrator of Springer's shows exactly. Just look at where the images were actually, the repetition of the images, and how there is a desensitizing process that I think he did, that was taking place on his talk show, where you know, the fact that someone is gay has become, finally, in some parts of this country, kind of dull. And for some generations and some populations, it is certainly not. We're not all the way there, but I think that's a great achievement, you know, and I think that's one of the things that talk shows contribute, that you could not go on a show now and just be a gay or lesbian professor or whatever. That's not interesting enough, and that kind of phenomenon has been a goal of the media activists for a long time, to be on the map but not have your gayness be much more than an incidental piece of you. Obviously we had lots of cultural visibility now without civil rights particularly. That is the game of overestimating the impact of cultural visibility. I mean, I think basically that cultural visibility helps in that you meet people who know that you exist. In other countries it has happened differently, where political rights preceded cultural visibility, but in this country I think that is pretty much the way it works, where in order to claim rights for the groups of people, you need to be established as existing as a group of people. Yet, just because people know there are gay people now, and because more and more people think that is just a fact of life rather than a moral flaw or disease, it won't stop the need for political organizing. What people do with the fact that they're visible is up to them. Just because you are on TV doesn't mean that suddenly everyone is going to rally behind antidiscrimination protection. You actually have to do political organizing to get that to happen. I think a lot of times people look at cultural visibility and somehow expect that it transfers (a) into tolerance, which it doesn't necessarily, and (b) into political change, which it definitely doesn't.

Alan Ross: I have been on about twenty talk shows. It just sort of spun out of control. I probably became somewhat of a "TV personality" in Philadelphia because there weren't a lot of gay fathers who were—I mean, there were only a few willing to appear. Each time I would take somebody new on with me. I'm out here willing to put myself on the line and take the risk. And I think if I'm able and willing to do it, I should do it because it is important to the rest of us. Every time I hear people saying, "Oh, I don't like the people who go to these Gay Pride marches," I tell them then you need to go and you need to be one of those people who gets in front of that camera. You have to outnumber the people you don't like. I like representing myself and nobody can represent me better than I can represent myself. So that's why I'm here.

Joshua Gamson: The new talk shows target a much younger audience, and so a lot of people see the history of the talk shows for gay people in a period of decline and of a sort of stereotyping. They perceive the shows of the last five years, the younger-oriented shows, as stereotyped, with gays presented as lowlife. I don't think that is really accurate. I think what has happened is sort of a replacement of one class dynamic for another. Because of the class dynamic of this new genre, it is a replacement of one set of class-based stereotypes with another set of class-based stereotypes, and that the object is again diversity of imagery. You actually get, for instance, in the more exploitative, louder kind of shows a lot more gay and lesbian people of color than you ever had on *Donohue,* and a lot more than you get in most mainstream organized gay communities, like gay urban centers and bars for gay men which are much less racially diverse than *Ricki Lake*—and so that is ironic because it is not the way people are used to thinking about it. And the same is true of seeing working-class gay and lesbian people—who you see almost nowhere culturally or at least not in media culture, except on the talk shows. And, you know, they suck. The shows suck, but the imagery is ironically very mixed up in a way that is different from most of what you get on TV. That is one of the important things I think about the change in the direction of the talk genre, for people not to mistake the fact that Donohue had middle-class, higher educated, white members of organizations as his guests in a nonstereotypical presentation—and that is also a very narrow vision of what gay and lesbian people are about.

Chapter Six

A Queer World

The International Outing of Queer Broadcasters

*In my dream, I would virtually be accessible on every station,
and this was before the Internet which is now. That's a whole
other amazing thing, now: the whole idea that somebody with a
computer and a modem can download and listen to our
program anywhere in the world, any time they want to,
on-demand, is just mind-boggling.*

—Greg Gordon, founder of *This Way Out*

The Gay Media Resource List[1] keeps track of radio and television shows targeted toward lesbians, gays, bisexuals, and the transgendered community in the world: indeed, the number of LGBT shows per country is as follows: Australia (24), Canada (26), Denmark (1), Netherlands (1), New Zealand (15), South Africa (2), Sweden (1), United Kingdom (3), and United States (259). Many of these shows air on community radio stations, like *Fruit Cocktail* on CHSR-FM in Canada. A search of the Web reveals a number of queer radio shows around the world, such as Japan's *Gay FM* and Canada's *Out and About Queer Radio* and *Queer FM*, as well as queer broadcast companies like Paris's techno-dance gay radio station Fréquence Radio Gaie (since the mid '80s) and the Dutch lesbian/gay radio-television company MVS Media.[2]

Queer broadcasting is fairly strong in Canada and Australia, and there is an increasing interest in such programming in New Zealand, South Africa, and the United Kingdom. On the other hand, the Thai broadcasting system ordered its television networks to restrict transvestites and transsexuals on soap operas and other popular shows, and the reaction among viewers has been mixed.[3] Over the years, Thailand programs have increasingly featured flamboyant transvestite and transsexual characters to the point that some gay and lesbian activists have complained about their stereotypical portrayal, while other viewers have objected on the grounds that impressionable youth might model sexual behavior after these characters.

Particularly significant is the fact that the United States is fertile ground for hundreds of queer programs, broadcast traditionally through radio and television and more recently via the Internet. *This Way Out International*, with its roots in

the *IMRU* days, represents an American effort to liberate gays and lesbians struggling for their civil rights and human dignity and to reduce homophobia through
education and information across the world airwaves and world wide web.

This Way Out, International

> *I very much appreciate the nice job you did [reporting] on*
> *that [Congressional] debate. My lover and I listened to it in*
> *the car as we were coming home from the gym, and we were*
> *both moved by it. I am honored to be on your Advisory*
> *Committee. You are doing excellent work and I'm glad to*
> *cooperate in this small way.*

—Barney Frank, U.S. House of Representatives[4]

Since its inception in 1988, the Los Angeles–produced *This Way Out* has become an
award-winning, internationally distributed, weekly, half-hour, gay and lesbian ra-
dio newsmagazine that currently airs over 100 primarily community and a few
commercial radio stations in seven countries, as well as across Europe on World
Radio Network's WRN1 and on Costa Rica–based global short wave station RFPI
(Radio for Peace International). *This Way Out* has won multiple awards from the
National Federation of Community Broadcasters, the Gay and Lesbian Alliance
Against Defamation (GLAAD), Parents, Friends, and Family of Lesbians and Gays
(PFLAG), and the Gay and Lesbian Press Association.[5] The program's accomplish-
ments over the years are even more impressive when you consider that its staff is
all volunteer.

Greg Gordon: We've just substantially expanded our potential listening
audience by about 22 million households through distribution across Europe
by World Radio Network (but they're also a nonprofit and can't afford to
pay for our program). In many ways it seems absurd that a globally distributed weekly LGBT radio show with only a mid-five-figure annual budget
(which has never been fully underwritten, by the way) can't get the funding
it needs, but that's the reality we've faced since we began distribution in
April 1988.

This Way Out also broadcasts in Real Audio on the Internet on PlanetOut Radio, in
exchange for a monthly licensing fee guaranteeing exclusivity rights. Each program is filled with interviews with authors, humor, poetry, and music recordings
by openly gay and lesbian performers rarely heard on commercial radio. *This Way
Out* has been praised by the queer community for "reaching into the closets and
countrysides where gays are painfully isolated."[6] Indeed, a number of listeners
write in to the show to express their appreciation:

I am just writing to let you know how important *This Way Out* has been in my life. I am now a junior in college and in the process of coming out to the world. During that time when I had no one else to give me courage and tell me stories about my past, it was *This Way Out* that did. I know that my experiences are not at all out of the ordinary. I just hope that you continue to provide the kind of service that you do. If you can help to give faith to one other young queer person to feel pride in him/herself you've done more than most.—Minneapolis, Minnesota.[7]

One of Gordon's favorites:

I'm a 44-year-old married male just confronting my homosexuality. I can't tell you what a moral boost your program is for me. I look forward to it every week. It's better than church.—Los Angeles, California[8]

This Way Out leads off each week with NewsWrap, a summary of some of the major news events in or impacting the lesbian and gay community. Stories are compiled from a variety of publications and broadcasts around the world. In addition to NewsWrap, other show segments include interviews with authors and performers, feature stories, AIDS updates, humorous poetry, readings from gay and lesbian literature, and self-produced recordings by openly lesbian and gay performers who rarely receive commercial airplay.

News and feature stories are produced by volunteers throughout the United States as well as from Canada, Australia, the Netherlands, Sweden, New Zealand, Great Britain, and Denmark. Responsible for *This Way Out's* news coverage is news director and NewsWrap coanchor Cindy Friedman and associate news director and NewsWrap coanchor Brian Nunes. Friedman has a long history of radio producing with *IMRU* and has worked extensively for a variety of women's and feminist causes for nearly fifteen years, including serving as the acting executive director of Haven House, a battered women's shelter in Pasadena, California. Brian Nunes became a volunteer staff member of *This Way Out* in 1991. He has a communications degree and works by day for Business Wire, an international media relations wire service.

Greg Gordon left *IMRU* in 1984. Four years later, *This Way Out* would debut on twenty-six stations. For Gordon, Lucia Chappelle, and eventually other *IMRU* volunteers, it seemed only natural to take this next step: the production and international distribution of a gay and lesbian radio program. In the late 1980s, National Public Radio satellite was beginning to connect public radio stations across the country. Finally, there was a way of distributing programming that had not been previously available for queer producers like Gordon and Chappelle. In a sense, Gordon's dream of a network of radio producers has been fulfilled, although he never fully parted ways with KPFK.

This Way Out is produced by the nonprofit organization Overnight Productions, and it is the sister show of *IMRU,* which is the starting point for many volunteers at KPFK. *IMRU* trains volunteers who eventually contribute to *This Way Out,* which accepts features from all over the world. Most of what they air on local issues in Los Angeles is produced by people who started at *IMRU*. Since both *IMRU* and *This Way Out* air on the same station, there's some programming overlap. Like many volunteers, Chris Wilson became hooked on gay and lesbian radio and considered it a creative way to give back to the community. Along with her partner Pam Marshall, she hosted an LGBT music segment called "Audiofile" for *This Way Out,* and it grew into its own entity over the years and is featured on PlanetOut.

Jon Beaupre: Chris Wilson and her partner Pam Marshall, developed their own franchise, "Audiofile," which was a five- to seven-minute monthly review on what's new in lesbian and gay music. It was superbly produced and beautifully put together. They received a Silver Reel from the National Federation of Community Broadcasters.

Chris Wilson: I was driving down the street listening to public radio when I heard that the local gay and lesbian radio show was looking for volunteers, and I thought I'd like to help them out. I don't have any radio background or experience but I bet I could go answer some phones for them or do something behind the scenes, and so I went to the orientation that they were offering and I learned what I didn't know then about public radio, and that is that just about everything in public radio is volunteer, and yes, volunteering did include doing on-air work, and so I was asked what I might like to produce a piece on— and one of the things at that point that was near and dear to my heart was my very own commitment ceremony. I wanted to explore different types of commitment ceremonies in the gay and lesbian community, and the next thing you know, I had done my first full-length show exploring different types of commitment ceremonies with excerpts and what have you. I was hooked. In fact, at the orientation session, I'll tell you how they hooked me. They asked me, my very first time, the very first time I ever walked into a radio station, they asked me to read the community calendar to be taped for broadcast the next day. I became so enthralled, and I recalled back to when I was a child and how I used to love to tape-record things and make little interesting stories on tape by taping clips of different songs and putting the lyrics together to tell a story with some narration, and it just all kind of fit together. It really met my needs for creativity and my need for service to the gay and lesbian community all at once, and I've been producing radio ever since. It's my volunteer work. The founder of *This Way Out,* Greg Gordon, was originally an *IMRU* volunteer, but he had a vision to create something more than a local L.A. show.

Greg Gordon: After almost ten years doing *IMRU*, I had reached the burnout stage, and I wanted it to expand and to go national. I took some time off after *IMRU*, and I was kind of frustrated that there wasn't a lot of other enthusiasm by the collective members to try to put together a national gay and lesbian program. There were, and are still, several locally produced gay and lesbian shows, and I really wanted to try to get some sort of tape exchange going at the very least with other local programmers, and then expand the programming possibilities of what we could put on *IMRU* by including material from other shows that might be of interest to all our listeners. But the problem was, and still is, that the producers of many of the local shows at community stations, particularly in small areas, but just about everywhere, I think, have offices in two or three local queer rights organizations, so it is basically all they can do to get into the station once a week and do a live show with phones or something, let alone get them on tape and to make a copy and then take it to the post office. Just the mechanics of a tape exchange proved very frustrating because not many programmers at other stations were able to do what I was hoping we could do. There had been two other attempts at national programming before what became *This Way Out.* One was the *National Gay Network.* I think that it was based in San Francisco. *NGN* failed for a number of reasons. I think it wasn't on for even a year. After that, I believe another guy in New York, based at WBAI, did a strictly gay men's show, and he was completely resistant to making it pro-gender. And it basically was phone reports from different people around the country, and at the risk of sounding immodest or whatever, the production value of both shows was not really good. *IMRU* approached them after hearing that the folks at the gay men's collective were having a gay day from 9 A.M. until midnight with all gay and lesbian programming. And so we started doing that, and at one point the guy at *NGN* in San Francisco had live radio coverage of the San Francisco Freedom Day parade. We let it run, and we stayed by the phone line and let it run for about twenty minutes, but the sound quality was just awful. We finally wound up pulling some archival tape and switching from the live coverage to whatever it was that we had on tape. I wondered from the beginning how can you do real compelling radio, live radio coverage of a parade, when the most prominent feature of a parade is what you can see, you know?

Lucia Chappelle: Greg and I thought that we should—somebody should—do this on a national level. We were busy doing a weekly show. So it took a while. We thought about it really before the idea actually became viable—like this could be done. This was probably in the late '70s, early '80s.

Greg Gordon: I had talked Lucia into being my coconspirator. I took a grant-writing class, a night class at Los Angeles Community College, just to sort of become familiar with the basics of getting funding. Actually, before

This Way Out, we started a community program named *Inside Out,* and our first program feed was April 1 of 1988, April Fool's Day. We sent out a postcard to all the U.S. stations that were able to download satellite-fed programming and announced its debut. Within the first six months, we got a letter from some group in Indiana; essentially it was a cease-and-desist letter because "Inside Out" was the name of some in-classroom video instruction series that they produced, and we didn't have any kind of money or lawyers or anything else to fight it. You know, why anyone would confuse a weekly queer radio show with an in-classroom video education series for students is beyond us, but we just decided on the path of least resistance, and so we changed the name of the show to *This Way Out.*

Chris Wilson: *This Way Out* originally started financially with grants, and it has managed to get grants for the last twelve years, but we've learned that there are a lot more worthy causes than there are grants available and we have to look at other ways. A lot of people don't realize when they listen to *This Way Out* what it costs to make it available to them, and when they support their local public radio stations, which we encourage them to do, that has nothing to do with the radio station's annual budget, nor do we receive any money from those fund drives on the local radio stations.

Greg Gordon: In 1986, there happened to be a conference of the international community radio association called L'AMARC, the world association of community broadcasters. They were holding their annual conference in Vancouver, British Columbia. I met a guy from London who wound up being one of our first international contributors to what became *This Way Out.*

Lucia Chappelle: I think what we do is a little bit different—carrying weekly news, particularly international. I think a lot of the shows that are available are mostly talk, and that's fine. I don't see anybody else really taking the global perspective that we try to have in our programs because most radio itself is local, and that's very, very important. That's part of the heart of radio, yet to take the global perspective is something different. It's something different for the gay and lesbian community, and it's something different for the TV media. Oh, it's all those distracting pictures, as we radio people say. Personally, it's not my medium. And I think radio can be a lot more penetrating. Radio is ambiguous. People have radio in their bathroom. You don't have your TV in your hip pocket, and maybe that will happen more and more. To be transmitted globally, radio is very, very important and very neglected.

Greg Gordon: We started with twenty-six stations that sent postcards back saying that they'd be carrying *This Way Out* in the United States and Canada, but mostly in the United States. We heard from the station in Melbourne, Australia, that they had read a little blurb about us, or about what became *This Way Out,* in a gay newspaper out of Vancouver, British Columbia. Somehow that paper winds up in Melbourne and they read about us, and contacted us, and so they started carrying our stuff. Then we started getting occasional programming contributions from them. I still marvel at the fact that we've done over 600 programs. We can't pay anybody. We can't pay for stringers or anything else, and, as I've jokingly said, all we can offer is international radio stardom because of our wide distribution. Even so, we have rarely been flailing about every or any week saying that we have nothing to run. It is just marvelous that volunteer producers, who do news and stuff—and good stuff—for their local programs or their local stations offer it for us to use. Of course they are getting much wider exposure for their work, but even with the fact that we can't pay anybody, it is wonderful that there's still people, younger students, helping us out, and it is also frustrating because I wish we did have the money to pay people.

Jon Beaupre: Their budget is probably a hundred times that of *IMRU* because it is sent all over the world. It's a show that could use a lot more money, but what it does with the little bit of money that it has is just remarkable and done on an absolute shoestring budget. It is just remarkable that the show gets the few grants that it does and manages to stay on the air, seemingly being ready to drop off the radio, almost at any moment, but Greg manages to keep it going.

Chris Wilson: What I do off the air is help with the incredible fund-raising that is necessary to keep the international show going up on the NPR satellite. As the president of Overnight Productions, my main responsibility is to increase the visibility of the show and to let people know that the only way we can go up on the satellite and be available free of charge is from the financial support of the people who feel this is a good thing and want to support the program. I love the creativity of producing radio, but the bottom line is that it will wither and die if we don't make our budget of, at minimum, between $36,000 and $50,000 a year, just to go up on the satellite and be available free to all the community and college radio stations. In her professional life, my partner Pam is a financial consultant. I'm an attorney. We wanted to do something creative. This is how we got involved. Then we became involved in the organization itself with respect to the fund-raising and the struggling with all of that. She's just recently taken over as cochair of the board of directors, and I took over as president, and we decided to really put our efforts into long-range financial planning for *This Way Out.* We'd like it to continue to grow and be there and not have to constantly worry about whether there is grant funding.

Lucia Chappelle: Funding is a continual problem, so it's hard to think of the next step. I think it's pretty significant that we're already on-line on PlanetOut so we've kind of tapped that market. We've gotten into shortwave and we've gotten into the distribution service in Europe, and more and more of those kinds of distribution opportunities are going to be coming. Our next step depends somewhat on what happens in the world of broadcast and netcast—on-line, off-line—it's hard to say what kind of turns the media is going to take in the next five to ten years to know where the really best place for us is going to be.

Greg Gordon: PlanetOut has been very helpful financially to us. We have the exclusive rights to carry the audio of *This Way Out* on their Web site, for which we are paid a licensing fee. Tom Rielly, who is the founder of PlanetOut and was the cochair and founder of Digital Queers, has sort of been our angel. He managed to get the very first computer system for *This Way Out* through Digital Queers because they had a grant-making program through the Gill Foundation. We used to drive to a different bookstore every week and pick up twelve or fourteen gay publications, and that's how we wrote the weekly news segment of *This Way Out.* Now of course, being on-line, it is instantaneous.

Lucia Chappelle: Now we can go on-line and find out what happened in Burma yesterday, and that's pretty remarkable. But I still think that we are bringing that information to a whole lot of people who not only are not on-line, but are not going to be on-line for an awfully long time, in places where radio really is the electronic medium that's available.

Greg Gordon: I also cannot tell you how many times I have contacted national organizations saying that I'm still waiting for the audio versions of the public service announcement that they just started with Judy Shepard. They never think about radio. I think that the work that programs like *In The Life* and local gay access shows are doing is wonderful, but radio doesn't take a lot of money. If it took a lot of money, *This Way Out* wouldn't be on the air. I'm not looking for fame and fortune or people to erect a statue in my honor. But I feel like the work that we do doesn't get the respect that it deserves from the national queer powers that be, with rare exceptions. We had a very nice letter from Barney Frank. And I've interviewed him a couple of times. Considering that we started with twenty-six stations in the United

States and Canada and we're now on the air on over a hundred stations around the world—without doing any one of my standard lines like if we had any money, we'd really be dangerous—we have barely scratched the surface.

Lucia Chappelle: Certainly, there's been a tremendous blossoming of gay and lesbian programming throughout Australia and New Zealand and the connections that we have with those people have been really promising. Clearly, *This Way Out* being there has helped them to put out the message. A lot of them use our material and we pass our material back and forth and around the world, so we've been a part of that and have also watched that and benefited from that. We've started to get our feet in the doors of Asia, and I think we will be seeing a lot happening in Africa, and radio is very important there.

Chris Wilson: I don't love anything, any organization, within our community the way I love *This Way Out,* and I see its value because it's the one aspect of the gay and lesbian community that can be made available to anyone with access to the radio or to the Internet and they can listen to it privately, and no one has to be aware, and they don't have to interact with any other person. They don't have to out themselves. They can just listen to this wonderful news from all over the world.

Greg Gordon: It is the whole notion of *This Way Out* being an activism tool, like when something happens and the community needs to be rallied on a national basis, what more likely outlet for that than a weekly gay and lesbian show to rally the troops, so to speak. It is one of Lucia's lines, and I can't remember who she borrowed it from, but radio is the community's tribal drum, and I love that line because I think it's true.

Lucia Chappelle: Oh, listen, we know people who are producing radio shows on community radio stations who grew up listening to us. That's pretty scary. Our role is the same because even though it's been twenty years, everybody's not out yet, you know? We don't have rights yet. We still get beaten and murdered, twenty years later. So the show continues to bring to our own community and to the wider community our stories and our voices.

Greg Gordon: At one point, I was at KPFK, more specifically the Pacifica Radio Archives. They archive all of our tapes and at one point they were duplicating and distributing the program on tape to some stations that couldn't get us off the satellite. And I was there on a Tuesday to drop off a tape—for maybe five minutes. And this was when I was still working full-time. I was there at the time when a phone call for me came into the switchboard. It just happened. I was there. A woman who was driving from Boulder to Denver, where she lives, happened to be listening to *This Way Out* off of a Boulder station because we're not on Denver. She tracked me down from an old job and happened to call up KPFK looking for me at the exact moment I was there. She said, "I heard your program, and I thought it was wonderful. Do you need any money?" Her name is Clarissa Pinkola Estes, apparently a very well-known feminist author. She has a small foundation, and she wound up giving us funding for about two or three years running. And when things like that [happen], if you don't believe in divine providence or God or something, you know, then something like that gets you to rethink your philosophy. Because I mean the odds of something like that happening are just too bizarre. And in some ways it is amazing to me that we've lasted as long as we've lasted. You know, our 600th program was just distributed. It's just something that I keep doing. The personal reward from doing it is the feedback we get from the show. Somebody once asked me, "Do you think there'll come a time when there will be no need for *This Way Out*?" And I think, hopefully, ideally, that day will come, but at the same time I think there will always be a need for us to talk to ourselves, to each other, in some sort of forum. I don't think the *Advocate* will ever go out of business—at least it won't be from a lack of a need for us.

Gay Talk and Queer Folk

> *The UK is not known for being the most liberal and forward thinking of countries, but it has worked for me. In fact, every time I want to step away from this gay bubble and enter mainstream broadcasting, I seem to get that call asking me to get involved in something gay again! And guess what? I am a consultant now on a new gay television series for the BBC.*
>
> —Paul Graham, host and producer of *Gaytalk*

Paul Graham began his broadcast career, immediately after college, in hospital radio, which he described as having "zero gay perspectives in the production content"—it was only a matter of time before he would seek other opportunities in gay media. Having grown up around Manchester, he easily decided to return home, so to speak. He soon began to work in recording studios and became part of the band the C30's for a while.

In the mid-1990s, an offer from a gay producer at KISS 102 in Manchester set into motion what would become a career in gay radio for Graham. Another invitation soon came along, but this time to produce and present a segment within *Gaytalk,* a new gay show at the local BBC station in Manchester, and this quickly turned into an opportunity to host what is now considered the longest running gay program in the United Kingdom (UK). And the rest is history.

Paul Graham: It all started when I complained to the then *Gay News* about its London-centric attitude. The reply was a bit standoffish: "Well, if there is anyone out there who wants to write about the gay scene outside of London..." Well, I did. Combined with my KISS radio work in the Manchester [northwest UK] area, I soon used the celebrity radio interview transcripts for written articles. Well, very few celebs would entertain an interview with a gay magazine.

About three and a half years ago, I was working for KISS 102 in Manchester. The KISS shows were, admittedly, littered with positive gay and lesbian references with no need to hide our sexuality. Though they were gay friendly, I did not see any sort of gay-specific show being aired. When I left KISS and moved to the BBC [British Broadcasting Corporation], I had within me the production values of KISS—fast, furious, and to the point. Although they did not fit in with *Gaytalk* immediately, those values have heavily influenced the current *Gaytalk.* I also learned how to produce *Gaytalk* from "the heart," that is to produce [pieces] that I would listen to, those that I really do like to hear.

Most local BBC radio stations throughout the UK tend to cater toward the older audience, completely the opposite of the market KISS goes for, so it was intriguing and surprising that they wanted me to come on board for their new show *Gaytalk.* Initially I was to write and present the "What's On" part of the show, right at the end. I watched and listened as the first few months saw changes in the weekly show.

The attitude of many at the BBC was one of open-mindedness—again, something which I had not expected. The great BBC was something I saw as being that bastion of conservatism. Were they just letting such a show go on in an attempt to prove that they cared about the community, only to watch the show dig its own grave and disappear quietly? I was full of enthusiasm but also full of skepticism and, I admit, saw *Gaytalk* very much as a little island in a big sea—an island that was not really connected to the mainland, nor really cared about. The management really supported *Gaytalk* though, much more than I realized at first. It was the only gay/lesbian show on local BBC radio in the whole of UK—and still is. Yes, there are and have been other gay shows on radio but never one to last three and a half years and be in an incredibly strong position and surviving very well! The show's creator, Matt Foster, left after two years, leaving me as the "other" presenter. A few producers stepped in to carry the show forward over a two-month period, but

I could see that ultimately I was continuing the original ethos/idea that Matt originally had: a magazine show for lesbians and gay men that covered news, local and national, celeb interviews, entertainment features, and a "What's On."

After taking over the reins of producer and asking a female colleague to copresent with me, I did stray close to that gray line—the one where management would step in and say, "No, that was too risqué/over the top/unnecessary, etc." You know, looking back at that period of *Gaytalk,* I can see that some would have had nervous and sleepless nights over the shows I was devising—themes such as S&M, fetish, casual sex, alternative comedy—I explored them all. And the BBC, God bless 'em, stood by me. I didn't really comprehend the situation at the time, not realizing that the typical audience was probably either turning off or smiling weakly at my production ideas!

But is there a compromise to be made in gay programming? Yes. Ultimately I did learn that a dedicated show like *Gaytalk* is of interest to the straight community and there is considerable crossover potential. Why bother? Well, I would bother because I don't see *Gaytalk* as a ghetto show. But nor do I see it as being a compromise—you know, a show where we cover gay issues in a straight way. We *have* to talk about sex and condoms and AIDS and death, but we also have a ball talking to Lily Savage and Jimmy Somerville and Boy George and Ian McKellan and Toyah and Barbara Windsor, etc. Of course, the BBC loves it when big names come onto the show, but I love it because gay men and women love it as well.

In April '99, I received a memo from the editor of the station. It went out to all presenters. It was time to have new photocards printed of all the station's presenters. It sounds weird, but although I know *Gaytalk* really did have a solid commitment from the great BBC for a gay show, this one thing really made me feel as though our little bit of gay broadcasting had made it. Our photocards were to be in the main reception area alongside all the other mainstream presenters. No special feature or separate container—"Mainstream Shows," "Community Shows" or anything like that. It made me feel sorta funny. A sorta nice queer feeling!

So what about the audience's opinion? Well, back at the start, *Gaytalk* was one of only two programs actually making "trails" to be broadcast in any show (that wanted to broadcast it). Ours were camp—spoofs on *The Wizard of Oz* or *Whatever Happened to Baby Jane?* And they really were played to death.

One listener wrote to the *Manchester Evening News,* the huge local daily, "Does BBC Greater Manchester Radio have no other show other than *Gaytalk?* Judging by their trails, it would seem not!" Then there was the man who rang in to complain . . .

Caller: All you talk about is sex, sex, sex. Don't you lot have nothing else on your minds?

Paul: Er, we don't always talk about sex!

Caller: Go on then—name something in tonight's show which isn't.

Paul: Well, there are the film reviews, and the London bombing.

Caller: Ah, there you go! If your lot didn't keep wanting sex all the time, that bomb wouldn't have happened!

Paul: Well, I think you are confusing sexuality with sex, sir. If you like, we can send you some stuff about being gay and lesbian, and support groups?

Caller: Yeah, but you would need my address and I am not giving you that. I wouldn't want you lot knocking on my door at all hours of the day and night!

Paul: In that case, Sir, I can see that there is no hope for you.

Nowadays, I can say that *Gaytalk* gets phone calls, letters, faxes, e-mails, etc., from all sorts of people, groups, marketing companies, record labels—you name it, they want us to interview this person/group, review this record/book/ theater play, give away Levis/vodka/videos, etc. Actually, I remember that we used to receive soft porn videos for review twice a month. Not that we actually could review them, or really wanted to review them, but one lady in the main office who opened the mail used to get so offended by the videos that she threw them straight in the bin. When I found out, I politely stated that if anyone were going to bin videos addressed to *Gaytalk,* it would be me. And you know what? She was given a right telling off from the management.

I give the idea that working on a gay show at the BBC is just so easy. It really has been, though. Easy from the point of view of no hassle and tons of support from the corporation. When I wanted to do a three-hour live show from the Mardi Gras, there was no objection at all. When I wanted to broadcast a show live via the Internet, the only objection was that we had to do it through the BBC Web site and not an Internet Service Provider (ISP) who had volunteered their services free. I have lost count of the number of people who have wanted to meet up and discuss how *Gaytalk* works, because they want to set up a version elsewhere. So far, I have heard stories that no other local BBC station will entertain a gay show for all sorts of banal reasons. Are we really that liberal in Manchester??? Or will those other stations really really combine the gay stuff into the mainstream shows?

There is a danger, of course, of creating a show like *Gaytalk,* which is ghettoized. We sometimes talk "scene-talk," without thinking for example. But mainstream broadcasting, in radio, tele, cable, Internet, or whatever, cannot cater for a specifically gay market. Even creating gay shows cannot work if the production team is not primarily gay—in my personal experience, at any rate! But a gay show can and does work, and work exceptionally well, if it does not alienate those who are not gay.

Queer As Folk in the UK

> *Too many think of the Gay Village as a cultural nexus, but at the end of the day my beloved Manchester contains a small to medium-sized gay ghetto that straight people find all too inviting. It offers a playground and nothing else. It's great to play, but don't expect any favors in an area devoted to hedonism!*

—Paul Graham, producer of "Village Voices"

Queer television in the United Kingdom has "never really had any weight thrown behind it," according to Paul Graham, neither by community leaders nor station management in terms of providing more than a superficial look inside the gay and lesbian community. In 1997, Graham submitted a proposal to Channel 4 Television to produce a special about Manchester's Gay Village—an area of the center city that contains around forty gay/lesbian businesses, including bars, clubs, taxi firms, shops, hairdressers, and solicitors. The station accepted it and "Village Voices" went into production—an hour-long documentary revolving around the lives of a number of real people in the Gay Village.

Paul Graham: I found this project more remarkable than any other I have done. People have a heightened opinion of a gay television show, much, much more than radio or the written word. Because we didn't always go for the "gay village is nice" person, we did take some criticism for not portraying the Gay Village in a glowing light, which I thought was a very sad attitude, but one I could understand.

During the last three years, the UK has begun to loosen its reins on acceptable content, and this change in attitude became evident when it aired the first program of an eight-part controversial series called *Queer As Folk* in the late 1990s. Coproduced by Russell T. Davies and Nicola Shindler, *Queer As Folk* revolves around the loves and lives of three gay males in Manchester's Gay Village—one of whom is only fifteen. The show promises its viewers

> No victims
> No martyrs
> No role models[9]

and that's what many viewers like about the show. As for the public outrage, there's been plenty of that too. Some viewers were concerned about the sexually explicit gay story line:

> Vince Tyler is in love with best friend Stuart and happily living in his shadow when along comes fifteen-year-old Nathan Maloney and nothing's ever the

same again. Stuart Jones is king of the world! You know those nights when everything's just magic? You're confident, hot and the boys think so too. For Stuart every night's like that because he says so. But for how much longer?[10]

The concerns did not halt the production of a sequel in the UK. A two-hour follow-up was filmed in August 1999—again in Manchester—for telecast in January 2000. The series spawned numerous Web sites, the initial video was among the Top Ten, and the double CD soundtrack rose to the Top Five. An American version—set in Pittsburgh—made its debut on Showtime on December 3, 2000, and has proven to be equally graphic in its bedroom scenes, according to British reviews.[11]

Paul Graham: The gay genre has always been played with, but never seriously. I remember gay shows from the '80s, but never has anything been particularly different as a series up until *Queer As Folk*. This was an eight-part gay drama, made and filmed in Manchester, that totally changed things in terms of broadcasting. It was hard hitting, dealt with underage sex, and showed full gay sex, more or less, taking place right on your telescreens. It caused a massive outcry in the press, with criticisms from straight and gay alike. It also was Channel 4's third most popular show during the weeks of its transmission. And I loved it. This was Queer slapped right in the face of Mr. and Mrs. General Public! I've heard that no U.S. stations will broadcast the [Manchester]series as it is too sexy/pornographic/ honest/lewd, etc., etc.! Strange to think that a series like this can come from a nation that is supposed to be more repressed sexually than the whole of Europe! It does seem that Channel 4 is the only broadcaster that will get its hands dirty in terms of gay stuff. They even have a subdepartment for gay and lesbian material—an offshoot of independent stuff.

Queer Under in Australia

> *I was lucky to have been going through the formative years, around sixteen, seventeen, at the height of glam rock. David Bowie, especially, made sexual ambiguity and sexuality itself not just acceptable, but absolutely enthralling. Bisexuality was readily accepted by my friends. However, I only knew two men who had always been confident and proud to be homosexual.*
> *One was the sixteen-year-old mail-boy at work, who considered himself married at the time and who told me that I should start getting sex now, because I would soon be over the hill (at eighteen!). The other was a friend's older brother. Parties at the friend's household, when the parents were on vacation, were a wonderful mix of dykes, fags, and straights. I could have easily fallen for a cute Canadian exchange teacher, who said I should*

come to see him, when I eventually decided that I was gay. I
was not sexually active at the time and found it easy to be
distracted by music, mild drugs and the other wonders of life.

—John Frame, host of *Queer Radio*

In 1993, after some serious introspection, John Frame decided that he wanted to become more openly gay, and get involved in queer issues. He became active with a very queer-friendly and sociable political party, the Democratic Socialists. This decision would lead him to an old acquaintance and a major role in the production of *Queer Radio.* Frame, host and coordinator of *Queer Radio* in Brisbane, Queensland, Australia, used his own coming out as inspiration to others struggling with the same identity issues. One of Frame's guests was Erin Shale, a dedicated high school counselor from Melbourne, who has edited a new book called *Inside Out: A Collection of Australian Coming Out Stories.* The book features thirty-eight stories, including those of footballer Ian Roberts, musician Monique Brumby, Senator Bob Brown, comedian Sue-Ann Post, and lots of young men and women. Shale spent two years on the project and had approached approximately a thousand people to find interview subjects.

Indeed, *Queer Radio* is a show driven by music and issues that speak to the LGBT experience.

John Frame: *Queer Radio,* the show that I've presented for the last five years, was instrumental in helping me deal with my sexuality—so I know how valuable and unique it is in Brisbane. I regularly meet activists who state that the show had been crucial in developing their self-acceptance. Sometimes they've happened on the show by accident while channel surfing—startled to hear someone actually saying positive things about being gay. I've seen the benefits of hands-on involvement with the show—not only in myself, but also especially with other long-term participants.

Our host, subscriber-owned community broadcaster 4ZZZ [Four Triple Zed], was the first FM radio station in our state. It was established and run by students at the University of Queensland in 1975, at the height of a regressive conservative period of government. Gay men and lesbians were involved from inception and since at least 1980 there has been continuous weekly programming aimed to support gay, lesbian, bisexual, and transgender listeners. No other radio station in Brisbane has a gay-supportive program—and even Australia's national "youth network"—Triple J FM—fails to give space, which I believe is a great wasted opportunity to increase visibility and to combat homophobia.

We alternate with our sister show *Dykes on Mikes* each Wednesday night from 7 to 9 P.M.—which makes us accessible to everyone who could want to listen, yet late enough so that frank discussions about sex shouldn't frighten the children. We present news, reviews, and interviews; promote local events and groups; discuss relevant topics and usually have invited guests—including workers from the Queensland AIDS Council and Queensland Positive People, who discuss current projects and strategies for dealing with HIV. Listeners are welcomed to join us in person. Recently a lovely man returned to Pennsylvania full of confidence, after being a regular listener and studio visitor, during his work assignment here.

I try to steer the show toward supporting those who are young and developing an awareness of their identity and sexuality, because they are the ones most likely to be suffering from the lack of support elsewhere in the media. There is a lot of fear that openly supporting youth will be seen as recruiting or even akin to pedophilia. Youth need to know *now* that they are valuable, just as they are, and that sex can be fun and safe, but that sexuality is not chosen.

We also cater to those who are closeted and/or dealing with coming out as a mature adult (as I did). When we had transmitter problems, a man in his late forties phoned to make sure we were still there, even if he couldn't receive us at the time. He said that he was isolated in a distant suburb and that we were a lifeline for him each fortnight. Just knowing that you are not the only gay man in town can be comforting. Aside from saying the right things, it's also important to actually entertain—a major factor, especially in radio (after all, we are in show business). Consequently we have a broad queer-friendly audience—our PFLAG of the future. Our current panel operator, Gordon, is a happy heterosexual man who has regularly tuned in for the last year or two.

The nature of the position of coordinator-presenter necessitates being aware of and interacting with a large range of support and social groups in the gay and lesbian community. I have come to know many wonderful and sincere men and women locally, as well as those I've interviewed from interstate and overseas for various reasons: writers, musicians, actors, directors, educators, performers, politicians, clergy, and activists. I'm sure it was the honesty and openness of those people which led to a point, about two years into presenting *Queer Radio,* where I became conscious of the fact that I knew, with every fiber of my being, that it was OK to be gay. Hopefully our listeners will all arrive at the same conclusion but, like me, they may have to talk it through—not just listen. That's why I actively encourage involvement with community groups.

Community radio has a huge advantage over commercially oriented operations because programming can be based on needs rather than profits. We have shows that cater especially for prisoners, women, youth, the environment, and anarchists—as well as for jazz, blues, heavy metal, ska, and punk rock enthusiasts. The other volunteers openly and positively support us. The station gave us the use of its basement to stage two "Pink Light Disco" dances for queer youth in '96 and '97. I spent as much as I could afford to have professional lighting, sound, and deejays but keep the door price low. I wanted those attending to know we take them seriously. There is no regular entertainment venue here for queer youth under eighteen and I think it's risky to have them trying to develop vital social skills at bars. The basement is being renovated as a bookshop/drop-in center and I hope to arrange regular evenings for movies, music, or discussion.

For the last two years I've been Four Triple Zed's official media representative at the Sydney Gay and Lesbian Mardi Gras Parade. With several thousand people from a huge range of groups marching, and all of them happy to talk about why they are there, it's a unique occasion to do "vox-pop" interviews. The statements define the times, and I'm quite sure I was the only person doing this style of recording on the day. Having access to the whole parade is a great privilege—one that I take seriously. Within a few days I had forty perfectly recorded interviews edited to compact disc and copies sent to Mardi Gras for its archives—as well as sitting in 4ZZZ's library. I heard selections played by several other deejays.

In 1999, *Queer Radio* had our first [parade] entry—a walking group of eight men and women with the theme "There is no substitute for equality." Even though this was my fourth Mardi Gras, it was especially exciting to be representing *Queer Radio* and our listeners in front of 600,000 enthusiastic supporters. It's a fun and effective way to do public relations. There are lots of angles you can use as a radio reporter on gay issues. We took part in this year's Labor Day parade and afterwards I asked unionists if they were aware that they worked with any gay men or lesbians and, if so, how well were they treated? I recorded many positive responses—even from big, booffy waterside workers. You get more confident with each situation you work in because you find that people really do respect honesty.

High-profile people such as local football player Ian Roberts, Jimmy Somerville, Julian Clary, Armistead Maupin, and Clive Barker have all been generous in sharing their feelings with our audience. However, I believe it's equally important to hear local men and women talk confidently about life, love, desire, emotion, and sex. I try to accentuate the value of seeing yourself as an individual, who has some things in common with others. The more people who can be open and honest on radio, the better.

We are just stepping into the arena of the Internet (see our home page at 4zzzfm.org.au) which I expect will be a great boost to the number of people we can reach and how well we communicate with our audience. In the last two years, independent gay [recording] artists Steve Cohen, Dave Hall, and Ed Diamond have contacted us via Internet and sent us copies of their work, which we've been happy to play. Our Web site will have a playlist for each previous show with full details of the music used. I hope this will lead to CD sales for those who are not only out and proud, but also talented and supportive.

Involvement with *Queer Radio* has certainly given me a greater understanding of myself, as well as those around me. I feel I have the skills and confidence to talk to just about anyone about anything (shutting me up may be the hard part). My interviews have been described as being more like informal chats—which is fine; I think we can all share something as we talk. The person I was most nervous about interviewing was Jimmy Somerville, because I was so much in awe of his status as a politically aware, gay musician. He quickly put me at ease with his honesty and humor and I had a great time.

Melbourne's Joy

I often think about my closeted days and think about how wonderful it would have been for me had I been able to listen to a local gay FM radio station and learn something about a lifestyle that had been locked away from me for so many years. I especially hope that my small contribution to the gay electronic media here in Melbourne will lead many of our listeners to a more open, happy, productive, and satisfying life.

—Allan Smales, host of *Pot Pourri*

Joy Melbourne 90.7 is a gay and lesbian volunteer-run radio station that began broadcasting on World AIDS Day, December 1, 1993. Allan Smales is one of the hosts of *Pot Pourri*, a show that appears to have struck a cord with Melbourne listeners who phone into the station, e-mail the staff, and stop to chat with Smales outside the studio on a regular basis. A marriage that failed as a result of his coming out in 1991, and his earlier interest in radio during his early twenties, eventually lead to Allan's involvement in Australia's first gay and lesbian radio station.

Allan Smales: The announcement that Joy Melbourne was now operational prompted me to immediately apply to become a supporting member. From the beginning of 1994, I started making representations to the then organizing committee about how I might be able to become actively involved. Quite by chance a few weeks later (April 1994), I attended a totally unrelated meeting of a group intending to plan a Melbourne entry for the 1995 Mardi Gras parade. At this meeting, there was the presenter of a weekly news review program from Joy Melbourne who was bemoaning the fact that his regular on-air cohost was unexpectedly in hospital. This meant that the following Saturday he was going to have to do the program solo. He was saying how he would have preferred a stand-in cohost. The rest is history. I volunteered on the spot, he accepted, and the following Saturday in May 1994, I found myself in front of a microphone in the Joy Melbourne studio. I have been actively involved in Joy Melbourne, Australia's first gay and lesbian radio station, ever since.

This was only shortly after the conclusion of the two traumatic years following my marriage breakup. As a result, even though I was trying to consider myself as now being fairly much out, I still found it slightly uncomfortable to even use (or have other people use) my first name on radio. It was to be about another year before I finally got to using my full (and real) name on radio. It's rather strange, when I look back now, how uncomfortable I felt in using even my first name on radio during my program. Now, it is a total nonevent.

In early 1995, a new station programming committee had decided that the station needed a lifestyle program and I, with Bill, my cohost of the time, was asked to plan and conduct that program. *Pot Pourri* went to air at midday on Saturday May 6, 1995. Initially this was a three-hour program later reduced to two hours. *Pot Pourri* has regularly rated as one of the most popular programs on Joy Melbourne, even allowing for the fact that we have had a few time changes in recent times. In May 1999, we not only celebrated the fourth anniversary of the program, but this anniversary also coincided almost to the very day with the 200th edition of the program.

Through *Pot Pourri,* we wanted to present a variety of different subjects each week, with a mix of middle-of-the-road popular music. Some of the regular segments in the program over the years have included insurance issues with a gay slant, gay medical issues with a local gay doctor, pets, health issues, gardening, show reviews, restaurant reviews, as well as interviews with people in the news, visiting celebrities, or people who were involved in the organization of local gay and lesbian events. But one of the most popular regular segments from the very outset of this new program has been one called Coming Out. This had been my idea from the beginning. I was well aware of the struggles I had been through over recent years and had wished that I could have heard other people's stories about their lives, their problems, family issues, and finally coming out. I decided that this was my way of putting something back into the community again. I wanted to be able to present something that other still-closeted people could listen to and be reassured that they weren't the only gay people in the world. I also wanted to be able to present coming-out stories from people from all walks of life and to show also that not all gay guys are effeminate . . . that they can be very successful in the business community and generally be your "boy next door" (although I hate that description).

One of the most satisfying things about including the Coming Out segment each week in our program is the feedback that we receive. These come in the form of phone calls to the station, e-mails, and discussions with people I meet. We know from phone calls and messages that teenagers and university students listen and are still living at home with Mum and Dad. They cannot take gay papers and magazines home lest they be found. But we know they can (and do) listen in on their Walkmans to our program (and to the station in general) and gain reassurance about their own sexuality. They get to find out about what it is like to be gay, where the clubs and bars are, what major events are coming up, and general information about the various social and support groups that exist around Melbourne. I find this to be one of the most satisfying aspects to doing gay radio.

I guess my other main objective was to be able to present a program that sounded professional, well researched, and that was interesting and entertaining at the same time, and hopefully went close to competing with the professionalism of the many commercial radio stations. I guess a secondary objective here also was to show that not all gay guys are hairdressers, chefs, actors, or air stewards. (And I have absolutely nothing against hairdressers, chefs, actors, and air stewards. I have many friends who are all of these.) This had been one of the things that had bothered me for many years . . . that I did not see myself as the stereotypical gay male. And in doing the many interviews during my program over the years, I have discovered that there are many, many more gay guys out there who had the same difficulty when facing their coming-out process. I wanted to be able to reassure these people.

I have now been actively involved in gay radio since early 1994 and have gained great satisfaction from it. It was a medium in which I had always had a casual interest, but I never thought I could ever have made a career out of it because of the perceived insecurity of that industry. That is why the concept of involvement in radio was always pushed to the background of my mind. But now I find that my coming out has opened up the opportunity again, even if just in a nonpaid voluntary role, as with all the on-air presenters at our station. But now, not only have I had the opportunity to get involved in doing radio work, but I find there is a community purpose to it as well. I am deeply aware that we have tens of thousands of listeners who are not presently so open about their sexuality. I hope that in my own small way I am helping those people, young or old, to feel more comfortable with their lot.

The *Eldoradio* Story

> *Gay and lesbian live in Berlin and continue without our radio station and it seems that nobody really misses it. That's life.*
>
> —Uwe F. Goetz, founder of *Eldoradio*

Uwe F. Goetz was one of the founders of *Eldoradio*, which was the first gay and lesbian radio station in Germany. In the mid-'80s, Goetz, a college student at the time, and a couple of his friends contemplated the possibility of a commercial gay radio station in Berlin, and subsequently the idea for *Eldoradio* was born. It aired on cable from 1985 to 1986 and later, from 1987 to 1989, as a gay and lesbian program at Radio 100, Berlin's alternative radio station. Meanwhile, Goetz worked as an editor at Berlin's public all-news radio station InfoRadio.

To appreciate the difficulty of actualizing such a dream, it is necessary first to understand the nature of the German radio and television system. After World War II, it was organized by the British, Americans, French, and Russians, who granted licenses for radio stations in their occupation zones. These stations became the nucleus for the German public radio and television system. The BBC stood as the model for the German stations, with stations controlled not by the state, but rather a board of representatives from political parties, employers, trade unions, churches, and other groups.

By 1968, just prior to Stonewall, the alternative movement challenged the conservative politics of the day, influencing the rise of the German Green Party, which was founded in 1979. Alternative organizations in Germany varied from human rights groups, pacifists and grassroots groups, women's organizations, and the politically left to the gay and lesbian spectrum. By the 1980s, the tide shifted toward conservatism and patriotism, and although the founders of the modern gay movement would continue to press ahead for civil and human rights, much of gay Germany was content to define itself socially, rather than politically. Even within this conservative political environment, the restrictive nature of Germany's media system was beginning to change—and be challenged, and audiences were provided choices in their station selections.

It was during this pivotal time in Germany's history, with the emergence of a national cable system, that Goetz and his small collective pushed forward with their dream of *Eldoradio*, a radio station dedicated to the concerns of the gay community. To make this station a reality, they were required by the Berlin Media Authority to obtain a cable broadcasting license, and to do this, they would need to form an association to which the license would be assigned. In the early summer of 1985, the *Eldoradio* collective leased a studio and worked to organize their new radio station together with other smaller broadcasters. In August 1985, the collective debuted *Eldoradio* on their assigned frequency on the Berlin cable network, yet only a small number of listeners tuned into it. Without an audience, the station would not attract sponsorship, no matter how unique the programming.

It is no surprise then that the *Eldoradio* collective jumped at the opportunity to apply for an FM license—it needed a larger audience base. The Berlin Media Authority sent out a call for applications for the first FM frequency of the city. In autumn 1985, it decided to split the only available frequency between two collectives—one that was politically left and one that was politically right. By 1985, the FM station was on the air, and in the process the *Eldoradio* collective had agreed to become part of Radio 100, a consortium of alternative media groups within Berlin. Over the next four years, the turnover among the *Eldoradio* volunteers was fairly high and, by late 1986, only three or four of the founders of the station, including Goetz, remained on staff. In 1990, *Eldoradio* went off the air.

In the final years of the show, *Eldoradio* had been whittled down to a two-hour show. The political attitude toward gays and lesbians in the German Democratic Republic (GDR) was still very restrictive. Radio 100 began to buckle to the conservative reaction against liberal programming, and *Eldoradio* had become increasingly politically correct. It was not until the first few AIDS cases were reported in Rostock and East Berlin that the government would begin to rethink its conservative attitude toward gay and lesbian programming.

Uwe F. Goetz: This is the not-so-glorious story of Germany's first gay and lesbian radio station. It begins in the mid-'80s in Germany, after nearly thirteen years of social-liberal government. In 1982, the conservative Helmut Kohl came into power in the Western Republic. Most Germans were well situated, the economy was growing, and there seemed to be no need for major social change in the society. From America and Britain, Germans learned that making money was the real thing. Reagan, Thatcher, and Kohl represented the philosophy of this era.

At this time, Germany's gay community began to change. Along with the founders of the modern gay movement that had risen since Stonewall, a new generation was growing. In the '70s, the gay movement saw itself as one part of a social emancipation movement. There were straight women and lesbians on one hand, gays on the other hand. They didn't have strictly the same ideals but their goal was clear: an open society that would accept different ways of life. Although nearly all of them were closely affiliated to left-wing groups and parties, there were deep differences between the different trends. From the beginning, West Berlin as Germany's biggest city had a strong gay and lesbian community. Since the founding of the HAW (Homosexuelle Aktion Westberlin), many other organizations had appeared.

Gays and lesbians organized themselves in their social context: university students, lawyers, members of the Social-Democratic party or of the Green Party and many others. They saw themselves as a part of Germany's alternative movement, mainly represented by the Green Party, which was founded in January 1980 in Karlsruhe.

In the mid-'80s, the picture began to change. New organizations rose, representing a broader spectrum of the political life in the country but also less ideological and more pragmatic. Although there were many gay or lesbian organizations who considered themselves fundamentally in opposition to Germany's political system, there were younger people who tried to change the situation within their social context—and who thought about creating common structures for gays and lesbians together. After the social liberalizations under the social-liberal government, there was no expectation that the conservative administration would start any new efforts to end discrimination. In the society however—and mainly in Germany's big cities—the understanding and acceptance of homosexuals was growing. It grew slowly, yet the situation was better than that of the prudish '60s and the early '70s.

It was in this situation that one of the first big projects of the Kohl era began. For the first time and still restricted to some pilot projects, Germany's media system was liberalized. From the founding of the Federal Republic in 1949 on, there was a strict separation between the privately owned newspaper market and the public radio and television system. Now, for the first time, Germans in selected areas had the choice between the traditional national and regional public radio and television stations and private stations—provided that they belonged to the few being connected to the cable system of the new Berlin authority. Berlin was one of the pilot cities where the cable industry was liberalized and, in August 1985, cable households received the first new stations.

In 1984, I was living in a Berlin apartment house with many gay neighbors. Most of them were students of journalism or working as freelance journalists, and nearly all of them felt connected to the gay movement of the city. We were interested in the media development and we often discussed the possible commercialization of the electronic media. One evening, Thomas, Toni, and I sat in my living room. We had an idea: why not run a gay radio station of our own? There was *Fréquence Gaie* in Paris and at this time it belonged to one of the most successful private stations in France. Basel in Switzerland was free "Radio Dreyeckland," and broadcasting over the German border—they had a gay show of their own. Why shouldn't we try to do such a thing here in Berlin? Wouldn't it be great to break the silence and to create a voice for gays and lesbians in the city—and talk about our cultural and political needs and show gay life from our own point of view? West Berlin is a city of 1.2 million and there are enough gays for a substantial audience.

Berlin's media law allowed an open channel with access for everyone who could hold a camera or a microphone. Very early, we decided that this was not the way we wanted to make radio. We wanted to start a professional station. Therefore, we needed a license from Berlin's Media Authority. The first step: we had to create an association that would be the holder of the license. Meanwhile, we started making our project public. There was an article in Berlin's new *Gay Review* and, following that, some new members joined our club. There was a reporter from Berlin's public broadcast station. There was a guy working in the PR department of a scientific publishing house, and there were others, students of journalism and other subjects. Founding the association was quickly done and soon we had a concept for our application for the cable broadcast license. Very soon, we learned that fundraising was one of the biggest problems for new projects in Germany. Nobody knew about the so-called new media and only a few could imagine that they would be successful some day.

In the gay community, there was no commercial infrastructure and to many activists, the project seemed very suspicious. Because it was the conservative government who liberalized the market and because the big media enterprises engaged in private radio and television, many of them refused to support us. For the Gay Pride Parade of 1985, we decorated my Volkswagen, recorded a promo tape, and made a lot of noise. But there was little interest in gay radio. The biggest discussion was why we were allowed to join the march with a car—at this point the Gay Pride March had been a strictly footwalking event.

Our own "office" was reduced to an answering machine on my desk and our pompous concept of a gay radio station had become two two-hour shows a week. We tried to stay in contact with the other gay organizations of the city, and *Eldoradio* became a member of the different board of gay and lesbian organizations of Berlin. The name came from one of Berlin's famous gay bars of the twenties, the Eldorado. Probably, most people looked upon us as "those crazy guys who want to start a radio station." In June and July 1985, we hired a studio and worked on a concept for a new radio station together with other smaller broadcasters. At the end of August 1985, during the Berlin International Radio and Television Fair, we started our program. Every Wednesday at 6 p.m. and every Sunday at 4 p.m., *Eldoradio* went on air via the Berlin Cable Network. About 300,000 homes were connected at the start, but who listens to radio via cable?

Eldoradio became a phenomenon. Many gays heard about it, but only an infinitely small number of them had ever listened to the show. For the most of us, this was the first real experience with real radio making. Some of us were interested in reporting, others more in music. So we decided to make an entertaining show with a lot of music, jokes, and self-produced radio plays on Sundays and a more political magazine program on Wednesdays. Our subjects dealt with the situation of the gay community in Berlin, AIDS, which had become more and more important to gays in Germany, the local elections, and so on. All of that was produced with a lot of enthusiasm and without money. After two or three months, the financial situation turned more and more to the worse. We hoped for advertisers and sponsors but only a few of them wanted to pay for a radio they and their clients couldn't listen to because they had no cable in their homes. We were not alone, because the majority of the other cable radio broadcasters in the city experienced the same problems.

During the following months, one broadcaster after another gave up. But the *Eldoradio* crew didn't. We even extended our shows to eight hours a week—space for experiments like our radio comedy series "Gay Pigs in Space," discussions, or a deejay show once a week. At the end of 1985, *Eldoradio* turned from a gay project into a gay and lesbian project. Two women contacted us and soon they had a show of their own. During this time, it became clear that cable radio would never work. The Berlin Media Authority invited entries for the first FM frequency of the city. Compared to other countries and to the west of the Federal Republic, Berlin was in a very delicate situation. The Allies controlled all the frequencies and the surrounding GDR had no interest in allowing new Western companies to broadcast into their territory. Nevertheless, in March 1986, the FM frequency 100.6 would be the first real private radio of the city.

All efforts to raise enough money for an application of our own failed. The requests from the media authority were many: all of us had to prove that we could finance a radio for a certain period. For us, that meant that we had to search for more money. We decided to convert *Eldoradio* into a cooperative where every listener could buy a part and influence the programming by his or her membership. For Germany, this was new. There were cooperatives but mainly in the agricultural sector or in the home construction sector. Nobody had tried to organize a radio station this way. After some months of recruitment, we had about a hundred members in our cooperative. And we hoped that we would find more when we went on air. It was clear that we would never have the opportunity to get the whole frequency for ourselves.

After long discussions of very differing points of views, we decided to join Radio 100. This is a consort of alternative media groups from the whole city, uniting women's organizations, third-world support groups, and the national left-wing newspaper. The *Eldoradio* crew began to change. Radio 100 saw itself as a political project giving a voice to groups who were not represented in the German media system. Some of the founders of *Eldoradio* withdrew from the staff—they had had the idea of a commercially working radio station for the whole gay and lesbian community and they feared that we would reach only a minority of our potential audience in the city. New people arrived. For them, the idea of a gay radio show was interesting and they brought in their own ideas.

In autumn 1985, the Berlin Media Authority decided to split the only available frequency. Radio 100 got the right to broadcast daily from 7 P.M. to 11 P.M.; the rest of the day went to a conservative local media group of the city. In March 1986, the new station started and this was the beginning of a local "radio war." In prime time, the Berlin audience had a strictly anticommunist local radio station, supported by the mostly conservative newspapers of the city and the city officials. At 6:58 every evening, they closed their program with the German national anthem and a confession to the traditional values of the society. Two minutes later, Radio 100 would take over the frequency. The reaction to the national anthem: instead of a show opener jingle, Radio 100 aired the sound of a toilet flush. Every Wednesday and every Sunday at seven, after the toilet flush, it was *Eldoradio,* the two-hour gay and lesbian radio show. There was uproar in the city's political establishment. Conservative politicians asked for a ban of Radio 100, but they didn't succeed.

The contents of our show changed. The makers of our satirical spots and radio plays had left the boat and others replaced them. Music changed. Radio 100 allowed only songs that were politically correct. We played less and less disco hits and replaced them with artists from small labels. In 1986, there were only a few gay and lesbian singers—not enough to fill the whole show. More lesbians joined our editorial staff but others preferred to join the daily women's program. Many radical lesbians of this time didn't want to work together with men, no matter whether gay or straight—which became an advantage for the *Eldoradio* staff because we all were convinced that our show had to be both for gays and lesbians so we became more radical and strictly left-oriented.

The reactions from the city were deceiving. There seemed to be only a few listeners—were we making radio for ourselves? Sponsors withdrew because they didn't like the political attitude of the program. The financial situation was worsening. Radio 100, including the *Eldoradio* show, stayed on air for another three years. Many people came, many went, and in late 1986, only three or four of the founders of the station (including me) stayed on the staff. The biggest projects were the Gay Pride Days in 1986 and 1987. Although everyone in Berlin and the surrounding areas of the GDR could listen to the station, there was little response. We had to learn that the majority of the gays and lesbians in the city were not interested in this kind of radio station. The majority of the crew members, however, wanted to continue this way. Our show seemed to be less important to the West of the city than to the East, from where we would receive letters about gay people in small GDR cities who had nobody to talk with about their coming out and who hoped to find contacts via our station.

More and more internal discussions had risen among the editorial staff. The majority had left and antibourgeois ideas and wanted to express them via the radio. All of them were investing a lot of time and energy but really only students had the time to do this. There was nearly no money to pay the bills for the studio rent—nobody earned money from working at the station. Many left the station after having finished their studies because they found jobs in public radio and television systems or in newspapers. Radio 100 was very good training for better jobs afterward.

I left the *Eldoradio* staff in 1989, shortly before the fall of the wall, because I had to decide whether to finish my own studies or continue to work for money and for *Eldoradio* while neglecting my university career. One year later, *Eldoradio* failed. There were too many debts to continue. Additionally, the situation for gays and lesbians began to change. Society became more and more liberal and confessing to be gay or lesbian was not too difficult any more. The public radio system was not broadcasting gay or lesbian radio or TV shows, but on Gay Pride Day, for example, they would produce a special live show covering the march. Maybe, this is one thing that *Eldoradio* changed. Gays and lesbians in the other media had come out in their staffs and they dared to bring it on air.

In other cities, independent radio stations worked better. *Radio Z* in Nuremberg/Bavaria, founded in 1987, continues on, and there is still a one-hour gay show every Wednesday. Other cities with free radios have their own show but the audience is small. In the German capital, there are initiatives for those who broadcast via cable, but the German gay and lesbian audience does not seem to miss its own radio station or radio show.

What is left of the first attempt to create "a radio of our own"? There are some tape cassettes left in the Berlin Gay Museum. There are some journalists in the city who started their careers at *Eldoradio*. There is a radio show called *Eldoradio* in Dortmund and one in Luxembourg. Both of them have nothing to do with our project—we just couldn't afford to save the copyright for the name. Gays and lesbians live in Berlin and they continue without our radio station and it seems that nobody really misses it. That's life.

In the end, the German Democratic Republic seemed to have understood that they could control the situation better if gays in the country could meet officially (under control of the state, of course). From 1987 on, groups developed—first under the roof and protection of the church. Later, homosexuality was discussed in TV and radio shows and the GDR officials showed their willingness to end discrimination. This doesn't mean that discriminations of gays and lesbians in the GDR ended. The population of East Germany was and is still very reserved towards homosexuals.

More Queer Radio—Out in Canada

The Canadian Lesbian and Gay Archives hold some of its nation's earliest LGBT music, media interviews, and special events, such as crowd reaction to the once-annual "flight" of the drag queens on Halloween night in 1969 along Toronto's Yonge Street. The archives also contains seventeen cubic feet of recordings, playlists, scrapbooks, and other material from Vancouver's pioneering *Coming Out Show,* dating from the late 1970s to 1986.

Within the Canadian Broadcasting System, there are approximately fifty licensed community radio stations and forty-three campus radio stations licensed by the Canadian Radio-Television and Telecommunications Commission (CRTC)—and still only a fraction of programming is dedicated to the LGBT community, even though Canada is one of the most progressive nations in such matters. Similar to American broadcasting, these stations are operated by not-for-profit organizations and rely primarily on volunteers for programming and other station operations.

In 1999, CRTC sought comments from community and campus radio broadcasters as part of a broader process it initiated in 1997 to examine all of its radio policies in an effort to simplify the regulatory process. As an independent agency, the CRTC is responsible for regulating Canada's broadcasting and telecommunications systems. The proposed policy also indicated the commission's desire to ensure that community and college broadcasters continue to strive for diversification in programming.

In response to the call for comments on the proposed policy for campus radio, Heather Kitching, cohost of *Queer FM* on CiTR 101.9 FM in Vancouver, addressed the need for stronger governmental commitment toward minority and marginalized groups. Here is an excerpt from her letter dated April 12, 1999:

> The purpose of my submission is to explore campus radio and campus radio policy in the context of section 3D(iii) of the Broadcast Act, which states that one of the purposes of the Canadian Broadcasting system is to:
> ... through its programming and the employment opportunities arising out of its operations, serve the needs and interests, and reflect the circumstances and aspirations, of Canadian men, women and children, including equal rights, the linguistic duality and multicultural and multiracial nature of Canadian society and the special place of aboriginal peoples within that society.
> Currently, campus and community radio stations are the primary source of programming in Canada serving minority and marginalized communities. Commercial radio, which has always been programmed for the tastes of the majority, is now at the point of showing open hostility towards minorities in the ongoing quest for ratings. Furthermore, women and minorities continue to be far under represented among commercial radio air-staff.

...Canadian Broadcasting Corporation (CBC) radio, while not intentionally hostile to marginalized communities, still provides no real discussion or analysis of the issues of those communities and tends to approach all subject matter from a decidedly white, heterosexual, middle class perspective. ... It could be said that campus and community radio programs are to minority and marginalized communities what the CBC and commercial radio are to the mainstream. They celebrate the culture of these communities in the music and content and provide in-depth analysis of relevant issues free from the influence of commercial interests.

For the last five years, I have hosted *Queer FM* on CiTR 101.9 FM in Vancouver. During that time, my cohost and I have probably spent over $5000 of our own money on such things as long distance phone interviews, road trips to cover events, and new music, all in an effort to develop the show into something that truly serves our community. In addition, my cohost and I have each purchased our own $165 EV professional microphones, I have spent $2700 putting a professional sound card and production program on my home computer, and my cohost has purchased a high-speed modem which allows us to upload and download radio programs on the Internet using MP3 files. Both of us work at jobs that give us some flexibility with our schedules so that we can attend press conferences and interviews during the day without giving up wages. At the same time as our program is thriving, I know another host of a gay radio program on community radio who finally gave up the show in frustration because he couldn't afford the kind of investment it would've taken to do the quality of show he really wanted to do.

From this experience, I have become aware of one of the great ironies of the Canadian Broadcast System: In order to do campus/community radio effectively, a person needs to come from a certain position of privilege and that's exactly where a lot of people from marginalized communities don't come from. Yet this is the sector most responsible for serving those communities. While mainstream commercial radio is able to sustain itself on advertising revenue and the CBC serves white, straight, middle class Canadians on the government's dime, those of us whose communities already experience a disproportionate level of poverty and discrimination can only be represented on the Canadian Broadcasting System if we can find those among us who have high paying jobs and plenty of free time. Furthermore, since funding shortages also force many campus stations to operate on low power signals and poorly positioned transmitters, these same communities require above average stereo receivers to hear their programs.

As the CRTC has duly noted, most campus stations are run by volunteers. As anyone who recruits volunteers knows, it's hard enough to get ANYONE to work for free, never mind a team of reliable people from diverse ethnic and cultural backgrounds and sexual orientations. If stations had the ability to pay honorariums to DJs and to cover their expenses, they could assess the needs in their community and address them proactively, rather than simply having to make do. Furthermore, if more stations had access to funds to pay program coordinators, a more aggressive recruitment and training campaign could take place.

I submit that, if the CRTC is truly committed to the ideals of diversity and multicultural representation outlined in the Broadcast Act, then the commission will immediately take steps to investigate funding options for campus/community radio, and in particular programs to ensure that Canada's diverse communities really are being served by the Canadian Broadcasting System.

Queer FM Playlist
May 9, 1999 http://queerfm.lesbigay.com/playlist.htm

Artist	Album	Song
Gloria Gaynor	I Am What I Am	I Am What I Am
Amr Diab	Camelspotting	Nour El Ain
Amampondo	Drums for Tomorrow	Terre Terre
Noa	Noa	Wildflower
The Guo Brothers	Yuan	Step by Step
La Bottine Souriante	En Spectacle	Sur La Route
Paris Combo	Paris Combo	Irénée
Krishna Das	Pilgrim Heart	Namah Shivaya
Doula	In the Garden	Qadduka-L-Mayyas
Sweet Honey in the Rock	"25"	Motherless

Queer FM's diversity is reflected in its music and more significantly through the variety of news and information presented for the lesbian, gay, bisexual, and transgendered communities. *Queer FM* is concerned about national and international human rights issues. It presents routine analysis of court decisions and legislative changes that impact the queer community, directly or indirectly. According to Kitching, "*Queer FM* is committed to being accessible and responsible to all members of the queer communities and to be free from content that could alienate or divide members of those communities." *Queer FM* provides a forum to discuss issues in the local communities, to inform listeners about resources within their communities, to discuss forms of oppression that affect queers, and to exchange information on other "progressive movements."

Chapter Seven

Empire Builders

Queer Convergence Within the Larger Community

Three men who have made major contributions to gay and lesbian broadcasting are Marvin Schwam, the founder of the Gay Entertainment Television Network; Joe Liberatore, the founder of the *Gay News Network;* and John McMullen, president of GAYBC—The Internet Empire. Here are the stories of their amazing journeys in queer broadcasting, as told in their own words.

Borrowed Time and Broken Dreams: The Marvin Schwam Story

A popular alternative to public access has been leased access, in which airtime is purchased from a cable company. The leased time allows the independent broadcaster to generate advertising revenue from the commercials. Leased access allows the producer to concentrate on quality programming, which is more likely to be sponsored than many of the low-budget *Wayne's World* shows aired now on public access. By January 2000, a South Beach, Florida, company, with ambitions of becoming the first gay cable network, had planned to distribute entertainment programming across sixteen markets in the United States. The network, called CI TV, debuted only one hour of programming on a leased access channel of Time Warner, Inc., in New York City. The idea behind the channel is to target gay urban viewers with shows that play off *Real World* and MTV-like lifestyle shows.[1] With several cable companies competing for a share of the gay audience—and without sufficient capital to remain competitive, the network is likely to experience the same problems that confronted its predecessors in gay and lesbian cable broadcasting.

One of the first attempts at building a gay network was by the Gay Cable Network (GCN), based in Manhattan. Impressively, it was the first television news organization to cover the AIDS crisis. Since 1984, GCN's gay and lesbian production crews have videotaped the Republican and Democratic National Conventions. GCN won the Outstanding Achievement Award from the Gay and Lesbian Press Association. What began as a local New York operation in 1982 evolved into the longest running and, possibly, largest gay-owned cable facility in the world. Its news magazine show is also one of the longest running gay and lesbian TV news magazines, with broadcasters from Japan, Italy, Great Britain, Canada, and Australia regularly contributing to the show.[2] Although GCN reaches across the nation into seven metropolitan cities on both public and commercial access cable, with plans for expansion, it faces a number of financial obstacles, as would any gay network competing for national advertising dollars. It takes a lot of money—investors and sponsors—to move from a locally based to a national operation. And it takes a lot of quality programming to meet the needs of a diverse audience, day in and day out, twenty-four hours a day. The bulk of GCN's programming is low budget and its focus has been on adult entertainment. With tapes dating back to 1972, it boasts of the largest gay and lesbian video archive in the world.[3] To solve some of these programming demands, GCN has partnered with the Manhattan Neighborhood Network on certain projects in the past.

Nancy Kirton: I did a show called *The Pulse*—for people of color, lesbian, gay, bisexual, transgender—for two and a half years on the Manhattan Neighborhood Network. The show was difficult to produce because a lot of notable talents came in, but the funding wasn't there to make use of the many resources and the many people that came on. So everything was pretty much out of my pocket. And as a result, programming suffered tremendously, especially as we went on. We even had the opportunity to air once a week, together with Gay Cable Network. We couldn't keep up their level of quality programming. It wasn't a full-time profession for many people, and we certainly did not have the resources that a full-time professional would have. We were working from people's homes. So I couldn't ask people to come into a studio to do their work; we had to hop around a lot. We still sustained ourselves for two and a half years, and it was interesting to see the caliber of the people that came in and out. We had actors who were regularly featured on *NYPD Blue*. We had people who were editors for the major networks come help us. Some people went on to professional video or TV careers. Not everyone was LGBT and many are to remain nameless, but kudos to Cathy Che, Dale Ogasawara, and Luis Ramon.

Industry experts say that it would take $20 million in private capital to launch a network equivalent to Black Entertainment Television.[4] Many have tried, and few have succeeded. Most independent producers must make a choice between getting their messages out and making money, a little of which comes in handy when trying to produce quality programs. In November 1992, Marvin Schwam took the first step toward his dream of a gay cable television network—a dream that he chased for six years. He started Gay Entertainment Television (GET) in New York City and became the president. His efforts were applauded within the gay and lesbian community, as well as within the broadcast industry. Yet, when it came to raising money, the financial support from the gay community just wasn't there—and the straight backers did not want to proceed without investment from the gay and lesbian community. That meant that he could not afford to create and deliver more than a few hours of quality weekly programming to cable outlets in New York, Chicago, Miami, Los Angeles, and San Francisco.[5] His dream slipped away, nearly one year after it had begun.

Marvin Schwam: I started the Gay Entertainment Television network in November of 1992. Surprisingly enough, here in New York City, there was no quality gay/lesbian programming. I mean there were one or two awful public access shows that were done with five-dollar budgets, and there was a sex show from the Gay Cable Network. It'd been around for twenty-five years . . . kind of your just pure gay porn films. So when we put our show on the air which was a half-hour variety show, the whole city really immediately embraced it. I went on leased access, not public access television. I bought the time and was able to use it to sell commercials, whereas on public access they give you the time but it is not a commercial venture. I wanted to at least cover our expenses and do a quality show. So you need money for that and the only way to do that was to pay the $300 for the one half hour of leased access time and sell commercials.

Then I just went out into the community and found kids who were hosting a drag show or somebody who was a popular bartender and somebody who wrote some columns for a local gay paper, and I brought them on as television stars, which they became after five or six years. I mean they were stars, but the point is this city or a city like New York had nothing of gay cultural value for the gay community until *Party Talk*. GET started a nucleus of something that started evolving into a nationwide entity because we were getting rates from San Francisco, Los Angeles, and other gay communities asking to broadcast those shows that we were doing here in New York in those towns. I could do it merely by buying leased access time in Chicago, Miami, Los Angeles, and San Francisco, and put the same shows on in these cities. Within three to four months, we had eighteen commercials from cleaning stores, drug stores, and restaurants, and half of them were not gay. They were just in gay neighborhoods. Anyway, it really became a terrific venture.

So now that we had a fairly sizable audience and started attracting advertisers like Jaguar, Sony, Warner Brothers, and every major movie company because now we had a national audience; it really looked like we were going places. It was five and a half years of basically funding this myself, plus the advertising money we received. Yet we just kept putting all that money back into better productions, more cities, buying more time, and using better studios. Within a year, I started two more shows because people were asking for more product. We extended one show to one hour. We started a one-hour talk show about serious gay subject matter. We started a half-hour-style program and had all kinds of celebrities who would come on the show. It was the only thing that was real, and in fact style is part of the gay community's background and there was nothing on television with regards to that.

There was never a point where we were able to make money. When you're not financed originally and you're not dealing off of a capital investment, when you're just doing it day by day, it becomes very treacherous. So anyway, we finally—after trying to raise money basically from the gay community for all those years unsuccessfully—found an underwriter. Actually it was a financial investment company in Florida who found the underwriter, and who thought out this would-be-genius plan to take public. Everybody thought it was remarkable. Everybody thought it was an incredible idea—a cable network.

Think about it: the industry's so gigantic and there is no gay/lesbian network on cable, which was amazing—and that's what cable was originated for, to serve the minority interest groups on television. So everybody got behind us and everybody was congratulating us, and they thought this was the most genius idea. We went forward with the project because we got such a great response and put in another half million dollars for the year that it took to actually write the plan and register the company with the Securities and Exchange Commission and I got approval from the Federal Communications Commission to go public with it. Then we applied to NASDAQ for a listing on the stock exchange. The word "gay" in the name of a company— Gay Entertainment Television—was listed for the first time in history. At first they refused us, and then I challenged them on the grounds of prejudice and that they had no basis for not allowing our company to be listed except prejudice. We, in fact, won the decision when we went back down to Washington to challenge them. And we got a listing on the stock exchange. Then the stock went out to the public and nobody bought it.

We went to every one of the gay communities that we were broadcasting in, and with which we had a great rapport and reputation, and that we had thrown parties for through the years. We had parties for all the gay millionaires. We built a management team for the company. I had the past CFO [chief financial officer] of CBS as our CFO. We had the president of U.S. Cruiselines on our board of directors. We had the senior vice president of CBS television, currently a woman, on our board of directors. We had executives from ABC and NBC. We had a terrific staff of people. We had more than ample qualifications in terms of management to bring this company into the mainstream. We had party after party—things in the hotels of San Francisco, Los Angeles, Miami, and New York, and every time we left these meetings we thought it was going to be a resounding success, but nobody bought the stock.

We couldn't get the gay and lesbian community to put their hands in their pockets. It wasn't worth it to them. They all applauded the effort that somebody else was making, but were not willing to participate in seeing that it happened. The underwriter had committed $5 million to the project and $10 million in corporate money backing it as institutional money—all straight, by the way—all straight companies, which is exactly what I told him to begin with.

I had said not to expect the gay community to fund this project, if the funding does not come from the straight community. It's just the nature of the beast. This was not unlike other cable networks. The Spanish cable network was all Korean money. Black Entertainment Television was all white cable money. The blacks didn't put BET on the air, and the Spanish community didn't put Telemundo on the air. The money was from other than the ethnic community that they were serving. They were funded outside that community. And the same thing applies here. I knew that the gay community was not going to raise $10 million for this project. But the underwriters didn't believe me. They thought that this was such an incredible concept that the gay community would absolutely flock to it. And even though they weren't expecting to raise $10 million, certainly they would raise a couple million. The gay community absolutely didn't spend a nickel on this. I mean, they spent a couple hundred thousand dollars and in fact, when the underwriters saw the dismal response from the gay/lesbian community, they said we made a mistake. If your community is not supporting this, we're not putting our money in, and after six months the whole thing fell apart. How many rich men in this country could have put that network on the air by simply writing a check. Dozens and dozens and we spoke to almost all of them and couldn't even get them to write a thousand-dollar check, let alone a million-dollar check. One half of them won't even talk with us. They thought this is a public business—your business, we aren't interested—for we don't want to separate ourselves from the community we got rich in, in spite of the fact that we're gay. We're not going to separate ourselves. And in fact that was the message that I got out of the whole thing.

Close to a million dollars was spent in an effort to put a gay network on the air and, when it came down to the reality of it, the gay community simply wasn't interested. And the underwriters started backing it all up with statistics, like you say it is 10 percent of the population, which means you've got like twenty-five to twenty-six million gay Americans out there. How come the subscriptions for *Out*, *Genre*, and *The Advocate*—all totaled—don't even add up to a quarter million subscribers, which is true. How do you answer those questions? The gay community is not interested. They are trying to assimilate, not separate. As much as we all stand on platforms and scream "I want recognition" and as much as we want to separate with our parades and Gay Pride days and everything else, when it comes down to putting money into a project that will give us a real identity, nobody wanted to identify with it. The company now is in suspension—we're just doing nothing. The money that we raised was all held in escrow and we gave it all back after six months because we didn't meet the minimal goal. The adjustment suspension is on the interest. If an underwriting company picks it up, then fine, but I'm not going out anymore asking one more person for money to help with this project. After six years, I've had it. But, you know there is a whole political side of this, a whole personal side of this. There is the whole intrigue with all the people and the effort that the gay kids put into this. I mean, the heartbreaks along the way, the effort along the way, is just an amazing story. And when it came down to the bottom line, there was no money. Nobody wanted to put any money behind it; everyone thought it was brilliant and nobody would invest a nickel in it. And it wasn't that I didn't know enough people—that wasn't the reason I couldn't do it myself. Once we went public, it was a whole different story. Then the whole world knew about it. Still, nobody wanted to invest in it.

As an interesting follow-up, the Gay and Lesbian Community Center in New York had a seminar called, "Will there ever be a gay and lesbian TV network?" in the summer of 2000. For some strange reason, I was not invited to speak on the panel, and when one of my GET vice presidents showed up, he realized why. Everyone on the panel, and it would serve no purpose to identify them except to embarrass them, were all people in positions to really support GET and help it launch. Each one refused for one basically selfish reason or another, made no effort to help us, and then sat up on the stage pretending to be interested in the possibility of a gay and lesbian network. Needless to say, my V.P. got up and reminded each individual what had transpired with GET and basically called them hypocrites for sitting up on that stage pretending to be interested in helping the community, when in fact that opportunity was presented to them in real terms, they all refused. . . . To make a long story short, my V.P. was the hero of the evening for being the only one present who actually made the only valiant six-year effort, with Marvin Schwam, to accomplish the intended goal of the panel's question, "Will there ever be a gay and lesbian TV network?"

Around the World on GNN: The Joe Liberatore Story

Other networking efforts have included the *Gay News Network* (GNN), the gay community's answer to CNN. It is a nationally distributed news magazine program that can be viewed on commercial and public access cable televisions in Alexandria, Virginia; Arlington, Virginia; Baltimore, Maryland; Boulder, Colorado; Fairfax, Virginia; Minneapolis, Minnesota; Montgomery, Maryland; Philadelphia, Pennsylvania; Prince Georges County, Maryland; St. Louis, Missouri; St. Paul, Minnesota; and Washington, D.C. The show is hosted by Joe Liberatore, Holly Landau,

Matt Hutchison, and Francki DiFrancesco. Its mission is to provide news and information to gay, lesbian, bisexual, queer, feminist, and straight audiences. Based in Washington, D.C., the all-volunteer network of writers, producers, and reporters has been long recognized by the gay and lesbian community for its award-winning segments. *Gay News Network* is the brainchild of Liberatore, who originally became involved in cable access by cohosting a show called *One in Ten People*. The show ran for twenty-three episodes, and aired in twenty-five markets.

Joe Liberatore: I think it was incredible when I went out to Fairfax before I had even produced *One in Ten People* that there were three other shows, all produced in the same facility—a local show called *Gay Fairfax, Gay Spectrum*, and a short-lived soap opera called *Inside Outside the Beltway*. And when I went and talked to some other producers, I said, "I want your help, and I want to work with you." I bought all the footage from *One in Ten People* because I knew I needed some kind of library of stories, news, and pictures. I wanted to be prepared.

Behind *One in Ten People* were some incredible folks, and you don't just go out and volunteer for a show. The folks who worked on it, who we called the crew behind the cameras—all had to become a member of the facility, which was maybe about ten dollars a year. You had to be trained to use the equipment, and then there was the personal sacrifice and dedication to come out there on a regular basis and contribute, so I knew they were good people so I said let's make another program, something new and completely and totally different, something the nation has never seen—a gay news show—and let's make it a national program. At the time, I was just the most uniquely unqualified person to do that. Hadn't taken marketing courses and I didn't know very much about the technical side of TV. Although I graduated with a minor in Radio-Television, I didn't know about the meat and potatoes of the thing, didn't realize how many thing could go wrong. I did not know enough to know it should be done quarterly, and that's how the program started.

I was on a panel about 1995 in Miami and we talked about the future of gay television—everybody was excited to have the first gay network like BET and they called it ACME Television down in Florida. We set up a lot of groundwork to work with these folks and it literally disappeared off the map within two and a half years; they had even done advertising, even a demo reel, and took it to some gay conventions and it was really exciting because they loved our product. They were ready to go with us because they had no news shows on their network and it didn't happen. You hear lots of stories saying there needs to be a gay network and there's no programming for the gay network. There's lots of programming for the gay network. Are we just going to show circuit parties or have old movies with gay people in them? I honestly don't know if a gay network will happen, but I would love to form an alliance/partnership in a strategic situation, go forward where I can still operate independently and put the show out there in these small towns where I can be original—and keep it in the major markets as well like Atlanta, Chicago, San Francisco, Los Angeles, by working with a startup network and go forward. Right now, there seems to be nothing else out there.

In 1997 or 1998, people said satellite was the way to go. I think somebody was supposed to work with Time Warner and to make a gay channel or the first gay network. You put it on satellite and all you'd have to do is lobby your local cable station and they'd pull it down, but I never heard any more about that. There's a lot more time and channel space available, but the problem is it's so expensive for cable folks to pull it down and as you can imagine they get a lot of flak because the right-wingers are extremely active and love to fight these things.

So we created, if you will, a business plan, and about six months to the day that the plug was pulled on *One in Ten People*, I was up and running announcements that we were looking for a crew and talent, just to supplement anyone who might fall out of the picture. Our first meeting was at the same place out in Fairfax, Virginia. We did a PowerPoint presentation that was pretty technically advanced back in 1994. And we did a great slide presentation, and the people who were better in the business said "This is really ambitious. Do you know what you're doing?" Sure, no problem, and six months to the day of that meeting or one year from the end of the other show, our first of the preproduction work was done. Three meetings, many local announcements—we created a name and logo, an animated opening to the show. We had put together a format for the show which was a thirty-minute news program with international news leading the broadcast, national news, and something called the Gay Agenda—which is a public affairs segment. The show closes out with a few soft feature pieces.

Since we were in D.C., we were uniquely situated to get hold of organizations and put them on the spot and ask, "Can you tell me why you are for and why someone else also in the gay movement is against a gay marriage, the upcoming march on Washington, gays in the military?" It was a great opportunity for them to speak up because we usually see a gay rights piece/civil rights piece backed up with someone who is religious and can't stand it and is intolerant. I didn't want to give part of my thirty-minute show to someone from the other side, bashing us. I really had an internal struggle with that. And I said, if I'm going to come out and do this, that was the last thing I wanted to think about. That's only two hours of programming in a year. Four thirty-minute shows. I didn't want to give valuable time to the opposition. Again, the Gay Agenda was fulfilled by having people in the movement just provide different points of view, which was a lot more interesting than saying we're all monolithic voting—all the same, all the time—that we're just one group, like sheep, who say let's follow whoever says this is the right thing to do. That's not necessarily the way it is.

GNN is networked on eighty channels in sixty cities, and now I'm building a network of reporters. I have these ten students from across the United States. The national office of GNN got together and decided it would work on a pilot program where they'd bring together interns at the convention—twenty interns—ten did print and ten did video production. Last year, the convention was in Las Vegas. GNN trained these ten folks in journalism school and I said, "Cover this convention, learn new techniques, and your footage will appear on my show." Instantly I got footage. We said when something good, bad, or exciting happens or something you care about, do a piece, send it in to me, and we'll reedit it as need be, and if possible we will show it on our network. Like CNN, we've got field correspondents, so it's a little less work for me now because in the beginning I was like the producer of *One in Ten People* and did it all. When you wear many hats from writing to editing your own stuff, there is less of an opportunity for other people to participate.

Our next step is we file for nonprofit status so we can be recognized as a nonprofit group and then we will go into the fund-raising mode. Up until this point, my boyfriend and I literally have spent every penny from our pocket and, as you can imagine, it was expensive. We've won awards from GLAAD and the Alliance for Community Media, which is the oldest group to recognize public access cable programs. This year alone, we won three awards from the Alliance for Community Media and it's strange, because last year, we also won "best gay and lesbian show." You kind of wonder after a couple of years are we the only ones entering? Are there only two other shows and we're the best? Well, I talked to folks and they assured me that there are many other shows that enter. In addition to that sort of narrower category, we also won "best news program" and it was nice to knock the straight competition out of the ballpark. We sort of surprised everybody when we won not just in our program category, but actually won in a much larger category in which there were many, many more news programs.

The Internet Empire: The John McMullen Story

> *I do think the Internet's a really important thing and I think*
> *that it's really valuable for the middle-class gay kids who want*
> *some privacy and can in fact get to the sites and not get caught.*

—Josy Catoggio, interviewer and producer

In September 1996, John McMullen envisioned using new streaming technology to broadcast a gay-themed talk show and newscast across the World Wide Web.

Under the wing of Progressive Networks' WebActive service, McMullen and his associates—a dozen community leaders, broadcast producers, and air talent—began weekly Webcasts of a talk show called *Hangin'Out* (Appendix 6A) and a daily news program called *Daily Dose*. McMullen severed his partnership with Progressive Networks in January 1997, and launched the GLOradio Corporation three months later, which he founded along with his partner Charlie Dyer and a small group of volunteers, including Lucia Regan, Chelle Gannon, and Tam Keltner.

GLOradio was the first to air exclusive and breaking news coverage on major news stories, like the murder spree and siege of Andrew Cunanan and the unlawful attempted dismissal of Master Chief Petty Officer Timothy R. McVeigh from the U.S. Navy. In 1997, GLOradio merged with PlanetOut Corporation, and they worked as one entity throughout most of 1998. By late 1998, the two companies mutually agreed to dissolve the partnership.

In October 1998, GLOradio Corporation announced the GAYBC Radio Network, the new brand name for its LGBT online radio service. The GAYBC Radio Network division, at that point, began to work toward the acquisition of broadcast station licenses in metropolitan areas throughout the United States. In spring 1999, GLOradio's board of directors voted to change the corporate identity to Stellar Networks, Inc. (Appendix 6B). Meanwhile, PlanetOut, former partner to GLOradio, consolidated its interests with competing magazines *The Advocate* and *OUT* in summer 2000, and this merger represented the largest of its kind for the gay media industry.

John McMullen: I started my broadcast career by the time I was twelve years old. I had family that owned a radio station in the northwest part of Washington state, and so I would spend my summers working there, and by the time I was eighteen I was program director of a major market station here in Seattle—a station that has become KUBE-FM. I eventually went on to do some network communication stuff around the country. I had radio in my blood from as young as I can remember because of being around family and the business.

It was in 1993 though that I kind of went through a little burnout stage and I wanted to see if there were anything else out there for me. And that led me kind of into the high-tech field. I went to work for a software company called Aldus Corporation that started desktop publishing with a product called PageMaker. I really enjoyed working in the high-tech environment, and it was after Aldus was acquired by Adobe Systems in late 1994 that I ended up considering my various options, and some of the things that I was looking at dealt with desktop video productions, things like that, things that can maybe bring some of my broadcast skills together with my high-tech skills. And even though I had been kind of shoved out the door with several hundred people in the merger with Adobe, I ended up coming back to work for them as a contractor for about a year.

During that time I had had several conversations with some people at Real Networks (then called Progressive Networks) that I had worked with at Aldus. The company had started the streaming media revolution with Real Audio. And I thought, this would just be the best of both worlds, to be able to go to work with a company where I would be able to totally utilize my broadcast background with my more newfound love of working in high technology, and so I ended up taking a job with Progressive Networks. It was just one of those get-your-foot-in-the-door-and-then-show-them-what-you-can-do kind of things. So I joined sales and dealt with high-end clients that were evaluating the Real Audio server, and I also worked with some of the Fortune 500 and broadcast companies to show them how to make initial application of the product in their own Web sites. That job eventually became more of an executive producer position within Real Networks.

I was producing a lot of different content for a lot of different companies, and core to Progressive Networks is to really show off the abilities of, at that time, Real Audio. Real Video wasn't around yet. In the early summer of 1996, there was an opportunity here to marry my work to my outside interest, which was doing some political and social activism, along with my friend who cofounded and cochaired the Pacific Northwest chapter of Digital Queers, a nonprofit organization that helps endow other nonprofits with computers and software and provides advice on complication services as it relates to all things high-tech. I thought originally that I could produce something using this Real Audio medium called DQ Radio or something like that. The more I thought, I really missed being on the air and I thought that I'd really like to produce something that would be like an ongoing program itself. I turned around the idea and decided to create a pilot while I was at Progressive Networks called *Hangin' Out* and this would be, initially we thought, a daily talk show, but we realized that it would be too much work because I also have this other day job at Progressive Networks. So instead it would be a two-hour talk show, that would deal with gay, lesbian, bi, and trans issues once a week.

I had a good relationship with Tom Rielly, who was the founder of PlanetOut and had also been a cofounder of Digital Queers. And I approached him and said, "You know, you guys have a news product that you're producing in a written format each day on the PlanetOut Web site. I'd like to be able to license the news and use it in the context of this audio program. In the exchange, we'll give you promotional announcements and things like that throughout the program. What ended up happening was I shared my idea with a few of my friends around Progressive Networks, and they shared it with a few of their friends, and the next thing I know Andy Sharpless—who is the senior vice president of Progressive Networks and was also vice president of Web Active, a division of Progressive Networks that has an online progressive issues publication—and Sam Tucker, who was the publisher of *Active,* came to me and said, "We've heard that you are thinking about producing this thing and doing this original content, and we think that this would fit really great into the mission of Web Active. We could work with you to provide you with a bandwidth and studios, in exchange for your producing this program. We thought maybe we could do a trial run for a few months and see how it goes, and if it all worked out, we could build a business model around it. We will work you into transitioning the company over to Web Active full-time and producing this and other progressive issues programming for the company."

And so, I was delighted. This was the best of all worlds, and I get to do a little bit of my activism. I get to produce again, and I'm doing it in a very new and exciting medium. I decided that this was going to take a lot more than just John McMullen doing this program. We decided that we would produce a weekly two-hour talk show that would deal with all kinds of issues and topics and have various features in it dealing with relationship advice and interesting Web sites, and arts and entertainment reviews and all that. So I began to assemble a team of people—both a combination of friends and other people referred to me who were active in one way or another in the community. And we brought together I think a troop of about twelve people who became involved. Everyone including myself at that point in time was a volunteer. There was no compensation for this unless we could get advertising sold, and then there was an opportunity for everybody except for me to be paid because Real Networks had a policy about not paying people basically to do two jobs.

Hangin'Out debuted on Sunday, September 30, 1996, as part of Web Active. We dealt with issues surrounding the upcoming presidential election and it was the first of fourteen shows that we would do in this kind of trial run through Progressive Networks, and later Real Networks. Over that first fourteen weeks, we had about seventy guests on a wide range of topics representing various national organizations. One of the cohosts was very well tied into the community at the time, along with her partner of six or seven years who was an openly lesbian Seattle city councilwoman.

In the first three weeks that we were producing *Hangin'Out,* we were at the first Gay and Lesbian American Music Awards (GLAMA) in New York City. Another week we were at the national display of the International AIDS Memorial Quilt on the Washington Mall in D.C., which also coincided with the same weekend that they were doing one of the last PFLAG national conferences taking place in Arlington, Virginia. So we kind of established early on that we didn't just want to sit in the studio and talk to people about things that were important. We also wanted to get out to community events and really have a presence there and really be this kind of global network that gave people front-row seats to things that were important in the LGBT community.

And, in addition to kicking off *Hangin'Out* on September 30, we began a broadcast of a daily five-minute news show that also continues to this day, called the *Daily Dose*. It was a five-minute news report each day on news affecting people in the community. Initially, we worked with PlanetOut to produce that because we were basically repurposing the stories that their news team was reporting in an online print form into a radio newscast.

So at the end of the year, at the end of 1996, we were coming down to the close of our first season. It was agreed up front that thirty days before the term ended, meaning at the beginning of December, we would decide where the show was going, if it had a chance of really succeeding on a business model because this was not to be necessarily a nonprofit thing. The intention was to make this a commercially viable program, and we received a great deal of kudos from Progressive Networks down to Rob Blazer, who really supported the program, as did Andy Sharpless and Sam Tucker and others there at Progressive Networks. But there was a decision by Rob Blazer to begin somewhat restructuring the organization, and Andy Sharpless wanted to return to the East Coast, and our entire business plan that we had worked on was kind of, not just for *Hangin'Out* but for all of Web Active, tossed out the window at the last minute. So right at the end of the year, Rob Blazer called me into his office and said, "Look, you made this show work on a bootstrap and it is a great program, and it really is the kind of thing we want to do, but I got to ask you to please put it on hiatus while we get a new business model put into place for Web Active."

It was a very difficult thing for me because I remember the audience the first week we did the show was only six people, and we had worked it up to, by the end of that time, about 2,500 people listening. I was like, oh my gosh, you can't break the momentum of what we've got going here. What we need to do is just keep the thing rolling on. We can't take it away. There's such a flake factor throughout so much of the gay and lesbian media—publications and whatnot come and go and you never see them again, and your credibility with the advertisers is gone. I thought if we shut this thing down now, would we try to bring it back in, you know, two months? Three? Six months? Who knew? And they weren't going to give me a commitment as to when they would resume that. My feeling was that people would say, "Yeah, and how long are you around for this time, and if we make an investment and buy advertising would you see it through?"

I made a very difficult decision at that point in time. I came back together with a team of people that were working on this, including my partner Charlie Dyer, and Michelle and Lucia and Malcolm McKay, who was doing a very popular feature called Dr. Ruthless, and I said, "I'm not sure we can continue to do this but this is now where my heart is." My passion was in doing this much more so than my other work that I was doing at Real Network. I had kind of worked myself into a situation where we'd kind of worked me out of the original job I had at Real Networks so that I would be able to transition into Web Active come January. All of a sudden I was kind of caught in this big crossfire of what do we do now. They want to keep on doing the stuff, but they want me to wait indefinitely while they put a new business plan together.

So I decided to do something really risky and I've always been kind of a risk-taker. I decided that I was going to walk away in the beginning of February—my one-year anniversary—with my first vesting of my stock options in Real Networks, or in Progressive Networks. I requested that the intellectual property rights and all of the content that had been produced be turned over to me at this time. I believed in what we were doing. We were getting e-mail from people all around the United States and all around the world, and got a letter from a fourteen-year-old kid who says, "I just came out of an attempted suicide and now I can tune in and realize there are other voices out there, people who are going through what I'm going through, and all of a sudden I don't feel so alone." How can you walk away from that opportunity? So this great group of people that I had been privileged to work with in that first fourteen weeks, we all said let's suck it up. Let's take a risk, and make this a viable commercial entity on its own.

All of a sudden, *Hangin'Out* that had been this two-hour show featuring interviews, having all these different features on travel, relationships, arts and entertainment, and commentary, evolved into a company called GLOradio Corporation. GLOradio was going to become an all out channel of gay and lesbian content. *Hangin'Out* was going to be reduced down to a daily fifteen- or twenty-minute show that would just be an interview with somebody in the community on different topics in which we talked to authors or entertainers. Other topics were tied to important events taking place, at that time, throughout the world as they related to the GLBT community. We ended up splitting *Hangin'Out* into a bunch of other shows: *Dr. Ruthless, One Man's Opinion,* and *Culture Corner.* We eventually came to add *Pittstop,* which was commentary by comedian Marilyn Pittman, and a show about financial planning for gays and lesbians called Fiscally Fit. We continued to slowly but surely add content to our schedule and kind of build up this entire channel of programs, which would work in conjunction with GLAAD to create a radio version of GLAAD.

We also began to venture into some live programming again because all of this programming was on demand. *Daily Dose* newscast continued through this time of daily features, along with *Hangin'Out,* Monday through Friday, and then the other minifeatures would be updated on a different day of the week, Monday through Sunday, always making it so there would be at least something new on every single day of the week. Eventually we added a program called *Friday Night Fever*, which was done live and people could interact with us and this was built into the programming schedule and began to get some good press. The *Advocate* helped us out immensely on a review that they had done that happened to coincide at the time we were launching the GLOradio service. Our audience grew swiftly, and we had partnered at the time with PlanetOut to be kind of their radio partner. We worked out of Seattle. They were based in San Francisco. As we worked in conjunction with them, our audience grew to 35,000. And so we were on top of the world.

In September 1997, we began some serious discussions with PlanetOut that resulted in an agreement to sell GLOradio Corporation to PlanetOut. By this time, we were also starting to do more live events. We had broadcast concerts by the Seattle Men's Chorus and we had done some stuff with the Cathedral of Hope in Dallas, and some other things. We started to really spread our wings out and do more shows from other places around the country. And so we agreed, effective October 1 of 1997, to become a part of PlanetOut.

In December 1997, I transitioned myself and Charlie Dyer down to San Francisco and we kind of integrated into the operation there and began to develop a lot more live programming, where we would do six hours a day of programming and then it would recycle, four times each day. *Hangin' Out* eventually worked its way back to being a two-hour show Monday through Friday with a lot of interactivity with the audience, and Charlie Dyer hosted a program called *P&O Weekday*. We were having a great time doing some fun stuff in the evenings, and comedian Kevin Show did a talk show then. A local San Francisco personality whose alter ego was "Fairly Butch" was doing a program very openly about his sexuality and particularly about women's sexuality, and things were flying high.

PlanetOut was at a place where there were always different things going on, and so their attention and the opportunity for really investing heavily into the areas where they needed help did not always share the same priority that they had company wide, even though our programming was resulting in our being able to participate in some very big things. We broadcast the first Human Rights Conference national dinner that the president of the United States addressed. We broadcast the Los Angeles Gay and Lesbian Center Women's Night. We covered LAVA, which is the Lesbians of Achievement, Vision, and Action Awards. We broadcast from the Gay and Lesbian Music Awards again. We also went to Amsterdam to broadcast the Gay Games for eight or nine days.

Things were going well but it was clear that there was so much competition for getting attention at PlanetOut. In order for this to really grow the way that we wanted to see it grow, as a radio and as a broadcast entity, and to have the kind of focus that it needed to have, we came to a difficult but a mutual agreement that GLOradio would spin back off on its own and would no longer be directly affiliated with PlanetOut. PlanetOut would continue to offer some radio products but their direction was to be all things to all people through an on-line community, and ours was that we really wanted to focus on streaming media. In September of 1998, the company became basically two companies again. We unraveled the entire earlier agreement because it had been primarily based on an exchange of equity.

At that point in time, our group regrouped, and people got more involved again in building up new programming and deciding what direction we really wanted to take this. Was there a way to start moving some of the content into mainstream radio? Do we want to just be doing gay and lesbian content, or do we want to try and move into wider markets? We knew that doing the gay and lesbian content was really the thing that was at the heart of all of our desires. In terms of professional goals and what not, we brought in some people who really were able to help us focus on developing our business model into something that was really going to be a worthwhile business venture, something that would do the necessary evil of delivering a good return to its shareholders, but at the same time would never compromise the level of commitment and coverage that we wanted to provide in the gay/lesbian/bi/trans community. We took about six months to get ourselves kind of back to, what I would say, growing—a place where we hadn't been. We kind of slipped off because of the severance between PlanetOut and GLOradio. We started moving forward again with a whole bunch of new programming. We had moved the company, incidentally, back to Seattle in November of 1998.

When we did the severance with PlanetOut, we decided it was also time to put our programming through kind of a rebranding, in terms of how people identified with us, to reduce the overall confusion of going from Real Networks or Progressive Networks to going to GLOradio, going to PlanetOut, going back to GLOradio. We decided in late September of 1998 that we were going to rebrand the product as GAYBC Network and that it would be a division of GLOradio Corporation. We launched GAYBC radio as its identity in the first week of October of 1998, and then over those next several months through March of 1999, we pretty much were getting our ducks into a row and building the core infrastructural team of GAYBC radio. We launched a new live channel, where we were doing live programming twenty-four hours a day, seven days a week, on March 15, 1999, and that included a series of talk shows and music programming. We had gone through all the licensing with Broadcast Music, Inc. (BMI) and the American Society of Composers and Publishers (ASCAP). We had a couple or so music programs, and one was a mixture of gay and lesbian music and the other was mainstream music in more of a call-in format for people to request their favorite songs. And then we added some talks shows in the evening and expanded others, including our Dr. Ruthless feature, which had dealt with love, sex, and relationship advice, and had been with us basically since the very beginning and had always been an extraordinarily popular feature. Malcolm McKay, who is a sex therapist here in Seattle, agreed to expand that program on our live channel to a nightly one-hour call-in program, which has been very, very popular. And then we also added another program like *Ed TV,* which features a lot of interactive conversation with a guy who had become something of an Internet gay celebrity via his Web cam. It pretty much focused on his life, both at work and at home, and we're going to continue to build up that channel.

In June 1999, we really got very serious about taking this company towards an eventual public float, or potentially selling it to a larger media. In fact, we had decided in April to change the corporate name from GLOradio Corporation to Stellar Networks, and as a kind of prelude to all this to start looking at other markets that we might get into niche content programming on the Internet. We've built a plan that basically will take the company to being a $100 million-plus revenue company, not just based on the gay and lesbian market but on some other niche markets within the next five years, and part of that is through strong strategic alliances. We've benefited from building audience with new partners, on-line partners in San Francisco which own Gay.com and AOL's OnQ.com service, and it's been a very good relationship. We will be doing some strategical things with other companies. PlanetOut is, even though we're not a part of them anymore, still potentially a company that we could be doing some special projects with and we've talked to them about that.

Our objective was really to become kind of a full-service radio network, offering a wide variety of both live and on-demand programs that people can access from anywhere in the world. We've been approached by people who produce mostly public or noncommercial shows with a lot of services around the world and they asked if we could help them to develop a strong presence on the Internet, so we will be creating an international channel—GAYBC International—where programming in different languages and different countries and cultures around the world will be presented. GAYBC will become a content aggregator and redistribution point for those people who don't really have the resources to put behind both the distribution and the marketing.

GAYBC Radio Network—founded by John McMullen, his partner Charlie Dyer, and a small group of associates—has continued to expand, and in fall 2000, it featured original content around the clock. GAYBC's parent company, Stellar Networks, hired Michael Kakoyiannis, former executive vice president of the radio stations group for Westwood One, as president and chief executive officer. McMullen stated, "I believe that, under his business leadership and my programming direction, GAYBC is really going to grow tremendously." GAYBCFM.com debuted an all-music network that streamed across the Web beginning fall 2000, and as a result GAYBC became all-talk news. GAYBC also made history when it became the first gay and lesbian broadcasting service to have access to the floor of the Democratic National Convention in August 2000. Unlike the other networks, its news team—John McMullen, Jeff Calley, Dr. Grethe Cammermeyer, and Michelangelo Signorile—delivered full live coverage during the convention.

Empires on the Horizon

With the onset of the 1990s, queer programming continued to meet resistance on mainstream radio and television stations. And providing programming for public access stations was expensive and its audience could not be easily accessed. The Internet provided the privacy of radio and immediate feedback via e-mail and chat rooms. A number of gay Internet providers have appeared on the World Wide Web over the past decade. The most notable have been PlanetOut, Gay.com, GAYBC Radio, the Gay Cable Network, and Gay Financial Network, and others.

Independent producers have benefited from the Internet's insatiable appetite for more and more programming, and new Internet stars have been created through the process—in some instances they merely hooked up a Web cam in a bedroom or living room. Most of the programming is as innovative and provocative as you would see on premium cable. Yet its greatest asset seems to be its ability to reach into the closets of Americans and to provide immediate access to services, information, and companionship. Although the Internet is primarily a national medium and is not affordable to everyone in the LGBT community, it is integral to the future of gay broadcasting.

Joe Liberatore: Web TV is a merging of the technologies. It's extremely interesting, active, and hot. My grandfather worked at Sears in the electronic department for fifty years at the only job he ever had. The interns at the National Lesbian and Gay Journalists Association (NLGJ) Convention are part of the MTV generation, and they have learned to demand stuff immediately—the Internet has changed the way we look at a lot of things. For example, if Gay News Network partnered with PlanetOut, I would have a reach of an automatic base of viewers that would take years otherwise to cultivate—it would take thousands and thousands of advertising dollars to hook people up and tell them about the show—where now I depend on re-

porters in different markets to pick up a story for us, and hope people remember when we're on, what channel, and remember to watch the show or
that we have a listserver.

Chuck Colbert: The beauty of electronic media is you can get clips from all
over the country and major dailies: more and more gay papers are getting
Internet Web sites so there is more information that you can access from
your home or office. That's a big advantage. It makes my research work
immensely easier. I don't necessarily have to clip newspaper articles anymore and get my hands all inky. The amount of information that travels on
the Internet is staggering.

Joe Liberatore: PBS's *In the Life* is on a number of stations and they had a
huge problem when their show aired at 1 or 1:30 in the morning. They've
enjoyed some success, coming back a little earlier. I think they're on at 11:30
now in a lot of markets. I don't see PBS taking any more gay shows, though.
They can't fill it all up with programming from gays, lesbians, transgenders,
and the bisexual community producers. So the really exciting thing that's
left and the only other option is the Internet, and clearly nobody knows what's
going to happen with this. AOL is always looking for new and innovative
ways. They have creative centers and one is dedicated to Internet programming, which in a sense is like creating their own ABC, NBC, UPN, their
own network, their own channel, but on the Internet. That's probably the
way things are going to happen whether it is with AOL or a starter company
where somebody says, "Okay, here is a gay TV channel on the Internet. You
can download this on real time whenever you want, watch as much as you
want, watch part of it, save it, watch it as often as you want." I really think
that's probably where things are going to go—that's how it is going to happen—we will watch gay programming over the Internet, which will be good
for us. Not only can anybody watch it whenever they want, but there's a way
to track numbers. With cable access, it is extremely difficult to track any
kind of numbers of viewers. I know we're in 10 million homes, but I don't
know if one to 10 million are watching. The Internet allows you to get around
that; it's extremely exciting and allows for two-way communication. Now
with a TV show, you have to put "Please drop me an e-mail" and hope that
the person watching gets something to write it down with and then rushes
back to the computer. When you're on-line watching, already you're seeing
it; it is fresh in your mind, you can e-mail, write back and say "This stinks"
or "This is great, here's the story idea I thought about—would you like to
cover this?" I think the Internet allows so much more interaction and immediate feedback.

Hilary Hamm: To get *Queer TV* or parts of our show on the Internet is definitely a few years down the road. The technology is there, but it is getting people to spend the money. Like the Internet Service Providers (ISP) that I work for, they are not about to buy a server just to stream public access television or any TV or whatever on the Internet. But maybe in the future, maybe it will become affordable and the right thing to do at the right time. We're waiting for things like that and for things to become cheaper so more people have access to the equipment that they need to do these things. If you have a vision to tell, it is possible now, especially with the Internet's role increasing and with more ISPs being able to video stream—even a five-minute video can really get a message out. It can maybe help some queer youth who might be confused about things.

Joe Liberatore: Going forward—the '90s were incredible so I can't even imagine what the next decade is going to be like, as computers get better, faster. Sometimes the server you're going through has so much video on it—it looks like Max Headroom. It jerks and bounces around a bit. Every couple of weeks, they come up with something new. Servers get faster, more streamline video, new ways to say the information; it's really going to be like watching television.

Chuck Colbert: The disadvantage I see in electronic media is Internet impulsiveness because you can get on there and stir something up pretty quickly. It's easy to sit behind a machine without a name per se—without a particular face or human contact—and write up something, and do so before you think about it and read it or have someone else look at it, and then zap it out on the Internet and then you've got a buzz and sometimes more than a buzz. There is an awful lot in my view or too much of a tendency for this impulsiveness that I think is not necessarily good, especially on controversial things. Hate crimes would be one example. An activist, journalist, or anyone can get on the Internet and cook up all kinds of things and zap it out on the Internet with virtually no responsibility. I've seen some e-mails that I think have been very inflammatory and have stirred up things—nothing major. I don't really know enough about the electronic media to know what the safeguards would be, but I certainly know that e-mail in organizational settings can be very deadly. People get on there and they think e-mail is a license to attack people. You know, you can put something out on the Internet and you can keep putting it out and the more you put it out, it becomes a reality.

Josy Catoggio: The Internet is big and anonymous and there's some value to that, to be able to talk freely and have a fake identity and change your gender or your age or your race or whatever you want to, but that's sort of pretend. But that's really different from helping kids connect with a gay teenage rap group, or a support group, that helps them deal with homophobia in school so that they don't drop out, or if they have to drop out to help them become involved in a local program for gay kids who can't fit in high school. Here there's the Eagles program, which is kind of an alternative high school for the queer kids that have been so beaten up that they have to leave their schools so they at least can get an education . . . and there's only three of those in the country. That's the problem for a lot of gay kids. I mean, there's all this talk about how we're this wealthy community, but I keep hearing about gay kids that can't even finish school because things are so bad. Either the harassment in high school is so bad that they have to drop out, or the harassment at home is so bad if they come out that they have to leave home.

The Internet cannot solve all the inequities of gay America, but it offers the possibility of more choices and more diversification of programming, and an opportunity to develop relatively affordable partnerships with other content providers and distribution servers within the LGBT community—when compared to the $20 million needed to create a gay TV network.

Chuck Colbert: I am a freelance syndicated columnist, penning a gay beat column handled through the *New York Times* syndicate as a part of the syndicate's "New America News Service"—a cultural diversity news, opinion, and features specialty. I'm a columnist in one of the local gay papers here. In *Newsweekly,* I've done a bunch of freelance stuff in the gay press, for example, the *Advocate, New York Blade, Philadelphia Gay News, Bay Windows, Out in the Mountains, Houston Voice,* and the *Gay and Lesbian Review.* Let's pause there. I think that the Internet is a very sophisticated news medium for more and more people, but I don't think that television or radio or any of the dailies are going to be replaced by the Internet. There may be a version of the *New York Times* on the Internet but there will still be the *New York Times* every day. I feel sure of that.

Chapter Eight

"We Are Your Children"

It Starts with Queer Youth

*In what will be looked back on as an eerie historical coincidence,
the fact that Matthew Shepard's body was found the very same
day the Family Research Council unveiled the TV version of their
"ex-gay" ads was impossible for the media to not take note of.*

—Cathy Renna, GLAAD Director of Regional Media
and Community Relations

"He has all these good songs and everything, American flag songs and all that stuff, and now he's a floating fag. You can quote me on that," said Bob Lucente, president of the New York City's Fraternal Order of Police, after the rock legend Bruce Springsteen played his unrecorded, unreleased song "American Skin (41 Shots)" live in concert in Atlanta on June 4, 2000. Springsteen sang the song again at Madison Square Garden eight days later. The New York police commissioner and the mayor denounced the song, which begins with Springsteen repeating the refrain "41 shots" several times, in reference to the February 1999 death of twenty-two-year-old West African immigrant Amadou Diallo, who was hit nineteen times by a stream of bullets when four white police officers fired forty-one times after they mistook his wallet for a gun.[1]

The epithet rallied the gay community against Lucente as well as other types of gay bashing—verbal and physical—the most extreme of which had resulted in the tragic deaths of Matthew Shepard; Scott Amedure (shot by a fellow guest of the "Jenny Jones Show"); Billy Jack Gaither, a thirty-nine-year-old gay Alabama man who was brutally beaten to death; and Private First Class Barry Winchell, clubbed to death with a baseball bat in the middle of the night at the Fort Campbell, Kentucky, army base, and many others who did not make national headlines. Lucente apologized for the "floating fag" reference a week later, explaining that it was a comment directed against Springsteen, not the gay community. However, many in the gay community did take it personally. The mixed public reaction to "American Skin" is, perhaps, a reminder of the struggle for civil rights by all people—of all colors and sexual orientation.[2] In 1992, the March on Washington provoked a scholarly debate on what exactly were the civil rights of gays and lesbians in the United States, and whether the participants of the 1963 civil rights march—nearly thirty years later—had envisioned the rights of gays and lesbians as part of the struggle for equal rights under the law.

Henry Louis Gates Jr. examined what he perceived as similarities and differences in the definition of and struggle for civil rights among gay Americans and black Americans in his May 17, 1992, essay published in the *New Yorker*: "What makes the race analogy complicated is that gays, as demographic composites, do indeed 'have it better' than blacks—and yet in many ways contemporary homophobia is more virulent than contemporary racism."

He concluded his essay:

> Actually it's curious that those who feel that the example of the 1963 march on Washington has been misappropriated seem to have forgotten about [one particular black gay man], since it was he, after all, who organized that heroic march. His name, of course, was Bayard Rustin, and it's quite likely that if he had been alive he would have attended the march on Washington thirty years later. By a poignant historical irony, it was in no small part because of his homosexuality—and the fear that it would be used to discredit the mobilization—that Rustin was prevented from being named director of the 1963 march; the title went to A. Philip Randolph, and he accepted it only on the condition that he could deputize Rustin to do the arduous work of co-ordinating the mass protest. Rustin accepted the terms readily. In 1963, it was necessary to choose which of the two unreasoning prejudices to resist, and Rustin chose without bitterness or recrimination. Thirty years later, people marched so his successors wouldn't have to make the costly choice.

It is interesting to note that Gates also pointed out that mainstream religious figures "continue to enjoin us to 'hate the sin': it has been a long time since anyone respectable urged us to, as it were, hate the skin."[3] Take for example the full-page ex-gay conversion advertisement featured in the *New York Times* on July 13, 1998. Anne Paulk had repented and accepted Jesus into her heart. Her diamond engagement and wedding rings glistened as she testified to her new life as a wife, mother, and ex-lesbian. The ad was underwritten by at least fifteen Christian-right and ex-gay organizations,[4] and it was part of a much larger nationwide campaign to "stop the sin."

In many instances, the decision to be openly gay has been a costly and dangerous one, as in the case of Matthew Shepard. That is why a number of LGBT broadcasters are committed to preserving queer-operated media outlets—where another perspective is considered, where prejudices and injustices are analyzed, and where legislation is often advocated.

Chris Wilson: When the Matthew Shepard incident occurred, I was curious to see if *This Way Out* was aired in Laramie, and it wasn't and I just found that interesting. Not that I think we can prevent hate crimes just by being there, but I think we're part of what chips away at that ignorance, the fact that anyone might turn on their radio and *This Way Out* might happen to be on the radio, and they're going to hear, well, these gay people. "These are those people I have all those stereotypes and ideas about, but wait a minute, they sound just like me and, God, I didn't know." Ignorance is not just hate crimes. I've met straight people who don't understand that we don't have marital rights. They assume that we do. But they see us getting married, and they don't get it, that we didn't have a marriage license and we don't have the same legal rights. That's the kind of thing we want to educate straight people about too, and there are wonderful supportive people who just don't know. So anyway, that's just another aspect of what we're all about.

Marle Becker: Imagine the Matthew Shepards of this world who are so afraid in small towns throughout the whole country, throughout the world. I was involved with ACT UP when it was in its heyday. Some things used to bother me. They would say, "Why don't we get the people in Columbus, Little Rock, or Houston involved in this." But New York is much different from Houston. The people who I had just the most incredible respect for are those out in the boondocks who were able to come out of the closet. I think there's a long road ahead for us.

Hate crimes against the LGBT community have strengthened the advocacy role of media organizations like the Gay and Lesbian Alliance Against Defamation (GLAAD). Its mission is to promote and ensure fair, accurate, and inclusive representation of individuals and events in all media as a means of eliminating homophobia and discrimination based on gender identity and sexual orientation.

In 1999, MTV aired a public service announcement called "Fighting Words," sponsored by the Gay, Lesbian, and Straight Educational Network (GLSEN). The PSA, aired exclusively on MTV, showed young men in a locker room shouting gay epithets as they rushed toward the camera, and it closed with a warning by Judy Shepard, mother of Matthew Shepard, to young people to think about what these words really mean and how they can lead to tragedy. GLAAD honored MTV for this public service announcement and others like it.[5]

GLAAD keeps a critical watch on all aspects of media, in part by providing its own coverage of events—to ensure that another perspective is presented to the American public. Cathy Renna, director of community relations for GLAAD, reported on the Matthew Shepard story from the day of the initial news report.

Cathy Renna: Why did Matthew Shepard's murder capture the attention of the media like no other? Phrased that way or similarly, this is the most common question I get from fellow activists, the general public, and even from media professionals themselves. We had just spent three months in the throes of a well-orchestrated and highly visible campaign to convince people that lesbian, gay, and bisexual people could "change" their orientation. We are convinced that the kind of rhetoric we face from groups like Family Research Council and the Center for Reclaiming America and others contributes to a climate of prejudice and violence. It was like a light bulb went off over the media's head—to hear about the brutal attack on Matthew Shepard upon leaving the Family Research Council press conference. I knew the impact it had on me, returning to the office to the initial news report and scores of e-mails and messages from concerned people.

Undoubtedly, the lesbian, gay, bisexual, transgender, and allied community is increasingly aware of the power of the Internet and related technology like few others. News of Matthew Shepard spread like wildfire and communities across the nation—and around the world—voiced their sorrow and outrage. Web sites popped up with information and soon vigils were being organized like never before around a single act of violence. Local media suddenly had a "local angle" for this growing story and this contributed greatly to the amount of coverage. That now-familiar photo of Matthew Shepard in the kitchen in a blue and white check shirt was in newspapers that rarely covered lesbian, gay, bisexual, and transgender issues, as well as appearing on national and local TV news.

Truth be told, there is no short or simple answer. I have no "sound bite" that does it justice. I vividly recall the first time I met Matthew's mother, Judy, in person. We were having lunch right before the GLAAD Media Awards in New York, and she asked me the very same question shortly after we sat down. It took an hour for me to answer her question. In truth, there are a lot of answers to this one—some more painful and difficult to discuss than others.

Love Your Neighbor: It's Elementary

> *There are wonderful opportunities to teach children and young people that it is so much easier to love than hate—and that's important. And through the eyes of children, kids really don't care: it's what they hear from their parents.*

—Marle Becker, WBAI-FM radio activist

On March 30, 1997, BBC TV announced the release of its major pre-school series called "Teletubbies," starring four colorful characters who live in a fantasy world of technology. Following the lead of the BBC, the series soon made its debut on PBS and became an instant hit in the United States. Tinky Winky, the purple one, is the largest and gentlest of all the teletubbies. With a triangle secured to his head and his red magic shiny bag in hand, Tinky Winky was viewed by many Americans as an icon of the gay movement.

The obsession with his sexual identity hints at a cultural struggle between individualism and narrowly defined social norms that begins, if not at birth, when a child is first plopped in front of the television. By the time the child grows into adolescence, the electronic media, for the most part, has further delineated gender roles in America. In an effort to counter antiqueer advertising campaigns, gay newspapers in Atlanta, Houston, and New Orleans ran "Tinky Winky" parody ads that mocked attempts by Christian conservatives to persuade gays and lesbians to go straight.

> "If you love a Teletubby, tell him the truth," the ads warn. "Uh-oh," as they say in Teletubbyland. There's more. "Toward hope and healing," the ads go on, for cartoon homosexuals....The ads in gay newspapers ... urge Tinky Winky—and a host of other sexually ambiguous cartoon characters—to go straight. And they name names: Bert and Ernie of "Sesame Street" (described as "urban bachelors"), Velma of "Scooby-Doo, Where Are You," Peppermint Patty of "Peanuts" and that cross-dressing Bugs Bunny. "If we can save Tinky Winky," the ad promises, "we can help others, too."[6]

Coincidence? Purple, triangle, and red bag. And what did Reverend Jerry Falwell say about this? There is an "implicit sexual preference" by Tinky Winky. Purple is the color of gay liberation and the triangle is its symbol. A PBS spokesman responded, "Out of the closet? They're not even out of diapers yet!" Appearing on NBC's *Today* show, Falwell explained that he was "simply saying that this is one more in many, many building blocks where we have little boys running around with purses and acting effeminate."[7]

It was exactly these types of attitudes and stereotypes that producers Debra Chasnoff and Helen S. Cohen wanted to address in their documentary film *It's Elementary: Talking About Gay Issues in School*. The documentary is designed to inform adults about the importance of talking with elementary school-age children about stereotypes and deals with how antigay prejudice affects all children. The film came through the combined effort of hundreds of educators, parents, children, filmmakers, and activists; it continues to be distributed to a number of schools and organizations.

Debra Chasnoff: *It's Elementary* is really for adults. When some people hear that we want to talk to children about gay people, it sets fire alarms off. That's the worst possible thing that they can imagine happening to their innocent little children. *It's Elementary,* for this reason, is very controversial in this country, and given the political climate we're at a cultural crossroads. We offered *It's Elementary* through American Public Television, which is one of the distribution systems within public broadcasting, and KQED in San Francisco was one of our sponsoring stations for the broadcast. And when we started, there was a huge campaign from several religious right organizations to try to censor the broadcast. And we were engaged in that campaign for several months. There were a lot of PBS stations that initially said that they were not going to air the film, but eventually many programmers changed their minds. In part, this was because they talked to programmers at other stations, and heard what their rationale was for airing the film, and also because of the tremendous outpouring of support from local communities, from people who told their stations that they really wanted to see the film on TV. That has made a difference. Also, the criticisms that the right wing organization have made of the film have really fallen flat and are not accurate. When programmers looked at the real film and compared it to the accusations that those groups were making, they felt like they needed to have a little bit of courage and go ahead and air the film even though some people might be outraged by that decision. They saw that *It's Elementary* is not about promoting certain sexual practices. Instead, the film shows (and what we the filmmakers are advocating) is that kids are perfectly capable of understanding that gay people should be treated respectfully, and it is appropriate to convey that message to them at a young age. In the end, more than 115 stations agreed to broadcast the film. We've done a phenomenal amount of media work, including newspaper, radio, and TV interviews to try to get the word out about the film. We've been able to put the idea out to the media that people should be doing much more to prevent antigay prejudice. We've had a platform with these broadcasts and have been able to articulate that point of view all over the country. However, the broadcasts on public television came after a lot of groundwork had already been laid. Thousands of schools, hundreds of school districts, and more than 500 schools of education at different colleges and universities are now using *It's Elementary.*

Debra Chasnoff is now a full-time filmmaker. Her documentary *Choosing Children* won her national recognition in 1984, and later she won an Academy Award for *Deadly Deception: General Electric, Nuclear Weapons, and Our Environment* (1991), a documentary about the health and environmental consequences of nuclear weapons. Since then, she has worked on a number of film projects and also worked as a publisher and editor in print media. She graduated from college in 1978 and spent some time in film school in California before dropping out to produce *Deadly Deception.*

Debra Chasnoff: I finished my first film in 1984. And I collaborated with Kim Klausner. We decided to make a documentary film at the time called *Choosing Children,* which is the first film to examine the ways that lesbians could become parents. We made the film to challenge the prevailing social belief that if you were gay, you couldn't be a mother or father unless you had kids from a previous heterosexual relationship. We didn't know anything about filmmaking and the way we were able to do that film was we had a wonderful mentor, Margaret Lazarus, who runs a small production and distribution company. She literally taught us how to edit, how to hire a good crew, and how to write fund-raising proposals.

So we made that film in the early '80s. It was actually before the whole video explosion. We made it on film and started distributing it on video, mostly to colleges and universities. In the course of producing the film, we organized many community premieres for the film and learned very early on that when you make documentary films half the job is making the film, and the other half is getting media coverage for the film—and that in the process you can generate a lot of publicity, a lot of media coverage for an issue that has been kept away from the mainstream media. What I mean by that is suddenly articles started springing up in papers saying lesbians could have kids, too. And probably more people saw the articles than ever saw the film. By producing the film and by releasing it, we found that you could play a role in influencing public opinion and public discourse in the mainstream media.

Then in 1988, a bunch of other people and I started a magazine called *Out/Look: The National Lesbian and Gay Quarterly.* And that was our attempt to create a publication that was offering thoughtful writing on politics and culture which brought lesbians and gay men together. At the time that we started publishing it in 1988, it was still highly unusual for there to be anyone writing in mainstream papers about lesbian and gay issues. It would be very unusual for a piece to be in the *New York Times Magazine* or in the style section of the newspaper or any other magazine. It's been amazing to see how things have changed since we first started publishing *Out/Look.*

From these experiences, we were really able to craft our image and our message when it came to getting the word out on *It's Elementary.* We really relied on print media tremendously to let people know about the film. When the film first came out in 1996, we had our world premiere right here in San Francisco, with an audience of 1,400 people. It was an incredible night when the film was first released. The emotional response of the audience really conveyed to us how we really had succeeded in making a film that opened up new territory, to go where people haven't gone before, which is to begin looking at when and how prejudices develop. If we can reach children at an early age, the prejudice that leads to many of the problems that lesbian and gay men have had to face could be prevented. We saw early on that we had something very, very powerful in our hands and that it really had the potential to open a lot of hearts and to move things forward in a very dramatic way. As a result, we have been working extremely hard the past few years to distribute *It's Elementary* and to get as many people as possible to see it.

The next step was to produce a film called *That's a Family!,* a documentary for children. It features kids talking about different kinds of families—children from lesbian/gay-headed families, to parents who are divorced, to kids who are adopted or have parents of different races and so forth.

That's a Family! had its world premiere on June 10, 2000 at the Herbst Theater in San Francisco. Chasnoff is the director and coproducer of *That's a Family!* And the executive producer is Helen S. Cohen. The other coproducers are Ariella J. Ben-Dov and Fawn Yacker. Chasnoff also directed and coproduced "Wired for What?" (1999) for the public television series *Digital Divide*, which takes a critical look at the push to put computers into the nation's schools.

Dedicated to Generation Q

> *What these people really want, hidden behind obscure legal phrases, is the legal right to propose to our children that there is an acceptable alternate way of life. . . . I will lead such a crusade to stop it as this country has not seen before.*

—Anita Bryant, antigay activist

It was 1977 and those words sounded the beginning of the religious right movement in the United States. Anita Bryant, former Miss Oklahoma, dedicated mother and wife, and devout Southern Baptist, started a revolution:

> It was called "Save Our Children," the start of an organized opposition to gay rights that spread across the nation, and the beginning of what came to be known as the religious right. The Rev. Jerry Falwell came to Miami to help her, but it was Anita Bryant who first led fundamentalist Christians into politics under the banner of a domestic social issue.[8]

In 1977, San Francisco queer activists fought back with a campaign slogan of their own—"We Are Your Children."[9] In the year 2000, the gay and lesbian community echoes those words. Today it is a plea to save the Matthew Shepards of the world from verbal and physical violence and to stop the high incidence of suicide among queer teens.[10] The idea that queer youth would not have to hide their gender identity and be free to experiment with sexuality without shame or recourse is the underlying goal of many of those who choose to work in queer broadcasting. The desire of these broadcasters is to make life a little easier for the next generation, as demonstrated by their conviction and commitment to queer youth issues.

Marle Becker: It is interesting to look at where we are in the community now. Colleges now have gay organizations and gay groups. I don't think there is a college in the United States that doesn't have a gay organization. When I was growing up, I couldn't even go to college. I gave up. I was so ashamed of who I was when I was growing up in a small town in Pennsylvania. I couldn't wait to get out of there because I was so ashamed of who I was or what I thought I was at the time. I was a straight-A student until I hit ninth grade. I thought I don't care. I just want to get through these next four years and get out of this town where I might find someone else like me. I didn't even know what like me meant back then. But I just knew that I had to get out. I didn't want to go to college or do anything. But those are big regrets for me now that I never got a college education. I don't think there's anything more important than learning. But it was what I had to do to survive.

Jon Beaupre: I found a writer from a University of Southern California paper—a young man who was and as far as I know is a dispatcher in the Los Angeles Police Department. I read a story of his about losing the first friend that he had ever lost because he was gay. The piece was a very beautiful rendition called "Losing Jason" and it basically had to do with being surrounded by a bunch of bullies in eighth grade or high school, and one of them was his best friend, Jason. And the story goes, with them kind of bullying and cornering him, and saying "you're gay" and him not being able to answer that. In the written piece, he reflected back to childhood camping with this kid and trying desperately but not being able to discuss these issues with him. On the school playground that day, he lost this guy as a friend and they were never friends after that. We radio dramatized that piece, with a five- to seven-minute reflection, with sounds of a school yard, sounds of crickets chirping, and some sweet music under it as well, and it was the kind of reflection that I think resonated with a lot of people and it won for us our third Golden Mike Award.

Marle Becker: I see youth today with a place to go and a place to learn that it is all right to be gay. That to me is extraordinary. I think that if I can give young people—not just me—all the gay broadcasters—some role models and a reason to say, "It is all right to be gay, and I have nothing to be ashamed of," that for me is the best I can possibly hope for. I couldn't hope for anything more than having young people feel good about themselves. Because I grew up when being gay was quite frankly viewed by the American Psychiatric Association as an illness. You don't go through life being made fun of and having people look at you as if you really are a freak without internalizing it. It took its toll on people my age, and certainly on older gays who ended up committing suicide. I know people who went through shock treatment because they were committed to psychiatric wards simply because they were homosexual. That is pretty frightening, so I think if we can as a group support young people and say you have nothing to be ashamed of and it is perfectly healthy who you are and what you are doing with your life, then that is just the greatest reward that anyone in gay broadcasting could possibly receive.

Greg Gordon: Here is a nice story. There's this guy who did the local gay show on KKFI in Kansas City, Missouri, and as it turns out he grew up listening to *IMRU* here in Los Angeles. I think he's not doing it anymore, but he was for a long time. So it was sort of like queer radio of the next generation. He would tell us how valuable *IMRU* was when he was a kid and growing up. So those are the rewards that you get from doing a program like this. Certainly nobody is ever going to get rich.

Josy Catoggio: Over the course of the years, I got really passionate about gay youths, especially when the statistics started coming out about the levels of suicide among gay youth, and so I would ask every author I ever talked to, "What would you have to say to gay youth? Or before you knew there was anything else out there, how would you tell yourself to survive, as a gay youth, to adulthood?" Gay kids couldn't get a publication at home or even buy magazines and bring them into the house. And they couldn't get into the bars and there weren't a lot of places for gay kids to go, and in California it's such a driving culture. I'm from New York originally and until you get a license and access to a car, it's really hard for gay kids to get to rap groups or centers or anything like that. I have mostly tried to find ways to give gay kids some sense of the big picture and tell them all you have to do is survive to adulthood, and then there is a world out there for you to join. When I was working at the center even back in the '70s, a large part of our client base were these teenagers, who had either been beaten up and thrown out of their houses or who had left home. And they all come to Hollywood or San Francisco, thinking that's the Gay Mecca. They go to a big city—it's like that's where they can connect. Instead, they get preyed upon, and they get into drugs and prostitution and sexually transmitted diseases and homelessness and poverty, and their health deteriorates. With a lot of these kids, we'd be trying to get them into job training programs and they'd go, "Why should I take a minimum wage job when I can make 300 bucks a night on the street?"

What kept me going all those years as a volunteer is that, literally, people would come up to me on the street or in a bookstore, because they recognized my voice, and they'd say, "You saved my life when I was a teenager. It was my only access to the community. I would go in my room, put on my headphones, or I'd drive around in the car and listen to the radio—so nobody would know."

Cindy Friedman: I was one of those suicidal teens and very committed to the idea of putting something out there that would be something positive that could reach down. I was really excited about having a chance to work in radio.

Marle Becker: I used to think and I still think that every time that I step out in the streets of New York, how different my life would have been if I had been raised in New York, or in a city where I could have been just a little bit freer or just got lost in the crowd. And by getting lost in the crowd, you have a certain amount of freedom that I didn't have. I grew up in a very small town. It was awfully hard being someone I wasn't and when you pretend to be something that you are not, I think that ultimately you smother. I guess that I was lucky that I had the drive and the fortitude in the inside—"I'll get out of this and I'll make the best of what I can out of the situation," and that is precisely what I was able to do.

Josy Catoggio: There's a million things out there that kids can connect to, other than the bars, that didn't use to exist. And unless they're really listening to local radio, they don't really find out about that stuff. I mean what really appealed to me about doing community gay radio is that, in addition to everything else we did, we had a calendar every week, so that people could find out when the demonstrations were and where the organizations were and they could find out what was happening. So from my point of view, as sort of a grassroots activist, I think local programming is much more important than the Internet in terms of connecting gay kids with a gay community that they can get involved with.

Marle Becker: One advantage of doing gay broadcasting for me is to share the history of the community with the young people who are coming out— and they are coming out younger and younger and younger and, boy, that is so exciting to see when I go to the Gay and Lesbian Community Center on a Sunday afternoon. They have a group called Gay Youth, and they are thirteen, fourteen, and fifteen. And many of these people are experimenting and not even sure of their sexuality, but obviously they have tendencies that are different from what straight people are considering their sexuality.

A friend of mine just said to me last week: "I hate to say this but all of my good times were spent in bars because that is all we had. That's all we had." And how it is just so different today because here you have organizations all over the place and the gay and lesbian community centers all over the country. Every single night, there are ten to twelve meetings of different organizations, and every year they are multiplying. And new groups are coming on. If you have an interest and you are gay, there is someone else who has the same interest—and those were things growing up I could never have dreamed of. So it is changing. I don't think fast enough, but certainly since the '60s, there have been enormous advances. It's funny because somebody was just saying to me at the meeting we had with the collective last week as we put our programming for November and December together, there are still people who don't know that gay programs exist.

Josy Catoggio: Radio used to be the only place gay kids could go privately and connect with the community. Now for many gay kids the Internet is more that than radio. But not everybody has a computer. Not everybody has sound capability even though you can download Real Audio for free on the PlanetOut site and they tell you how to do it and all that kind of stuff. For now, I think the Internet reaches less people. *This Way Out,* for example, goes all over the world and there's a lot of little public radio stations in little towns at little universities that either use its news or use the whole show. So there's a lot of local volunteers here and there and all over the world that do locally originated programming, which helps people connect with the community in their community as opposed to this Internet community that's much more widespread and anonymous and doesn't really help people get involved.

Chris Wilson: We want to be there for the young kids who want the connections to the gay and lesbian community. It is certainly not a money-making enterprise. We want to be available to everybody and particularly for the kids who don't have the money and resources or contact with the gay and lesbian community. I mean, that is our mission. That's what we are really all about.

Josy Catoggio: More and more kids are coming out younger and younger because there is much more public information out there—*Ellen* and the sitcoms and *Will and Grace* and all that kind of stuff, but I think that for kids in small towns it's still really difficult to find anybody to connect with, and for a lot of kids, it's not safe to come out until they're away from home. So I do think radio is still really vital for that reason, and in many towns maybe there's a support group at the university or a local church or community center or one therapist or one priest or minister or something or a parents' and friends' group that will connect them with whatever is there. And in fact, you know, we used to think the calendar was the most boring thing we did, but also the most important thing we did because it was the one thing that let them know what all their options were about groups and organizations.

Marle Becker: I think gay programming is going to become very popular. I think people ask, "Why is there a need for gay programming?" We never really get equal time with issues that are important to the gay and lesbian community. It wasn't until AIDs came around that the heterosexual community started to say "Wow, this is what is happening to the gay community." And it was never anything good. So what I think we'll see in the future of gay broadcasting is positive images of the gay community. I see younger people becoming involved in gay programming. I see it as a respectable career for younger people to look forward to. I think that Alan Amberg, for example, is doing extraordinary things and he's in drive time; that is just phenomenal. And certainly there are also people in general broadcasting, like on the major networks, who are coming out of the closet too.

Josy Catoggio: Rather than informative or thought-provoking or deeper or more philosophical or political, which is always what I was passionate about, I think more and more what's happening is even commercial stations are now beginning to see a gay audience as a potentially lucrative market. There's all that mythology about how we all have this disposable income, which completely ignores the fact that most of us are pretty poor and marginal, and there's a few of us that have a lot of money, but it doesn't include all the kids that get tossed out or leave home and don't end up finishing high school. There's a belief out there that the MTV generation has no attention span. They don't read books, they don't care about authors. They don't care about big ideas. They bore easily. They don't like talking heads. You have to change the sound every few seconds. You have to keep it fast-paced and highly produced and quick-moving so that even if you're talking to an author, in that five or six minutes that you're interviewing this author, you also will include snatches of music or maybe of a film made from one of their books, you know a couple of lines of dialogue from the film. I mean just on and on and on and more and more and more entertainment and less and less and less depth.

Chris Wilson: I honestly believe if there were more shows like *This Way Out,* there would be a lot more education in society at large which might discourage in turn a lot of the hate which is based on misunderstanding and ignorance. I welcome straight listeners to listen to *This Way Out,* to understand what is going on in foreign countries, with respect to gay and lesbian rights, to hear the kind of music that members of our community are putting out on "Audiofile." Overnight Productions has a mission statement, but not specific to *This Way Out,* that it is really important to us to be nonprofit, noncommercial, and just try to get what we need to be available. That's really all we want.

Joe Liberatore: At the second annual National Lesbian and Gay Journalists Association Convention, we trained more students and more field reporters and all that kind of good stuff, making sure kids understand. I was flabbergasted when one student actually told me that there are no gay role models. Coming back from the convention, I said, "You're crazy, it doesn't have to be all these other people you see here at the convention. It's the person that supports [CEO] Megan Smith at PlanetOut, the person who's doing the internship program for NLGJA, and lots of other people. It doesn't have to be those you see on magazines." I was taken aback somewhat by this comment. I'm actually going to follow up with him. He was really out there, just questioning things like, "whether he was in the right major" and questioning about civil rights in a gay and lesbian group at the convention, and so on. I'm just so excited and energized by the things that I see.

Epilogue

The Senate approved the Hate Crimes Prevention Act (HCPA) on July 22, 1999. The purpose of the legislation was to add crimes motivated by sexual orientation, gender, or disability to the 1968 federal hate-crime protections covering race, color, religion, and national origin. It would allow federal prosecutors to pursue a hate-crime case if local authorities refuse to press charges, and to provide assistance to local law enforcement agencies in investigating hate crimes. To some, this bill is an attack on their right to free speech. For those who have lost loved ones and children to hate crimes, freedom is not so easily defined and espoused as a noble end. Freedom is perhaps relevant to one's particular point of view and standing in society. At the very least, however, broadcasters should contemplate their role in society, and the impact of their decisions on the youth of America—the future of America. On May 23, 2000, rapper Eminem released *The Marshall Mathers LP*, which contains the words "fag" or "faggot" in many of its songs and describes acts of violence against gay men.

To no avail, GLAAD made a plea to Interscope Records, Music Television (MTV), music retailers, and others to reconsider whether they should promote a product that elevates hate speech and dehumanizes gay men and women. The struggle within the LGBT community to be heard over the mainstream is not easily won. On November 1, 2000, GAYBC Radio Network, which was ranked by Arbitron as number two in Internet-only talk radio only months earlier, made a "Save Our Station" plea. The network, the on-line voice of the LGBT community, suffered a significant setback in its funding and was forced to cease normal operations on October 27, 2000. Within days, GAYBC Radio Network resumed its daily on-line operations, after having raised approximately $50,000 in that one weekend.

And the beat goes on. . . .

Appendixes

Interview with Allen Ginsberg (1926–1997)

By Matthew Rothschild, *The Progressive*, August 1994 Issue

"I'm banned from the main marketplace of ideas
in my own country."

—Allen Ginsberg

I arrived at Allen Ginsberg's apartment on the lower east side of Manhattan at noon on April 15, two months before his sixty-eighth birthday. The Beat poet, icon of the 1960s counterculture, gay pioneer, had just published a new book of poetry, *Cosmopolitan Greetings,* almost forty years since he shattered the poetry scene with *Howl.* I wanted to talk to him about his latest work and his current political views.

The narrow passageway leading into Ginsberg's small living room was clogged with equipment from a WGBH/BBC crew that was there to interview Ginsberg for a film on the history of rock-'n'-roll. I'd been told ahead of time that he'd be doing other interviews that afternoon, so I sat on a small squishy futon under the sole window and looked around. A framed and illustrated copy of Blake's "The Tyger" was at the entranceway. A large bookshelf stood against one wall, with an oversized volume about Lenin lurking on top. Poetry filled the top two shelves, and then nonfiction, including *Citizen Cohn,* and *J. Edgar Hoover,* and Edward Herman's and Noam Chomsky's

221

Manufacturing Consent. Tapes of Bob Dylan and CDs of John Trudell, along with videos (*The Panama Deception*) gathered on another bookshelf.

After about half an hour, Ginsberg came out of his tiny bedroom. He was dressed in a deep blue shirt, gray slacks, black slip-on shoes, and a red-and-black tie. He introduced himself to me, and then engaged the filmmakers. They wanted his recollections of meeting Bob Dylan and John Lennon, so he dutifully performed in his kitchen through numerous takes as the film crew fidgeted with the sound and the light—a process that took about two hours. A framed, if slipping, portrait of Walt Whitman hung on one wall, along with a print of St. Francis in Ecstasy. On the refrigerator, next to low-fat food lists and Buddhist chants, was a leaflet: Teenagers! Tired of Being Harassed by Your Stupid Parents? Act Now. Move Out, Get a Job, Pay Your Own Bills . . . While You Still Know Everything.

As the film crew was cleaning up, Ginsberg and I retreated to his bedroom for the interview, Buddhist shrine next to the bed, writing table nearby, and bookshelf of poetry at the front. Ginsberg was alternately impassioned and professorial, even occasionally disputatious as he resisted being labeled a political poet. There was one magical moment when he took down an old hardback copy of Whitman and started to read passages he had marked up. Halfway through the interview, Ginsberg broke to go upstairs in his building to Philip Glass's apartment to work with the composer on a memorial for a mutual friend who had died of AIDS. When Ginsberg returned, we talked for two more hours, and I left exhausted at 6:30 in the evening.

Q: In *Cosmopolitan Greetings,* you have a phrase, "radioactive anticommunism." What do you mean by that?

Allen Ginsberg: Well, the bomb was built up beyond the Japanese war as a bulwark against communism. The extremist anticommunism went in for mass murder in El Salvador and assassination in the Congo, when we killed Lumumba and put in Mobutu. The military extremism was not much help in overthrowing communism, except maybe in bankrupting both sides, but that only left the communist countries helpless when they switched over to the free market.

But beyond that I think as much was done to subvert Marxist authoritarian rule by Edgar Allan Poe, blue jeans, rock-'n'-roll, Bob Dylan, the Beatles, modern American poetry, and Kerouac's *On the Road*—that was more effective in subverting the dictatorship and the brainwash there than all the military hoopla that cost us the nation, actually.

Q: Why did these works undermine communism?

Ginsberg: The authoritarian mind—Maoist, Hitler, Stalinist, monotheist, Ayatollahist, fundamentalist—shares a fear and hatred of sexual libertarianism, fear of free-association spontaneity, rigid control over thought forms and propaganda, fear of avant-garde and experimental art. The Stalinist word for this kind of avant-garde is "elitist individualism" or "subjectivism"; the Nazi word was "degenerate art"; the Maoist word was "spiritual corruption"; the fundamentalist word is "spiritual corruption and degenerate art"; the Jesse Helms argument is why should the average American taxpayer have to pay for this "elitist individualistic filth"? It's exactly what Stalin used to say: "Why should the Russian people have to pay for the avant-garde to display their egocentric individualism and immorality and not follow the Communist Party line?"

The whole authoritarian set of mind depends on suppression of individual thought, suppression of eccentric thought, suppression of inerrancy in the interpretation of the Bible, or of Marx, or *Mein Kampf,* or Mao's "little red book" in favor of mass thought, mass buzz words, party lines. They all want to eliminate or get rid of the alien, or the stranger, or the Jews, or the gays, or the Gypsies, or the artists, or whoever are their infidels. And they're all willing to commit murder for it, whether Hitler or Stalin or Mao or the Ayatollah, and I have no doubt that if Rush Limbaugh or Pat Robertson or Ollie North ever got real power, there would be concentration camps and mass death. There already are in the police-state aspect of the "war on drugs."

Q: In one of your new poems, you mention your frustration that Jesse Helms and the FCC have banned your works from the airwaves except during the wee hours of the morning. How did that happen?

Ginsberg: As part of the totalitarian political-correctness mind-control movement on the fundamentalist Right, the makers of beer, Coors, funded the Heritage Foundation, which presented a position paper and the legal technical language for Jesse Helms, who is subsidized by the tobacco interests, to direct the FCC to forbid all so-called indecent language from the air twenty-four hours a day. It passed in October 1988 when the Senate was empty, and was signed by Reagan. I found out about it because there was a column in the *Village Voice* by Nat Hentoff in which the head of the Pacifica stations said they used to play my poetry quite a lot but now it was controversial—not that they didn't like it, not that it wasn't popular, but they were afraid it would be too expensive to defend in court. They couldn't afford an argument for free speech. So I helped organize a consortium of the Emergency Civil Liberties Committee, Harvey Silverglate, the then-head of the ACLU in Massachusetts, the Rabinowitz and Boudin law firm, and William Burroughs, myself, and the PEN club as friends of the court, and we helped bust the law.

Q: You won?

Ginsberg: Well, we won once. The FCC was directed to hold hearings as to whether or not it was legitimate to reduce the entire population of America to the level of minors, because the law was supposedly to protect the ears of minors. They agreed to define minors as eighteen, eliminating youth, teenyboppers—everybody's a minor now. The FCC came up with a home-made prejudiced thing, saying, "OK, the ban's not for twenty-four hours, it's only from 6:00 A.M. to midnight. And you can have sort of open passage, midnight to 6:00 A.M., when nobody is listening, for your art, your poetry, and your filthy books."

Then I participated in a roundtable discussion at an FCC lawyers' convention with James Quello, the oldest member on the FCC, and Quello pulled out a copy of *Howl,* and said, "This is a perfectly good poem you could broadcast on the air—all you have to do is eliminate a couple paragraphs." That was his idea of art! It was like a Soviet bureaucrat's statement. There's no difference between that Stalinist bureaucratic mentality and what's going on with these fundamentalist bureaucrats.

So we took it to court again. And the court said there was not sufficient proper scientific sociological investigation of when the kids were listening, but that it might be legitimate to protect their ears. So the FCC made it from 6:00 A.M. to 8:00 P.M. And that's being fought in court still on constitutional grounds.

Q: How does this censorship affect you?

Ginsberg: I'm a poet who specializes in oral recitation and performance. I am pleased that my work is good on the page—it should be solid on the page—but there is a dimension of sound, which Ezra Pound emphasized. I'm a specialist in that, I'm very good at vocalization, I'm famous for that around the world, and yet I'm banned from the "main marketplace of ideas" in my own country—radio, television, and God knows what they can do when the FCC gets hold of the information highway. That means the entire brainwash is all under the control of the FCC so that "who got fucked in the ass by handsome sailors and screamed with joy" will be banned from electronic media. People don't read as much these decades but they hear. Like John Lennon heard my poetry on radio before he read it and was moved by it. That means that a main avenue that I would have for articulation of my own thinking, my own ideas, whether social or political or aesthetic, is closed off.

Q: Do you see the Far Right gaining power in the United States?

Ginsberg: They have power. They've got control of television now; they've censored television and radio. They already have power. You've already accomplished your censorship of the media, and intimidated them as well as legally censoring them. You got it. You have this organized gang of listeners who will write in at the drop of a hat—you know, they'll say, "Write in and denounce this or that politician, or this or that abortion, or this or that poem," then bam, you've got it. They mobilize all these relatively innocent people to be writing in denouncing art. It's demagoguery, and the media caved in to it.

Q: One of my favorite poems in *Cosmopolitan Greetings* is "After the Big Parade"—about the American public's reactions to Bush's Iraq war. Were you actually at one of those parades here?

Ginsberg: I was down in the parade with a tiny group of people protesting it in front of City Hall. There was a group of maybe ten people amid the millions that were out there under the confetti, and the bunting, and the bands, and the police.

Q: How did the crowd respond to you?

Ginsberg: They ignored us, or they threatened us. So I saw it first hand, the mob hysteria, as in the old Roman mob. And then within two days the entire enthusiasm had evaporated, and within a few months, people realized more and more that the Iraq war was one of the most successful instances of brainwashing ever turned out by Madison Avenue and Government—by control of the airwaves and mass-media censorship.

In hindsight, people realize that they were taken in, that alternative views weren't presented, and that in order to present this war as heroic, you had to ignore some very obvious things—like the fact that we were building up Saddam Hussein until the very day that we bombed him, and that we had played one gang against another in the Iran-Iraq war.

In a way, we were responsible for the whole Middle East situation. We had overthrown Mossadegh, as I've got in my poem, "Just Say Yes Calypso." Norman Schwarzkopf's father was directly involved in the overthrow of Mossadegh and the training of the Savak. People weren't aware of that. People thought Schwarzkopf was some sort of country bumpkin from the Midwest who got to be general rather than a sophisticated Persian-speaking son of a man who trained the Shah's secret police.

So it was some kind of American karma we were bombing, and people weren't really aware of the historical relevance of the land they were bombing, that this was the Garden of Eden we were bombing, the land of Ur and

Abraham. And they didn't realize in a way that it was child molestation, because the average age of Iraqis at the time was only sixteen. The people being bombed were kids!

Trying to concentrate all that information into rhymed stanzas takes ingenuity, and interest, and curiosity. I think it's a really good poem because it's totally understated and it's a fact. "Have they forgotten the corridors of death?"—which was the boastful phrase that was used when we bombed the Iraqis. And "Will another hundred thousand desert deaths across the world be cause for the next rejoicing?" is a strangely sardonic compassionate touch—I don't know where I got that tone. It's not Pound; it might be Herman Melville's poetry. Melville has something like this in his poem, "On the Slain Collegians," who rushed into the battle and perished, "enlightened by the volleyed glare."

Q: The specter of AIDS is in many of the poems in your latest work. How has the AIDS plague affected you?

Ginsberg: There's this decimation of genius, particularly in theater and film and music and poetry. One of the greatest modern poems is called "Ward 7," written by Jim Dlugos, who was dying of AIDS. It's one of the most humane, heartfelt, sincere poems I've ever read. It's one of the great poems of this part of the century. So there's been a lot of loss.

My taste tends to be for young men and straight young men, so in a way in the early days of AIDS that sort of kept me a little bit safe. Now I'm very careful. It hasn't affected me all that much in terms of my love life, though lately I must say I'm getting older, I'm less successful in bedding young men and young straight men. And I like to be screwed, or screw, but I can't get it up anymore anyway (because of diabetes and other things that I mention in this book) unless there's a great deal of stimulation and rapport and real interest, so I'm not inclined to screw anybody because it's hard and I'd be a little scared to be screwed—though with people that I know real well and I know their situation and their history and have been tested, I wouldn't mind. But I don't know anyone that I like that well or that likes me enough to get it up.

Q: Even in these days of AIDS, you're like the last apostle of desire. You still celebrate sex.

Ginsberg: Safe sex is just as good as unsafe sex. And with safe sex you get something which I always liked anyway—you have these long pillow talks about what you're going to do with each other, how you're going to make love to each other, what you should do, and what you want to do, and who's going to be on top, and who's going to be on the bottom. You have a chance to talk it over if you're verbal at all, and that's fun because it's like opening up your secret recesses of desire to each other.

Q: You seem to suggest that there's something not only human but liberating about sex.

Ginsberg: I think it is. I always remember Kerouac saying, "Woe to those who deny the unbelievable joy of sexual love." The joy, the exquisite joy. I've found sexual communication to be one of the most thrilling and exquisite experiences in my life. With people I love, all shame is gone, everybody is naked, as Hart Crane said, "confessions between coverlet and pillow." And I think the best teaching is done in bed also, by the way, as did Socrates. It is an old tradition: transmission in bed, transmission of information, of virtue. I think Whitman thought so, Whitman pointed out that "adhesiveness" between the citizens was the necessary glue that kept democracy from degenerating into rivalry, competition, backbiting, dog-eat-dog. I think that's true. One of the problems of the Reagan-Bush era was the lack of cohesiveness, the competition, the rivalry, the Darwinian dog-eat-dog, which fed egocentricity, exploitation, and cruelty and indifference and left three million people out on the streets homeless.

Q: Are you hopeful about the lesbian and gay rights movement in the United States?

Ginsberg: Oh, sure. Everybody's gay in one way or another. "Everybody's got a big dong." Everybody's sexualized, and everybody's sex is somewhat repressed, and no one can really do any fingerpointing anymore. Everybody's a freak, so to speak, and I think people understand that. Certainly the younger generation does. I mean how long can you keep it secret that Cardinal Spellman was a flaming queen? How long can you keep it secret that J. Edgar Hoover was a transvestite blackmailed by the Mafia? How long can you keep it secret that Jesse Helms is overobsessed with homosexuality and is politically addicted to alcohol and tobacco interests? Even the press is sooner or later going to catch up with the hype.

What is the hype? The hype is hypocrisy, double standard, people coming on in public less intelligent than they are in private—say on something like marijuana. Everybody knows that marijuana is more or less harmless, but they won't say it in public. Everybody except maybe some crazed fundamentalists has smoked some grass or knows someone who's smoked some grass.

There's a schizophrenia between private knowledge and public knowledge. On sex, there's a schizophrenia between what people do in private and the way they talk in public. There's a schizophrenia about stimulants. A schizophrenia about politics: The contradictions are so big that it's a kind of public schizophrenia that people aren't in on what, say, the CIA in-group knows. The public never knows what the consequences of the hidden deals are. No one knows the ecological consequences or the political cause or consequences of an H-bomb, a Lumumba assassination, a Panama invasion—and the Government is supposed to be a democracy. That's schizophrenia.

Schizophrenia is no way to run a government or a society. You can't have a schizophrenic society without the results we're seeing: pollution of the air, pollution caused by conspicuous consumption, the very schizophrenia of thinking that we can continue to consume the vast amounts of raw material that we do disproportionate to our population, and saying everyone should aspire to be like us. If everybody were like us, the Earth would burn out overnight.

Q: What's your assessment of President Clinton so far?

Ginsberg: Bush was pretty much a sourpuss, a depressed and depressing person. I think Clinton is much more cheerful; I think that's always a help. I don't know that he can climb out of a pit that Reagan and Bush have dug in terms of national debt and exhaustion of national resources. But I like his attitude and I like his attempt to do something—I like his trying to do something about health, trying to do something about gays in the military. So I think he's a better person in terms of being more honest and inquisitive. At least he had the amusement to put a stick of grass between his lips. He's dealt with some real problems—like health, smoking, and ecology—which were being avoided or even subverted by Reagan and Bush.

Q: In the book, you have a couple of criticisms of 1960s activists, New Leftists—"peace protesters angrier than war's cannonball noises," and you talk about "the scandal of the '60s"—people carrying pictures of Mao and Che and Castro.

Ginsberg: It seems to me that the extreme one-dimensional politics of the New Left—which had no spiritual or adhesive element or direction but relied on "rising up angry" rage, which was considered by some to be the necessary gasoline or fuel for political action—was a great psychological mistake. Any gesture made in anger is going to create more anger. Any gesture coming from rage and resentment creates more rage and resentment. Any gesture taken in equanimity will create more equanimity. The 1968

Chicago police riot was, after all, to some extent provoked by the attitude, behavior, and propaganda of some of the members of the New Left, who had promised a Festival of Light but delivered an angry protest. The original Yippie idea, as announced, was to have a festival that would be cheerful, affirmative, ecologically sound, and generous emotionally so that it would outshadow the "Death Convention" of Johnson's war.

Before the Chicago thing, Jerry Rubin came over to my house, and I wanted reassurance that he didn't have any intention of starting a riot. I didn't want any blood. He swore, "not at this time." I should have suspected it then and there, but actually I do think unconsciously or consciously some wanted to precipitate an "exemplary" riot.

The result of the riot was to knock out Humphrey. And then many Leftists out of their hatred of Humphrey and their parents and their liberal middle-class background refused to vote and dropped out and so Nixon squeaked in by half a million votes. Millions of people didn't vote on the Left, angry at Johnson and his war, angry at Humphrey for going along (although every-body knew that Humphrey wanted to end the war, but it was just this totali-tarian insistence on having it your way, the way you wanted to end the war, the method you wanted to end the war, rather than let the war decline in a way that was politically possible). In 1968, the Gallup Poll reported that 52 per cent of the American people thought the war was a mistake. The question is, how come the Left could not lead America out of the war when the middle class was already disillusioned? I think it was because they were threatening the middle class with anger, because one motto was Kill Your Parents or Bring the War Home. They weren't leading the middle class, they weren't providing space for the middle class to change, they were threatening the middle class.

The Left, by not voting, let Nixon in. The Left, by discrediting the Demo-crats, let Nixon in. And once Nixon got in, the war got much worse—the bombing was escalated beyond the imagination of Johnson and Kennedy, the bankruptcy of the Treasury and the moral bankruptcy was escalated way beyond anyone's imagination.

It doesn't mean that the Left was wrong. The antiwar stance was correct. It's just that the method, which involved aggression and anger, was an un-skillful means. The blood of the Vietnamese from 1968 on rests primarily on the right-wing conservatives and the Nixonites, but there is some blood on the Left for their ineptness in politics. That's what I meant by speeches "an-grier than war's cannonball noises." It was the mistake of waving a Viet Cong flag—and half the people who did it were FBI agents anyway. In New York City, I remember parades being taken over by extremists, who later turned out to be FBI provocateurs. People don't realize the enormity of the infiltration of the Left by the FBI in the form of extremist provocation, which the neurotics of the Left went along with thinking it was more macho, holier than thou, "more revolutionary than thou."

Q: To what extent does your Buddhism contribute to this attitude of yours about the need for equanimity?

Ginsberg: The original Beat idea was a spiritual change, an attitudinal change, a change of consciousness. Then, once having achieved some reform of one's own, begin with yourself and work outward. Not quite Buddhist, but Eastern thought and "Beatnik" thought is pacifistic.

Q: Do you consider yourself a pacifist?

Ginsberg: Well, I haven't found a war I liked yet.

Q: You write in one of your new poems about being offended as a Jew at violent Zionists. What was your reaction to the Hebron massacre?

Ginsberg: The extremism among the Jews refusing land for peace and insisting upon that piece of dirt being theirs—you know, fighting over a piece of ground— seems to me to be some kind of awful chauvinism, creating a karma that may never end, like the Irish-English fight. Who knows where it will end now? They've started a circle of violence that may never finish until Armageddon.

Q: You say in one of the new poems that "all the spiritual groups scandal the shrine room."

Ginsberg: That's true, especially the monotheist religions. By their very nature, the Jews, the Christians, and the Islamic people claim that they're talking for God. As a Buddhist I don't even believe in God, much less talk-ing for Him if there were one. But all these guys have the chutzpah or the brass or the egocentric anthropomorphic totalitarian idea that they are the mouthpiece of God. The Ayatollah could tell Salman Rushdie to get killed, or the reactionary Israelis can say the Arabs are inferior, the Christians can create a holocaust. That's why I wrote "Stand up against governments, against God"—the monotheist domination of consciousness that insists on its own party line.

Q: What is your assessment of the state of poetry, or political poetry, right now?

Ginsberg: I myself don't believe in so-called political poetry. I think what a poet does is he "writes his mind." And like everybody else, his mind is concerned with sex, dope, and everyday living, politics included, whatever his experience is, so the personal experience of the poet will differ from the media representation of reality. As far as I'm concerned, my interest in poetry is in representing my actual mind as distinct from the official party line of the media, which is to say, the *New York Times,* the *Washington Post*, even *The Nation,* and from the official party line of the White House and the Establishment. So, private experience is different from the way it's recorded in the newspapers and on television. We have our own real worlds, and then there's the pseudo-event of newspapers. As Pound says, "Poetry is news that stays news," which is our actual emotions, our feelings, thoughts—Kerouac said "the unspeakable visions of the individual."

The subject matter is the nature of my consciousness, and the texture of my consciousness, and what passes through my mind spontaneously, not what immediate effect can I have on PR or public politics or day-to-day polemics.

Q: Yet more than almost any poet in the mid-century and the late century, you've written in your poems about America.

Ginsberg: It's not that I'm specializing in America. I've also written a lot about my sex life, I've also written about my family, and I've also written about food, and I've also written about meditation, and Buddhism—because those are the participating elements of my life, so I write about what I'm involved with. Which is not much different from anybody else. Maybe the Buddhism is a little more specialized and maybe the homosexual content is a little more specialized but everyone has their own sex lives.

Q: There is a strain of contemporary poetry that is shorn of politics, that is hyper-private.

Ginsberg: Who? Who? Mine is hyper-private, is what I'm saying. I'm just writing about what I think about privately. I'm amazed that more people don't write about what they actually think about privately, day after day.

Q: I'm not trying to pigeonhole you into this little box called political poetry, which you don't want to be shoved into.

Ginsberg: No, I don't mind that, but there's a distinction I'd like to make. I grew up in the '30s and '40s during the controversy between the socialists and the communists and the Trotskyites about political poetry. Now the theory that they laid down, both Stalin and the Maoists, and Hitler for that matter, is that poetry should serve the nation. And Jesse Helms and Pat Robertson also believe this; it's all the same, the dictatorial monotheists from Pat Robertson to Stalin. They all believe that poetry should be moral, defined in their own terms whether serving Christ, or the People, or the Central Committee of the Communist Party—that poetry is the vanguard of the revolution and since the will of the revolution and of the people is represented by the Central Committee of the Communist Party, therefore the poet should take his politics from what the Central Committee says is the proper party line, or what Pat Robertson says the Bible says.

You've got to remember the inheritors of that political Left tradition, the Students for a Democratic Society up to the Weathermen, the New Left, also first disapproved of psychedelics, also disapproved of rock-'n'-roll poetry, also disapproved of individual cocksucking poetry—you know, and thought that "no, this was not advancing the cause."

The primitive notion of a one-dimensional political poetry, up through Abbie Hoffman, even, maintained dominance over the notion of political poetry, especially reinforced by the poetry of the anti-Vietnam war. So I think it's important to make a distinction between poetry which is (and should be, as far as I'm concerned) Ivory Tower, the politics of which come as a secondary reflection or concomitant potential but not as the central purpose, and the distinction between that and deliberate, intentional . . .

Q: Polemical poetry?

Ginsberg: Yeah, but what you're nice enough to call polemical was the basic idea of political poetry all along. "Why aren't you taking responsibility for writing about blah, blah, gays, the blacks, or women?" Still, political correctness, party line. "Is your poem politically correct, Mister Mayakovsky?" That's where that notion, that phrase, political correctness comes from originally, from old Stalinists and Maoists. That still has a minor voice in poetics now, both from the Right and the Left.

If you want to go to the root of things and move people's consciousness, you can't do it in that vulgar or blunderbuss way of the Stalinists of the Left and the Right.

I'm more in the lineage of Poe. Why is Poe interesting? He gives you this sense of paranoia, modern Twentieth Century world paranoia, world nausea, "The Pit and the Pendulum," "The Telltale Heart," "The Descent Into the Maelstrom." He's the first, you could say, psychedelic poet.

Now who was Poe? He was the most Ivory Tower, art for art's sake, beauty for the sake of beauty, isolated, unpolitical poet in the world, yet he penetrates everybody's consciousness all over the world and is the first maybe adult poet prose writer people read from Russia to China to England to America. He has more influence on people's consciousness, and individuating them, and making them conscious of their individuality and their isolation than any other writer, and yet he's the least political.

Dig? I'm addressing myself directly to your question. It turns out that the one who went for the jugular of pure aesthetic beauty is the most politically influential in certain ways in terms of individuating people, empowering people, and making them conscious of themselves as individuals as distinct from members of a mass under hypnotic mass control—whether television or Hitler or American co-optation.

So there is no real distinction between political and unpolitical poetry, and I would advise a poet to avoid politics and get to what is his or her most deeply felt perception or impulse—that's way more politically effective than writing sonnets about the Republicans.

Q: In a way, you seem to claim yourself as Whitman's heir.

Ginsberg: I don't claim myself as Whitman's heir. I'm inspired by Whitman, but I wouldn't be so presumptuous. I don't think I'm as good as Whitman at all. He's much more ample. In my last book the Whitman influence is not the famous Whitman of "Song of Myself," but his Old Age Echoes, the little gay poems, and the poems talking about "my aches and pains" and all that. Whitman wrote geriatric poems that were quite interesting. There's a poem from *Sands at Seventy:* "As I sit writing here sick and grown old,/ Not my least burden is that, dullness of the years, querilities,/ Ungracious glooms, aches, lethargy, constipation, whimpering ennui/ May filter in my daily songs." Whitman is a very good model for the glooms and the delights of growing old and being energetic, aware, and vigorous and going on toward death, looking back and looking forward.

"Garrulous to the very last," do you know that phrase? "After the supper and talk—after the day is done,/ As a friend from friends his final withdrawal prolonging./ Goodbye and goodbye with emotional lips repeating./ (So hard for his hand to release those hands—no more will they meet,/ No more for communion of sorrow and joy, of old and young,/ A far-stretching journey awaits him, to return no more,)/ Shunning, postponing severance—seeking to ward off the last word ever so little,/ E'en at the exit door turning—charges superfluous calling back—e'en as he descends the steps,/ Something to eke out a minute additional, shadows of nightfall deepening,/ Farewells, messages lessening—dimmer the forthgoer's visage and form,/ Soon to be lost for aye in the darkness—loth, O so loth to depart!/ Garrulous to the very last." It's the last poem of *Sands at Seventy.* Isn't it charming?

Q: In some passages in the latest book, you write that you're bored with fame. Do you ever get tired of being Allen Ginsberg?

Ginsberg: No, there's no Allen Ginsberg. It's just a collection of empty atoms.

Q: But in several of your latest poems, you seem to be wrestling with immortality.

Ginsberg: No, I'm not wrestling. I'm saying, "Immortality comes later," by definition. It's a joke.

Q: Well, in one poem, you say, "I missed my chance."

Ginsberg: For salvation. Artistically I've got it made, but in terms of spiritual salvation, who knows? I certainly haven't taken advantage of all the good teachings I've been given, I must say. Otherwise, I wouldn't see anybody these days, and be on a three-year meditation retreat.

Q: I can understand the need to feel that your life's work was worthwhile, but to feel the need that people will be reading you when you're gone I don't understand. You're not going to be around to enjoy it, anyhow. What's the big deal about immortality?

Ginsberg: There's no total immortality. "The sun's not eternal, that's why there's the blues," as I wrote in a previous book. Even the sun goes out. There's "immortal as immortal is," which is temporary. However, it is important if you have the impulse of transmitting dharma or whatever wisdom you've got, writing "so that in black ink my love might still shine bright"—Shakespeare.

There is a Buddhist reason for fame and for immortality, which is that it gives you the opportunity to turn the wheel of dharma while you're alive to a larger mass of sentient beings and after you're dead that your poetry radio continues broadcasting dharmic understanding so that people pick up on it and the benefits of it after you're dead.

In a previous book, I wrote: "While I'm here I'll do the work. And what's the work? To ease the pain of living." You can ease the pain of living for people after you're dead through your artwork by creating a thing of beauty, like Poe, by creating a thing of political understanding, by creating a thing of psychological self-recognition like Walt Whitman, by making the ground safe for gays like Gore Vidal, Burroughs, and Jean Genet, by making the ground safe for straight people like Henry Miller and D.H. Lawrence.

Those works continue raying out wisdom even after the author's gone, and to the extent that your ambition is to relieve the mass of human sufferings, that can be accomplished with art, whether or not the planet survives. Even if it is in extremis, at the edge of death, as an individual or as a planet, there still is the consolation of insight and wisdom that you might get from a work of art that will ease the pain of passing from this life to whatever emptiness comes, and alchemize that sorrow into blissful recognition.

Rothschild, Matthew, "Allen Ginsberg," *The Progressive,* August 1994, http://www.progressive.org/ginsroth9408.htm. Reprinted by permission, *The Progressive,* 409 East Main Street, Madison, WI 53703. Copyright 1994.

Appendix 1B
Time Line: *Out and About*, Queer Radio

1948   Kinsey Report findings are released. First major survey of homosexual behavior informs Americans of the number of men who engage in same-sex sexual relations.

1950   Mattachine Society forms in Los Angeles (more than 100 discussion groups in Southern California by 1953).

1967   Following violent New Year's Eve police raids in Los Angeles bars, several hundred gay men and lesbians rally on Sunset Boulevard to protest arrests.

9/5/67   First gay character appears in a network TV series on *NYPD*.

1968   Metropolitan Community Church founded by lesbian and gay Christians in Los Angeles

6/27/69   Police prepare for a routine raid of the Stonewall Inn, which turns into a riot in the wee hours of the next morning. Riots over a three-day period in response to police harassment at the Stonewall Inn in New York City signal the transition from the more moderate homophile movement to Gay Liberation and more progressive activism.

1970   The '70s saw an explosion of books on lesbian theory, history, politics, and fiction. This came as a result of the rise of feminism and included Rita Mae Brown's *Rubyfruit Jungle,* Jill Johnston's *Lesbian Nation,* and *Sappho Was a Right-On Woman* by Abbott & Love.

6/28/70   First gay march in New York City.

1971   Connecticut, Colorado, and Oregon repeal sodomy law statutes.

1971   NOW acknowledges "the oppression of lesbians as a legitimate concern of feminism."

1971   Maxine Feldman releases the first lesbian-themed record—a 45 called "Angry Atthis" (Atthis was the name of one of Sappho's lovers).

1972   First lesbian drop-ins organized at The Woman's Place in Toronto.

1972   Lesbian journals *Spectre* and *Furies* declare that lesbians have to organize separately from both straight women and gay men, heralding lesbian-feminist separatism.

1973   The National Gay Task Force was formed.

1973   Metropolitan Community Church (MCC) gives first mission status in Canada. Begins holding services at Holy Trinity Church in Toronto under Reverend Bob Wolfe.

1974   *Lavender Jane Loves Women,* the first all-lesbian album is recorded by Alix Dobkin, Kay Gardner, and others.

1974   Representative Bella Abzug introduces H.R. 14752, proposing that the categories of "sex, sexual orientation and marital status" be added to the 1974 civil rights act; it was the first time gay civil rights legislation was proposed at the U.S. federal level.

1975   *Time* puts U.S. Air Force Sgt. Leonard Matlovich on its cover with the headline "I Am a Homosexual."

1976   The first Michigan Womyn's Music Festival.

1977   Billie Jean King, a tennis player, is sued for "palimony" by a woman.

6/7/77   Referendum, forced by pressure from fundamentalist Christians Anita Bryant, her husband, and their "Save Our Children" organization, repeals county ordinance prohibiting discrimination on basis of sexual orientation. First major battle, and defeat, in struggle for gay and civil rights in United States.

9/13/77   *Soap* debuts on ABC-TV with Billy Crystal in an ongoing gay role.

11/8/77   Harvey Milk elected to San Francisco Board of Supervisors.

12/16/77   First gay civil rights law in North America is passed in Quebec.

1978   California voters defeat the Briggs Initiative (58 percent to 42 percent), which would have expelled lesbians and gay men and those who support equal rights for them from school systems.

1978   Hour-long *Gay News and Views* begins on local station in Canada. First regularly scheduled gay radio program in Canada.

1978   Gilbert Baker of San Francisco designs and makes a flag with six stripes representing the six colors of the rainbow as a symbol of gay and lesbian community pride.

7/29/78   The Village People's first hit single "Macho Man" debuts in *Billboard*'s Top 40 Hits chart.

11/27/78   Ex-Supervisor Dan White assassinates Harvey Milk and San Francisco Mayor George Moscone at City Hall in San Francisco.

1979   "We Are Family" by Sister Sledge becomes a lesbian (and gay) anthem.

3/31/79   The Village People's final hit single "In the Navy" begins a thirteen-week run on *Billboard*'s Top 40.

5/21/79   The "White Night Riots" occur outside San Francisco City Hall, as gay community reacts with anger after Dan White, murderer of gay City Hall supervisor Harvey Milk, is given lenient sentence after the "Twinkie defense" in jury trial. Dan White found innocent of murder in assassination of Milk. Protest turns into riot.

10/14/79   More than 200,000 attend first national march in Washington.

5/30/80   Teenager Aaron Fricke takes a male date to his senior prom in Rhode Island.

1981   First reference to AIDS (under the name Gay-Related Immune Disease, or GRID) in medical journals and mainstream media.

7/27/82   The Center for Disease Control replaces "GRID" with "AIDS."

8/28/82   The first Gay Games are held in San Francisco, in the midst of a lawsuit by the United States Olympic Committee to ban the games from using the name "Gay Olympics."

11/26/82   First openly gay or lesbian musical act to play Carnegie Hall: Cris Williamson and Meg Christian.

6/5/83   Harvey Fierstein wins two Tony awards for his *Torch Song Trilogy* in a nationally telecast ceremony.

2/28/84   Boy George accepts Culture Club's Grammy for Best New Artist by telling Americans "You know a good drag queen when you see one."

1985   Gay & Lesbian Alliance Against Defamation (GLAAD) founded.

1985   Rock Hudson's death is turning point in the media awareness of AIDS; President Reagan publicly mentions the epidemic for the first time.

1985   Martina Navratilova releases her autobiography. She comes out.

4/1/85   First classes held at New York's city-founded Harvey Milk School for gay, lesbian, and bisexual youth.

11/9/85   Debut of first openly gay performer on network TV: Terry Sweeney on *Saturday Night Live.*

1987   The Bear Movement marks its beginnings in S.F. with the publication of a photocopied magazine called *Bear.* Essentially a way for hirsute, mature gay men to meet each other in S.F. *Bear* soon grows from its initial forty-copy run to the largest publication in North America for this subculture.

10/11/87   More than half million attend second national march on Washington.

11/15/87   Randy Shilts' *And the Band Played On* debuts at #12 on the *New York Times* best-seller list.

1988   The National Education Association adopts a resolution calling for every school district to provide counseling for students struggling with their sexual orientation.

10/11/88   National Coming Out Day is founded.

12/1/88   First World AIDS Day.

5/28/89   The Leather Pride Flag is first displayed at the Mr. Leatherman contest in Chicago. Featuring black, blue, and white stripes with a red heart, it is a symbol for the leather community, which encompasses those who are into leather, Levis, SM play, bondage and domination, and other fetishes.

10/1/89   First state-sanctioned gay marriages are performed in Denmark.

11/7/89   First network portrayal of two gay men in bed together on *Thirtysomething*.

1990   The U.S. Congress passes and President Bush signs the Hate Crimes Statistics Act, the first federal law to include the term "sexual orientation."

1990   Backlash against art with gay or lesbian content seen in an obscenity prosecution against a museum showing Robert Mapplethorpe's photographs and the rescinding of National Endowment for the Arts grants for four performance artists whose work is sexually explicit, three of whom are openly gay or lesbian.

2/7/91   The controversial lesbian kiss airs on *LA Law*.

1992   The Lesbian Avengers is founded in New York, and a year later, they lead 200,000 lesbians on the first Dyke March.

1992   Colorado passes Amendment Two, prohibiting civil rights protection for lesbians and gay men; a similar ballot measure in Oregon is narrowly defeated. One year later, a state district court overturns the Colorado measure, ruling that it violates constitutional guarantees of fundamental rights. The Supreme Court upholds this decision in 1996.

1992   k. d. lang comes out.

6/18/92   Billy Douglas becomes the first openly gay teen character on network soap opera on *One Life to Live*.

1993   President Clinton promises to lift ban prohibiting lesbians and gays from serving in military. After much controversy, Congress adopts legislation that leaves virtually all discriminatory restrictions in place. Clinton signs it into law.

1993   Melissa Etheridge comes out.

1993   Radical religious right groups push through antigay measures in Cincinnati; Lewiston, Maine; and Portsmouth, New Hampshire.

3/15/93   *Out and About* radio hits the airwaves on CKWR as a forty-five-minute once a week show. At first, it is a show for gays and lesbians, but after six months, it becomes a news magazine for gay men only. After the death of Dave Grant, the show's originator, the show becomes a regional show for the entire LGBT community once again.

4/25/93   One million attend third national march on Washington.

1994   The first ever prom for gay youth sanctioned by a school district is held in Los Angeles.

1994   Gay Games IV convene in New York.

1994   The twenty-fifth anniversary of the Stonewall uprising is commemorated with a march on the United Nations in New York City.

1998   Ellen DeGeneres comes out.

10/12/98   Matthew Shepard, an openly gay twenty-one-year-old University of Wyoming student, is murdered.

2/19/99*   Billy Jack Gaither, a thirty-nine-year-old gay Alabama man, was brutally beaten to death. Steven Mullins and Charles Monroe Butler were sentenced to life in prison without parole in August 1999.

7/6/99*   Private First Class Barry L. Winchell, a twenty-one-year-old native of Missouri, died in a hospital on July 6, 1999, after being forced outside his barracks at Fort Campbell Army base in Kentucky only six hours earlier. He was brutally beaten with a baseball bat. Three days later, Fort Campbell, Kentucky, officials charged Private Calvin N. Glover, 18, with premeditated murder in connection with Winchell's death.

7/22/99*   U.S. Senate approved the Hate Crimes Prevention Act (HCPA). The purpose of the legislation was to add crimes motivated by sexual orientation, gender, or disability to the 1968 federal hate-crime protections covering race, color, religion, and national origin. It would allow federal prosecutors to pursue a hate-crime case if local authorities refuse to press charges, and to provide assistance to local law enforcement agencies in investigating hate crimes.

5/13/00*   During Eleventh Annual Media awards, the Gay & Lesbian Alliance Against Defamation (GLAAD) presented awards to Billie Jean King ("Capitol Award") and Dennis & Judy Shepard ("Vision Award"), parents of Matthew Shepard, for their contributions to the ongoing battle to ensure fair, accurate, and inclusive representations of the lesbian, gay, bisexual, and transgender community in the media.

5/23/00*   GLAAD denounced the release of rapper Eminem's *The Marshall Mathers LP,* which contained the words "fag" or "faggot" numerous times in many of his songs, and described acts of violence against gay men.

8/3/00*   *GAYBC Radio Network* was ranked by Arbitron as number two Internet-only talk radio webcaster, ranked number nine of all Internet-only radio channels and number thirty of all channels and all formats, including traditional broadcasts on the Web and Internet- only channels.

11/1/00*   GAYBC Internet radio made a "Save Our Station" plea. The network suffered a significant (but temporary) setback in its funding and was forced to cease normal operations on October 27, 2000. The network hosted a series of special "Save Our Station" Webcasts during the weekend of November 3–5.

12/3/00*   *Queer as Folk,* based on the British hit series, debuted Sunday, December 3, 2000 on Showtime.

Source: Reprinted with permission from http://www.outandabout.on.ca/timeline.html
*Timeline was updated by the authors of *Queer Airwaves.*

Appendix 2A
The Gay Show's Memorial to Larry Gutenberg

There were teary eyes in the studio, Sunday, June 18, 1995, when Larry's regular program, *The Gay Show,* devoted an hour to his memory. As his illness advanced, Larry continued to do the show, coming in first with a cane, then in a wheelchair, and finally, unable to come in at all, instead calling in by phone. Bob Storm hosted, and was joined by Marle Becker, Eddie Goldman, Nelson Jewel, R. Paul Martin, George Reilly, Bill Miranda Salzman, Randy Wicker, and Rick X. Some of their remarks were:

"Larry epitomized what it meant to be living with AIDS. He wasn't dying with AIDS, he was living with AIDS."

"We remember Larry. Stay proud."

"He was a rock foundation here for gay radio at WBAI."

"I will always love him."

"Let's fight for what he stood for."

"You were teaching me, Larry, and I learned from a master."

Rick X: [When Larry called in a theater report to the show] he was being infused at the time, he was gasping for breath, and he was damned if he was going to be pulled down by this disease, and he did what he wanted to do for this show anyway.

Randy Wicker: We all give up so much to volunteer here. Larry did so much work. I started here in 1962 [at WBAI], with the first show featuring homosexuals speaking for themselves. Since then, Larry and others like him have kept gay programming on the air. Larry was extremely fair, and included everyone, and treated everyone fairly, and was so widely loved in our community.

Nelson Jewel: He was the most unprejudiced person I've ever known. He was a great humanitarian and a wonderful friend.

R. Paul Martin: Above all, Larry always remembered that we are in radio to serve, and he took great pains to insure that information important to the lesbian, gay, and bisexual community got out, and that our listeners knew that they were part of a community, even if they were temporarily isolated from it by circumstances of age or situation. In his later years Larry was also a member of the People With AIDS Coalition and did many fine, responsible programs about the tragic disease which finally took his life. Many listeners learned a lot about AIDS, and living with AIDS, from Larry and I'm certain that he brought both comfort and vital information to many listeners during his private and public battle with both the disease and the social obstacles which have grown up around it.

Source: Reprinted with permission from http://www.wbaifree.org/folio/guten.html

Appendix 2B
Bob Storm Obituary

STORM—Bob, 53, died of AIDS November 24, 1997, in New York City. Since the late '80s, Bob was heard regularly on Sunday nights as a host of WBAI-FM's gay-themed programs, first on *The Gay Show* and later on its successor, *Out-FM*. Storm's activism took root in early 1962, after he left Ohio to join the U.S. Army's intelligence unit. When his friendship with a gay German man was discovered, the military discharged Storm as a "suspected homosexual." He then moved to New York City, where he became active in the civil rights and gay liberation struggles. He soon became known as "Flash Storm," and with his lover, Ralph Hall, who died of AIDS in 1988, published *The Gay Post* and *Ain't It da Truth*, post-Stonewall gay magazines that featured Allen Ginsberg and Harvey Fierstein as contributing writers. In recent years, Storm counseled people on parole and at-risk youth with Offender Aid and Restoration.

Source: http://www.thebody.com/poz/gazette/4_98/obits.html
From POZ, April 1998. Reprinted with permission. Copyright 1998. POZ Publishing, L.L.C.

Appendix 3A
And the GLAMA Goes To . . .

Chris Wilson, Pam Marshall, and Christopher David Trentham produced the following *This Way Out* segment on the first GLAMA:

Pam Marshall: Webster Hall, a trendy art deco concert hall in New York City, was the venue for the first annual Gay and Lesbian American Music Awards.

Chris Wilson: Conceived by musicians Tom McCormack and Michael Mitchell, GLAMA celebrates and recognizes the musical contributions of artists who are not afraid to be identified as gay, lesbian, bisexual, and transgendered.

Pam: The event began with nominee Catie Curtis singing "Radical," a song which garnered a GLAMA in two categories: Out Song and Out Recording.

[Brief excerpt from "Radical," fades down and out under:]

Chris: Catie, congratulations on your award for "Radical." Tell me, what made you decide as a performer to break the barriers and try to make it as an "out" performer right from the get-go?

Catie Curtis: Well, first of all, I had this song about an alternative relationship and I figured people might guess that I was gay anyway . . . and then, you know, I'm out in my personal life . . . and there is the Internet you know, so I figured that people, if they wanted to find out, they could through all this sort of gossipy, personal stuff that goes on the Internet and . . . I wanted to be finally because it's who I am and it's just a small part of who I am, and I feel like when you hide it, it becomes a sort of overblown part of who you are instead of just, you know, as important as the fact that I'm from Maine and I play the guitar and you know, other things that are significant but not like the big thing about me.

[Brief excerpt from Melissa Etheridge's "Your Little Secret," fades down and out under:]

Chris: The GLAMA for best female artist went to Melissa Etheridge for "Your Little Secret." Etheridge could not be present but sent a videotape acceptance speech thanking supporters as well as the producers of GLAMA.

Melissa Etheridge: Thank you all very much. You're doing wonderful work. Keep it up, and thank you very much for the honor.

[Brief excerpt from "They Are Falling All Around Me," fades down and out under:]

Pam: The late Michael Callen swept the awards with wins in four categories for his album *Legacy*. Callen was recognized for Album of the Year and Best Male Artist, as well as Best Choral Group and Best Duo Group for his song "They Are Falling All Around Me," which was recorded with Cris Williamson, Holly Near, Arnold McCuller, and John Bucchino.

Chris: Callen's CD, *Legacy,* was produced by his partner in life as well as in music, Richard Dworkin, who was on hand to accept the multiple awards.

Richard Dworkin: I'm really glad that Michael's work was recognized, and of course, I'm sorry that he's not here to enjoy this . . . but he had a great time doing it and he got to work with some of his musical heroes, people he'd always admired, and it was a great thing for him, and I'm really glad that other people appreciate it as well.

[Brief excerpt from David Clement's "Eat It," fades down and out under:]

Pam: David Clement picked up the Best Debut Artist GLAMA for his album *Be More Like Me,* an independently produced compilation of songs such as "Angry Young Fag" which are meant to be provocative as well as entertaining.

Chris: The "Outmusic" award is a special award given to a recording artist, group, or songwriter who has advanced gay and lesbian music through their work as an out musician. The recipient is described as a musician with a steadfast commitment to speak openly and specifically to the lesbian/gay experience through music. This year, the honor was given to Ferron, who, for almost twenty years, has been uncompromising in her personal honesty.

[Brief excerpt from Ferron's "Alice Says Yes," fades down and out under:]

Chris: Congratulations, Ferron, on winning the Outmusic award.

Ferron: Thank you very much.

Chris: Could you have envisioned something like this when you started your musical career?

Ferron: Well, you know . . . yes! I mean, that was my vision—that all of this would be happening, and that we would be able to have children and have families and be doin' our work and be out. That's what I started for myself when I was eighteen years old. I'm just happy that it's happening and I like that we can give each other awards and acknowledgement for the work that we've done, with pride and honor.

Chris: What do you see as the future for gay and lesbian musicians? Do you think an event such as this will enhance the ability of people to be out in the music world?

Ferron: You know, in or out, you're gonna do that on your own. It's your own emotional track, it's everything that you have to work out. People have family stories and things that they're protecting. . . . I think the question is: What can out musicians do to help other people have the courage and the protection to be out in their lives?

Chris: The Michael Callen Medal of Achievement is given to an individual, group, organization, or business committed to the courageous and important work of engendering, nurturing, and furthering gay and lesbian music. This year, the Callen Medal was awarded to Tom Robinson, who has shared the stage during his musical career with such notables as Elton John and George Michael, and who has recorded on a variety of major as well as independent labels.

[Brief excerpt from the Tom Robinson Band's "Glad to Be Gay," fades out for:]

Chris: Congratulations on winning the Michael Callen Medal of Achievement. Can you tell our audience a little bit about what that means to you?

Tom Robinson: The fact that the award exists at all means an enormous amount to me. The GLAMA Awards would have been unthinkable even ten years ago . . . and certainly, when I started out twenty years ago, if you were gay you did not say that you were gay, and the out gay artists you could count on the fingers of one hand, rather than from a huge field from which you then select enough people to have an awards ceremony. It brings gay and lesbian activity and lifestyle and culture into the mainstream, so we get reports on MTV, we get reported in *Billboard.* Each year is going to grow in importance as more and more people come out in their writing and realize they don't have to hide, they don't have to live a lie, that people prefer you for who you are rather than the pretense of who you aren't.

Pam: The highlight of the evening was a show stopper which began with Men Out Loud, a Los Angeles-based a cappella quartet, who were later joined on stage by the Lavender Light Black & People of All Colors Lesbian and Gay Gospel Choir. The choir filled the stage with spiritual energy and had the crowd swaying and clapping to the rhythm of their gospel sound.

[Brief excerpt from on-scene musical performance, fades down and out under:]

Chris: Appropriately, the grand finale brought all of the nominees and performers on stage to accompany performer Keith Christopher and songwriter Marsha Malamet in singing Michael Callen's "Healing Power of Love."

[Brief excerpt from on-scene musical performance, fades down and out under:]

Pam: The audience seemed pleased with the debut ceremony. We spoke to executive producers Tom McCormack and Michael Mitchell as they look to the future of the Gay and Lesbian American Music Awards.

Tom McCormack: We're very pleased. Everybody seemed to have a good time and the show went off well, people liked the music and we got all the awards out, so we're happy.

Pam: Michael Mitchell . . .

Michael Mitchell: I'm speechless. On one hand, I feel completely spent, and on the other hand, I feel so alive. It really accomplished what we wanted to accomplish, which was that it really created, I think, a family tonight.

Pam: What are you hoping for next year? I think we can all safely say we will see a second annual GLAMA awards . . .

Michael: You will definitely see a second annual. . . . I think next year will be bigger and better.

Chris: The Gay and Lesbian American Music Awards are here to stay. Next year's event has already been announced for October 5, 1997. Reporting from New York, this is Chris Wilson . . .

Pam: . . . and Pam Marshall, for *This Way Out.*

[ends with an excerpt from "The Healing Power of Love" from Michael Callen's multiaward winning *Legacy*].

Source: Reprinted with permission. Chris Wilson, Pam Marshall, and Christopher David Trentham, "And the GLAMA goes to . . ." *This Way Out,* 447 (3), October 24, 1996 (transcript).

Appendix 3B
Amazon Radio Playlist/Archive,
November 7, 1995

SWEET HONEY IN THE ROCK / Every Woman / BELIEVE I'LL RUN ON . . . / Redwood Records

KAREN LESLIE HALL / Walkabout / ON THE DREAM WORLD Seadance Music

TRACY CHAPMAN / New Beginning / NEW BEGINNING / Elektra

PATTY LARKIN / Dear Diary / STRANGERS WORLD / High Street

LISA KOCH / The Curve Of No Return / YOU MAKE MY PANTS POUND / Tongueinchic Records

SALLY FINGERETT / TV Talk / Four Bitching Babes / FAX IT, CHARGE IT . . . / Shanachie

CAMILLE WEST / Your Family's Dysfunction / MOTHER TONGUE / Mother Tongue Music

DEBBIE DIEDRICH / Paternity Suit / GOING THE DISTANCE / West Broadway Music

k.d. lang / If I Were You / ALL YOU CAN EAT

KATIE HENRY / Bridges To Green / BEARS IN THE CITY / Katie Henry

MARY PAULSON / Lilah / JUST BECAUSE / Palmay Music

WORD OF MOUTH / Courage / SOMEWHERE IN THE WORLD / Trova Recordings

LAURA KEMP / Language of a Gun / VOLCANO / Rain Water Records

An interview with Caring Cuisine / AIDS Project, New Haven

251

CASSELBERRY-DUPREE / Foolish Attitudes / HOT CORN IN THE FIRE / Ladyslipper Records

GABRIELLE ROTH / Tongues / REST YOUR TEARS HERE / Raven

LIBBY RODERICK / If The World Were My Lover / IF THE WORLD WERE MY LOVER / Turtle Island Records

CROW JOHNSON / Fly Away Sweet Misery / PAINTING STORIES ACROSS THE SKY / Zassafras Records

ELIZA GILKYSON / Calling All Angels / PILGRIMS / Gold Castle Records

ASE DRUMMING CIRCLE / Shangoya / SOULS A' GATHERED / Tu Spearitz Records

SWEET HONEY IN THE ROCK / I Remember, I Believe / SACRED GROUND / Earth Beat

MAHOTELLA QUEENS / I Shall Be Released / WOMEN OF THE WORLD / Shanachie

ZAP MAMA / Take Me Coco / ADVENTURES IN AFROPEA I / Luka Bop

HORSE / Natural Law / GOD'S HOME MOVIE / MCA

WIMMIN ON THE EDGE / Keep On Getting On / HERSTORY FROM THE EDGE / On the Edge Productions

JUSTINA AND JOYCE / Sip of Water / RHYTHMS, RHYMES, AND TIDES / HSP Records

SANDY ROSS / If You Miss Me / This Train / PORTRAITS OF INNO-CENCE / SLR Productions

C2H / Blues in the Pink / A RADICAL BAND / Locust Lane Music

SAFFIRE The Uppity Blues Women / Tain't Nobody's Business / OLD NEW BORROWED & BLUE / Alligator Records

SARA HICKMAN / In the Fields / SHORTSTOP / Elektr

JESSE HULTBERG / My Friend Wants a Baby / JESSE HULTBERG / Wild Monk Records

JUDY FJELL / Reaching Out For Heaven / LIVIN' ON DREAMS / Honey
Pie Music

JULIA FORDHAM / River / FALLING FORWARD / Virgin

DIANE ZIEGLER / Sting of the Honeybee / STING OF THE HONEYBEE /
Philo

ALIX DOBKIN / Some Boys / LOVE AND POLITICS / Ladyslipper Music

CONNIE KALDOR / I Am a Believer / OUT OF THE BLUE / Coyote
Entertainment

DISAPPEAR FEAR / Sexual Telepathy / LIVE AT THE BOTTOM LINE /
Philo

LIBBY RODERICK / How Could Anyone / IF YOU SEE A DREAM /
Turtle Island Records

THE FLIRTATIONS / Your Children / THE FLIRTATIONS / Significant
Other Records

Source: Reprinted with permission. Amazon Radio, Bridgeport, CT: WPKN. (*http://
www.wpkn.org/wpkn/amazon/index.html*), 2000.

Appendix 3C
What's Normal?
An Exploration of Homosexuality and the Gay Subculture in Our Society

A thirteen-part radio series produced by KUT-FM and
the University of Texas at Austin.
Each program is twenty-five minutes long.

List of Programs and Guests

1. **Homosexuality in Cultural Context:** Dr. Mary Sanches, Asst. Prof. of Anthropology, UT Austin; Dr. Bonnie Freeman, Director, Cultural Foundations of Education Program, UT Austin. A cross-cultural discussion of sexual roles and attitudes, and a look at the new sexual freedom in relation to the feminist and gay movements.
2. **The Psychological Establishment and the Gay Client:** Dr. Wylie Jordan, psychiatrist; Ms. Miriam Kaye, psychoanalyst; Mr. Bill Shinder, alcoholism counselor. A detailing of some of the psychological problems the gay client may have and how they can be dealt with.
3. **Gay Rights and the Legal Status of Homosexuals:** Ms. Bobbie Nelson, attorney, Austin, Texas. A progress report on gay rights concerning laws in employment, housing, and marriage. Some special legal problems, such as lesbian child custody, and police harassment, are discussed.
4. **Parents and Gay Children:** Ms. Mary Milam, organizer of Parents of Gays; Ms. Betty Banner, transactional analyst. The pressures created when a gay person tries to gain acceptance from family, peers, and co-workers are covered as well as a description of the work done by Parents of Gays.
5. **The Homophile in Literature:** Ms. Jody Benson, author; Mr. Randy Conner, teacher and author. An examination of gay authors and gay characters and how they can create or explode gay myths.
6. **The Motivations and Means of Gay Activism:** Ms. A.K. Campbell, Austin Lesbian Organization; Mr. Ken Carpenter, Gay Community Services, Austin, Texas; Mr. Woody Egger, law student. A rap session with several members of Austin's gay community detailing some specific problems such as discrimination in real estate purchasing, housing rentals, and newspaper advertising, and how these gay activists chose to deal with them.

7. **The Lesbian Separatists:** Ms. Glenda Tokastein, Ms. Sheila Sisson, and Ms. Robin Birdfeather, all of Austin Lesbian Organization. Three lesbian women explain what separatism is and why they consider a society without men the only real alternative.

8. **Racism and the Gay Community:** Ms. Anna Escamilla, a member of the Chicana lesbian community and a well-known public speaker on the topics of racism and sexuality; Ms. Faye Roe, a black lesbian author and actor. The difficulties of maintaining a cultural-ethnic identity in the predominantly white, middle-class gay community.

9. **Gay Men's Movement:** Mr. Art Addington, member, national board of directors of the Gay Academic Union and coordinator for Texas Gay Task Force; Mr. Marc Sancers, former coordinator of Gay People of Austin. Some of the special societal pressures on gay men, and talk about ways changes can occur through a grass-roots political level.

10. **Grass-Roots Gay Counseling:** Mr. Dennis Milam, and Mr. Ron Loessin, counselors, Gay Community Services; Ms. Scotty Scott, counselor, Womenspace. A description of gay peer counseling services and programs provided by members of the gay community, and a few of the recurring problems of their clients.

11. **Bisexuality—A Door That Swings Both Ways:** Ms. Marti Kranzberg, counselor, Womenspace; Mr. Pete Williams, active in communications and music. Bisexuality as a broad avenue for increasing experience and toward self-awareness, with its inevitable stresses on identity, provides the topic for discussion.

12. **Gays and Role Playing:** Ms. Boby Mae Conners, Gay Women in Texas; Ms. Jackie Merrill, Board of Directors, South Central Region of Gay Academic Union; Mr. Randy Conner. An explanation of roles in terms of dress, sexual, and social behavior; and discussion of how they have been translated into the gay world.

13. **Gay Bar Scene:** Ms. Frieda Werden, Austin journalist; Mr. Alfred Rubio, doorman at a gay disco bar. An exploration of the social and sexual needs filled by the gay bar.

Reprinted with permission from Frieda Werden, radio producer, WINGS: Women's International News Gathering Service, P.O. Box 33220, Austin, TX 78764 USA, *http:/ www.wingsorg*, (512) 416–9000.

Appendix 4A
10%-Qtv: Season Five, Episode One, Summaries of Original Broadcasts

Monday, October 4, 1999; Saturday, October 9, 1999;
Sunday, October 10, 1999

1999 AIDS Walk Toronto

We kick off our fifth season with a few thousand people at the 10th annual AIDS Walk Toronto. We also chat with AIDS Committee of Toronto Chair Michael Battista, Toronto's "Mayor Mel," and former mayor Barbara Hall about what this day means to people living with AIDS.

Homo History

Since we're celebrating our fifth year, we decided to take a look back at other history-making events in queer history. This month we revisit 1969 and the decriminalization of homosexuality in Canada.

SciFi Expo

Space Cadet Enza takes us on a journey to the Canadian National SciFi Expo to explore new worlds, seek out new civilizations, and boldly go where no man in a dress has gone before. We visit the huge rolling pecs of Lou Ferrigno (The Incredible Hulk), the bright star Jeri Ryan (*Star Trek Voyager*'s "Seven of Nine"), and other lesser but no less colorful bodies.

"Dragging It Outta' You"

Back for a second season, we tour out to straightsville to ask the hets some skill-testing queer questions. This time we asked them to name three famous gay people (with extra points if they could go beyond Richard Simmons).

Wyoming One Year Later

October marks the one-year anniversary of Matthew Shepard's brutal beating and death in Wyoming. With all the media coverage and vigils a distant memory, we went out into the Village to ask if society's learned anything from his bashing. We also got an opportunity to meet with some nice folks at the United Gays and Lesbians of Wyoming to get their side of the story, and maybe dispel some myths about the "wild west."

"Village Voice"

In another new series this season, we camp out on "The Steps" on Saturday nights to hear what queer folks on Church Street have to say about . . . whatever. And that's what we got!

Source: Reprinted with permission from http://10percent.interlog.com/

Buchanan Wimps Out in Interview:
Candidate Bails on Gay Hosts at KFI

By Tomm Looney, September 24, 1999

Anybody who knew Pat Buchanan as a child, a teen, or an adult knows that the guy never used to back down from a fight. Pat even spent time in the poky as a youth for throwing down with a cop. Well, that all seems to be in the past.

It became obvious the other day that, in presidential candidate Pat Buchanan's old age, the estrogen seems to be kicking in big time. As I drove on the congested freeway Wednesday afternoon in Southern California, I was tuned to KFI/Los Angeles, L.A.'s top-rated talk station. All of a sudden, I heard the voice of former macho CNN *Crossfire* man-on-the-right Pat Buchanan on the *Karel & Andrew* show on KFI!

As those of you familiar with the local radio scene are aware, Karel and Andrew are an openly gay couple. For those of you familiar with right-wing politicians, Buchanan doesn't seem all that crazy about homosexuals.

Seems as though Buchanan made the mistake of his life getting into a sparring match with two gay guys! When the crossfire of jabs and hooks started snapping, it was pansy Buchanan who lisped a lame fairy tale about having to leave, grabbed his purse, and found an excuse to throw in the towel à la Roberta Duran. *No más, no más!*

As RadioDigest.com subsequently found out, Karel and Andrew, KFI's unambiguously gay spousal afternoon-drive talk team, were lucky to even get the very short interview with the presidential hopeful Buchanan. According to my KF-eyes, earlier in the week, when the Buchanan for President staff got word that an afternoon-drive radio talk show in Los Angeles was interested in having Pat on as a guest, the answer was, "Yes! Of course!"

During the course of the week, when Buchanan got wind that Charles Karel and Andrew Howard were life partners for over ten years, Buchanan wanted nothing to do with them and attempted to cancel the interview. KFI threatened that should Buchanan back out, the station would send out a press release letting the world know that Buchanan was a big fat homophobe who wasn't macho enough to handle an interview with two gay guys.

The Buchanan team relented, and Pat was dragged kicking and screaming to the interview by what would formerly be known as his political "man" handlers.

Most of the interview was perfectly calm and diplomatic. The two asked Buchanan about his controversial comments about World War II in his new book. Then, when the discussion got the tiniest bit testy—about Buchanan's open support for discrimination against gays in public accommodations such as hotels and other public places—an uncommonly flustered Buchanan nervously tongue thrusted, "I have to go, guys. I have to do *The Today Show!*"

Buchanan was booked on KFI until the top of the hour, but ended the interview at 5:45 P.M.—at least ten hours before any *Today Show* interview could conceivably take place.

"Wow, did he wimp out in that interview or what? Maybe instead of hollering 'Go Pat Go' at the next rally, they should start hollering, 'You Go Girl,'" said a disappointed former Buchanan supporter.

Isn't our next president supposed to stare down Saddam Hussein on one side and the Chinese menace on the other? Seems like this Pat Buchanan character was afraid to take on two gay radio clowns 3,000 miles away. "If a presidential candidate can't handle a couple of radio farts, the world is in grave danger," said a former well-known major-market talk-show host.

Reprinted with permission from RadioDigest.com (www.karelandandrew.com)

Appendix 5B
Opening the Vent: Thoughts on Frontiers, Al Rantel and Such

By Charles Karel Bouley II

No one expected us to do well except the powers-that-be at KFI. And, to everyone's surprise, we are doing well. The gay guys make good. Who knew?

Then on September 17, 1999, one of the largest gay and lesbian publications, *Frontiers,* landed on my desk. Great! I thought. Given all the rumor and conjecture about the sale of KFI, a story focusing on the positive inroads made by gays and lesbians at talk radio would be refreshing. After all, Andrew and I are the only openly gay male couple to have a radio show, one that is not gay in content, just in presentation. History made at KFI. I thought the story, the press, would be happy about this. Alas, again I was wrong.

A quote from me about Dr. Laura. That's riveting. Laura is Laura. I hear through the grapevine she thinks we're quite hysterical. An inroad made. But it doesn't matter. Another quote from me used to denounce KPFK's *IMRU* and *This Way Out,* two shows I not only support but admire for their tenacity and longevity. Misquoted? No, just not fully quoted. I simply said they do a good job, but don't do much to progress our movement because they are preaching to the masses.

Then comes Al Rantel, a closeted gay male on KABC. I say closeted because the few times I've heard him, he seems to downplay his sexuality. There he was again, saying things like "they won't last because the gimmicks and novelty of a gay couple won't baffle people for long. . . ." He's made other derogatory statements about us that I've just laughed off. But you have to wonder why. Shouldn't he be proud of us? We don't compete with him. I was proud of him before I saw his true colors. Now, I am ashamed of him. I have never spoken negatively of him in public. Even in the article, no negativity from me about him.

—excerpt

Source: Reprinted with permission from www.karelandandrew.com

Appendix 5C
Must There Be A Great Divide?

By Charles Karel Bouley II

KFI doesn't have to care about the gay community. Cold, hard fact. They are a very small part of their demographic. In fact, Orange County, the bastion of conservatism, is one of their main audiences. The fact they even agreed to participate in Pride, to hire us, immediately alienates some of their targets. Yet, they did it. And to show those 90 percent of non-supporters that KFI is supporting this cause just might change a few minds, or open a few doors.

Who's a better black activist, Al Sharpton, or Bill Cosby? Think about it. Cosby is beloved by 80 percent of America, black or white. He's the quintessential father figure even though he's black and had an affair on his wife. Yet, more non-Black Americans accept him in their homes, listen to him, know him than they do Al Sharpton, Jesse Jackson, Martin Luther King III, or any other. Cosby is not a professional black man, he's not seen as one thing. And thus he does more to bring a positive image of African Americans to the masses that need that positive image than the others.

Who's a better gay activist, Elton John or Larry Kramer? Who reaches more, who is seen as something else first, and then gay? The answer is clear. While I love Larry Kramer, Elton does more to normalize gay and lesbians in the fabric of our culture. But why must there be a division between these two factions? Why do activists and organizations in our community, and others, seemingly want to divide instead of unite the communities they serve? There is room for all kinds of activism, as long as the goal is acceptance, equal rights and all the other laundry lists.

Look at our track record. We fought for gay marriage. Lost. Fought for gays in the military. Lost. Fought for increase in hate crimes bills. Lost (most). Gay and lesbian voter participation, according to a recent poll, is down to 4 percent. So, 4 percent of the 10 percent of the 100 percent vote. No wonder we can't change much.

We continue to fight on our enemy's terms and follow leaders steeped in either the "in your face" activism of Stonewall or the corporate activism of the huge gay organizations that collect millions and are much ado about nothing. We get bogged down in battles that are unwinnable, and won't move to the areas we can create greatest change.

The fact is the community leadership hasn't supported us because we aren't the activist they want. We don't sit every day, for three hours, preaching about gay causes because that would turn off our listeners. They would tune out. And keeping them tuned in, learning to be tolerant of us through association is the key. MAKING them care about us, and interjecting things along the way. I call Andrew my husband on air, in drive time. When we do a subject about cheating spouses, we talk about how we'd feel if either of us ever cheated on each other, in drive time. When we do stories on the government using polygraph tests for job hirings, I undergo one on air and am asked if I've ever cheated on him, or which of our two dogs I love more, or if I really like my mother-in-law (his mom). When we do the commercial for Ortho Mattress, we say "We sleep in an Ortho, our bed is an Ortho" in drive time L.A. radio. Call me crazy, but that does more than demanding an apology letter or picketing some organization.

—excerpt

Source: Reprinted with permission from www.karelandandrew.com

Appendix 6A
Previously on Best of *Hangin'Out,*
June 2000: Guests and Topics

- Rochelle Diamond, chairperson of the National Organization of Gay and Lesbian Scientists and Technical Professionals, de-mystified cloning and stem cell research

- Filmmakers Randy Barbato and Fenton Bailey, whose new documentary *The Eyes of Tammy Faye* has been the smash hit of film festivals nationwide

- Comedy writer Richard Day talked about his new comic play *Straight Jacket,* about a '50s closeted Hollywood star

- Director Jose Miguel Arteta discussed his second feature film, the disturbingly compelling *Chuck & Buck*

- Canadian same-sex marriage applicants Judy Lightwater and Cynthia Callahan

- Kief Hillsbery, author of *War Boy,* the story of a gay, deaf, punker skateboarder hangs out in hour one

- Author Jane Summer, whose new book *The Silk Road* is a lesbian coming out story set in the '70s

- *Chutney Popcorn* filmmaker Nisha Ganatra and her costar Jill Hennessey discussed their story of an American lesbian surrogate mother who confronts the cultural and familial traditions of India

- Congressman Barney Frank checked in on the issues of intolerance on military bases for gays and discussed his letter to Secretary William S. Cohen on accountability for base commanders

- *I'm the One That I Want:* comic, actress and self-described "fag hag" Margaret Cho speaks about her new film

- *It's Time's* Lori Buckwalter discusses landmark transgender prisoner rights in Oregon

- Yvonne Welbon and Ruth Ellis (oldest living out, African American lesbians) discuss their film *Living With Pride: Ruth Ellis at 100*

Source: Reprinted with permission from www.gaybc.com

Appendix 6B
GAYBC / Stellar Networks Staff

John McMullen   Founder and chief programming officer; host,
                             The John McMullen Show

Charlie Dyer   Cofounder and senior vice president of Music
                             and Special Events; host, *TraQz*

Jeff Calley   Executive producer; cohost, *Hangin'Out*

Dr. Grethe Cammermeyer   Cohost, *Hangin'Out*; host, *The Dr. Grethe
                             Cammermeyer Show*

Christian Grantham   Host, *GAYBC Today*

Jeremy Hovies   Music director; host, *All Mixed Up*; host,
                             Electric Brunch

dj Kirby   Host, *NightGroove*; host, *dj Kirby's Dance
                             Mix*

Michelangelo Signorile   Host, *The Signorile Show*

Marilyn Pittman   Host, *The Marilyn Pittman Show*

Rex Booth   Host, *Rex's Rants*

Michael Wengert   News director, Anchor, *GAYBC News on the
                             Hour*; Anchor, *GAYBC Week in Review*

Tim Curran   Washington, D.C. news bureau chief

Jennifer King   Producer

Tom Hawken	Associate producer
Michael Bisogno	Youth programming producer
Chelle Gannon	Host, *The Chelle Gannon Show*
Michael Thomas Ford	Host, *My Queer Life*
Peter Berkery	Host, *Fiscally Fit*
Nancy Nangeroni	Cohost, *GenderTalk*
Gordene MacKenzie	Cohost, *GenderTalk*
Ann Northrop	Host, *Point of View*
Christian de la Huerta	Host, *SpiritWave*
Aubrey Sparks	Host, *Aubrey's Playroom*
Don Romesburg	Host, *Times of Our Lives*
Andrew Thiessen	Director of operations
Michael Kakoyiannis	President and CEO

Notes

Notes to Chapter One

1. "Gay Liberation: We're Here, We're Queer, Get Used To It!," *Time* 100 (Special Issue), 153 (23) <http://www.time.com/time/magazine/articles/0,3266,26412,00.html>, June 14, 1999. Also see Barry D. Adam, *The Rise of a Gay and Lesbian Movement* (Boston: Twayne, 1987). In 1961, Kameny started the Washington, D.C., chapter, which radically revolutionized and modernized the movement.

2. Matthew Laser, *Pacifica Radio: The Rise of an Alternative Network* (Philadelphia: Temple University Press, 1999), and Adam, *Rise of a Gay and Lesbian Movement*.

3. Laser, *Pacifica Radio*.

4. Edward Alwood, *Straight News: Gays, Lesbians and the News Media* (New York: Columbia University Press, 1996).

5. Mike Wallace and Harry Morgan, "CBS Reports: The Homosexuals" (TV news special), March 7, 1967.

6. Larry Gross, *Contested Closets: The Politics and Ethics of Outing* (Minneapolis: University of Minnesota Press, 1993).

7. Chris Hawke, "Beat Poet Ginsberg's Health Declines," United Press International (http://c-level.com/news/new26.html), April 4, 1997.

8. Matthew Rothschild, "Allen Ginsberg: Interview," *The Progressive* <http://www.progressive.org/ginzroth9408.htm>, August 1994.

9. Stephen Brophy, "What's News: The June Pride Special from *In the Life*, Gay and Lesbian TV Newsmagazine Is One of the Best Yet," *Bay Windows* <http://content.gay.com/whatsnews>, May 28, 1999. Also see "The 1999 Gay Pride Special!—Judy Garland, and more. . . ," *In the Life* (New York: New Life Media, Inc.).

10. "Lesbian and Gay Solidarity" (Sydney, Australia: <http:www.zipworld.com.au/~josken/lgs.htm>, November 1999.

11. Aart Hendricks, Rob Tielman, and Evert van der Veen, eds., *The Third Pink Book: A Global View of Lesbian and Gay Liberation and Oppression* (Buffalo, NY: Prometheus Books, 1993).

Notes to Chapter Two

1. Matthew Laser, *Pacifica Radio: The Rise of an Alternative Network* (Philadelphia: Temple University Press, 1999), and Barry D. Adam, *The Rise of a Gay and Lesbian Movement* (Boston: Twayne, 1987).

2. David Lamble, "How We Are Seen; How We See Ourselves: The Lavender Airwaves," *San Francisco Bay Reporter*. Also see, Eric Jensen, "Dykes on the Air: How We Are Seen; How We See Ourselves: The Lavender Airwaves," *San Francisco Bay Reporter* (personal collection, Jon Beaupre).

3. Allen Ginsberg, *Howl and Other Poems* (San Francisco, CA: City Lights Publishing, 1956).

4. Lamble, "How We Are Seen."

5. S. Carter and Larry G. Burkum, "Tongues Untied: Public TV Managers and Potentially Objectionable Programming," presented to the Media Management and Economics Division, Association for Education in Journalism and Communication, Kansas City, KS, August 1993; also see *Pacifica Foundation* 36 FCC 2d 147 (1964).

6. Lamble, "How We Are Seen."

7. Ibid.

8. Guy Raz, "Radio Free Georgetown," *Washington Free Weekly* (DC: http://www.washingtoncitypaper.com/archives/cover/1999/cover0129.html), January 29–February 4, 1999.

9. Ibid.

10. Ibid.

11. Program Transcript: "A Conversation With Don Belton, Editor of 'Speak My Name: Black Men On Masculinity & The American Dream,'" *This Way Out* (Episode 2 of three-part series, Segment 4), March 1, 1977. Josy Catoggio was the interviewer.

12. "Alternating Currents," WAIF (Cincinnati, OH: <http:// www.alternatingcurrents.org/about.htm>), July 10, 2000.

13. "Q'zine," WXPN-FM (Philadelphia: http://pobox.upenn.edu/~qzine), June 2000.

14. Alan Ross, personal Web site <http://www.geopages.com/WestHollywood/1001/1001–p3.html>.

15. R. Paul Martin, personal Web site (New York: http://www.wbaifree.org/folio/guten.html), June 2000.

16. "OutFM," WBAI-FM (New York: http://hometown.aol.com/Out FMradio/index.htm), July 2000.

17. "The Tenth Voice," KKFI (Kansas City, KS: <http://www.kkfi.org/main.htm>).

18. "Sin Fronteras," KNON-FM (Dallas: http://www.knon.org).

19. "Lambda Weekly," KNON-FM.

20. Lambda Legal Defense and Education Fund (New York: http://www.lambdalegal.org), July 2000.

21. Ibid.

22. "Lambda Weekly," KNON-FM (Dallas: <http://www.know.org>).

23. Ibid.

Notes to Chapter Three

1. Various, *Club Verboten*, DCC Compact Classics, 1997.

2. Harriet L. Schwartz, "Rockin Gay at the Hall of Fame," *Southern Voice* <http://www.rockhall.com>, September 5, 1996.

3. Gay and Lesbian American Music Awards (New York: <http://www.glama.com>), 2000.

4. Lesbian and Gay Country Music Association (San Francisco: <www.lgcma.com>), 2000.

5. Chris Dickinson, "Country Undetectable: Gay Country Artists," *Journal of Country Music* 21(1) (1999): <http:// www.country.com>.

6. Mark Weigle, *The Truth Is* (Vallejo, CA: M. Weigle, 1999). All songs by Weigle in this chapter are from his debut album *The Truth Is*. His latest album is *All That Matters*. Both albums are available through songs.com.

7. "Bring Gay Music Out of the Closet," *Billboard*, June 18, 1994, 4.

8. Outmusic, (New York: <http://www.geocities.com/outmusic usa>), 2000.

9. Michael Callen and Marsha Malamet, *A Love Worth Fighting For* (Durham, NC: Ladyslipper, 1995).

10. Gay Wired Music Source: The Global Gay and Lesbian Network 10. <http://www.gaywired.com/streeter/love-lyr.htm>, 2000.

11. Jay McLaren, *OutLoud: An Encyclopedia of Gay and Lesbian Recordings, Limited Edition* (Amsterdam, Holland: J. McLaren, 1992, 1998).

12. Susie Bright, "Sexpert Opinion: Lilith vs. Dyke-o-rama," *Salon Magazine* <http:/salonmagazine.com/columists/bright.html>, July 18, 1997.

13. Jennifer Earls, "Michigan Womyn's Festival Gears Up," *The Washington Blade* <http://www.washblade.com/>, 1999.

14. Michigan's Womyn Festival, <http://www.michfest.com/General/general.htm>, 2000.

15. "Timeline," *Out And About* (Online Canada: <http://www.outandabout.on.ca/timeline.html>), 2000.

16. Ibid.

17. Ibid.

18. Sarah Schulman, *My American History: Lesbian and Gay Life During the Reagan/Bush Years* (New York: Routledge, 1994).

19. "Timeline," *Out And About* (Online Canada: <http://www.outandabout.on.ca/timeline.html/>), 2000.

20. "Face the Music," WCUW (Worcester, MA: <http://www.splusnet.com/wcuw/facethemusic/>), 2000.

21. John Dinges, "What's Going On at Pacifica? A Special Report," *The Nation*, <http:/www.thenation.com/issue/000501/0501dinges.shtml>, May 1, 2000; Guy Raz, "Radio Free Georgetown," *Washington Free Weekly* <http://www.washingtoncitypaper.com/archives/cover/1999/cover0129.html>, January 29–February 4, 1999.

22. Yolanda Retter, "The Lesbian History Project: Los Angeles Lesbian Chronology, 1970–1990" <http://www-lib.usc.edu/~retter/main.html>, 1996.

23. Ibid.

24. Schulman, *My American History*.

25. Ibid.

26. "Holly Near," GayGate web site: Interactive Strategies 27, <http://gaygate.com/media/pages/hollynear.shtml>, 2000.

27. Meg Christian, "Ode to a Gym Teacher," *I Know You Know*. Olivia Records, 1973.

28. "Amazon Country," WXPN (Philadelphia: <http://pobox.upenn.edu/~amazon/>), 2000.

Notes to Chapter Four

1. *Electric City"* press release, San Francisco, CA: City Visions Cable, *<http://members.aol.com/narle/pressrelease.html>*, July 2000.

2. Ibid.

3. Ibid.

4. *The Fresca Vinyl Show*, Gay Wired, The Global Gay and Lesbian Network (West Hollywood, CA: http://www.gaywired.com/frescavinyl/), June 2000.

5. Snow is featured in the July 2000 issue of *Genre Magazine* (also see <http://www.gaywired.com/ttownqueer/tv.html>).

6. Gay Cable Network (New York City: <http://www.gcntv.com>, 1997. The Gay Cable Network is the parent company of *Gay USA* and GCN-TV.

7. *Outlook Video*, Mountain View Community TV (Mountain View, CA: <http://www.outlookvideo.org/>), July 2000. *Outlook Video* was founded in 1987.

8. Joseph L. Casadonte Jr., *Gay Media Resources List* <http://www.netaxs.com/~joc/gaymedia.html#List>, February 2, 1998.

9. Ibid.

10. *10%-Qtv*, Southern Ontario: Rogers Community Television Network. The Hometown Video Festival is the largest and longest-running video festival for local cable programming in the northern hemisphere. In 2000, 1,472 entries were submitted from across North America in various categories. <http://10percent.interlog.com>/

11. *Dyke TV* (Manhattan, New York: <http://www.dyketv.org>, June 2000.

12. Ibid.

13. Bonnie Burton, "TV Shows Unlock the Closet Door for Gay Characters," University of Colorado in Boulder: <http://bcn.boulder.co.us/campuspress/jan201995/mail.html>, January 20, 1995.

14. Ibid.

15. Queer TV, Santa Cruz, CA: Santa Cruz Community Television. The "QTV" Web site is <http://www.rainbowway.com>.

16. "Youth Speak Out," *Queer Youth TV*, Episode C (Santa Cruz, CA: Santa Cruz Community Television).

17. "Camp Tolerance," *Queer Youth TV*, Episode C (Santa Cruz, CA: Santa Cruz Community Television).

18. Ibid. Christian Left, unpublished song.

19. *In The Life*, <www.inthelifetv.org>.

20. A documentary account of black gay life in the United States. *Tongues Untied* (1989) was directed by Marlon Riggs, and it aired on PBS stations in 1991. The broadcast of the documentary resulted in a few indecency complaints to the FCC. A number of PBS stations refused to air the controversial documentary.

Notes to Chapter Five

1. "Trends in the Making," *Advertising* 11 (8), August 1998, p. 7.

2. Michael Wilke, "Commercial Closet: Advertisers Battle Dr. Laura," *Gay Financial Network* <http://gfn.com>, May 29, 2000.

3. Scott Giordano, "Orlando TV Stations Refuse to Air the Rights's Anti-Gay Ads," *Bay Windows*, June 3, 1999, pp. 3, 27.

4. Susan Schindenhette, "Straight Up," *People Weekly* November 30, 1998, pp. 117–118.

5. Giordano, "Orlando TV Stations."

6. Pam Belluck, "Gay Church Sues TV Station for Rejecting an Infomercial," *New York Times*, Chicago Metro edition, p. 1 <undated, http://www.outnow.com>.

7. Gay and Lesbian Alliance Against Defamation <http://www.glaad.org>, June 2000.

8. Wilke, "Advertisers Battle Dr. Laura."

9. A Coalition of Hate was founded by several groups who want to stop Paramount from airing Dr. Laura Schlessinger's TV show <http://StopDrLaura.com>.

10. Michael Wilke, "Commercial Closet: Awkward Advertisers' Gay Themes," *Gay Financial Network* <http://www.gfn.com>, March 13, 2000.

11. Michael Wilke, "Ads Targeting Gays Rely on Real Results, Not Intuition: Marketers Pay to Research Return on Investment," *Advertising Age*, June 22, 1998, p. 3.

12. Paul D. Poux, "Gay Consumers MIA from Media Surveys," *Advertising Age*, April 20, 1998, p. 26.

13. Michael Wilke, "Commercial Closet: Abercrombie Boys Hit TV," *Gay Financial Network* <http://www.gfn.com>, August 17, 1999.

14. Michael Wilke, "Commercial Closet: Budweiser's Controversial Gay Ad," *Gay Financial Network* <http://www.gfn.com>, May 3, 1999.

15. Cliff Rothman, "Big Companies Are Openly Courting Gay Consumers," *Los Angeles Times*, May 18, 1999, p. C1.

16. Michael Wilke, "Abercrombie Boys Hit TV."

17. Michael Wilke, "Commercial Closet: Gay Ads Promote MTV," *Gay Financial Network* <http://www.gfn.com>, November 9, 1999

18. Michael Wilke, "Commercial Closet: Lesbian Fantasy Ads," *Gay Financial Network* <http://www.gfn.com>, December 28, 1999.

19. Michael Wilke, "Gay Ads Promote MTV."

20. Eric Boehlert, "Gay Radio Comes Out Commercially: New Shows Give Voice to Ignored Demo," *Billboard*, pp. 64, 66.

21. Ibid.

22. Randall Bloomquist, "Format Feverishly Springs Forward," *Radio & Records*, March 18, 1994, p. 41.

23. Boehlert, "Gay Radio."

24. Dale Eastman, "Media With a Message," *New City*, August 5, 1993, pp. 10–13.

25. Boehlert, "Gay Radio," p. 66.

26. Eastman, "Media."

27. Bloomquist, "Formats," p. 41.

28. Phylis Johnson, Chuck Hoy, and Dhyana Ziegler, "A Case Study of KGAY: The Rise and Fall of the First Gay and Lesbian Radio Network," *Journal of Radio Studies* 3 (1995–1996), p. 176.

29. Johnson et al., "Case Study," pp. 162–181.

30. Ibid., p. 170.

31. Ibid.

32. *This Way Out*, Program 288 (Los Angeles: Overnight Productions), October 4, 1993.

33. Steve Nidetz, "LesBiGay Radio," *Chicago Tribune*, May 22, 1994, p. 5.

34. Charles Karel Bouley II, "Opening the Vent: Thoughts on Frontiers, Al Rantel and Such" (Los Angles: http://www.karelandandrew.com), September 1999.

35. Karel Bouley II, "Must There Be a Great Divide?" (Los Angeles: <http://www.karelandandrew.com>).

36. Karel, "Opening the Vent."

37. Also see Michael Biocco's Gay Television Home Page (formerly Carol Mortimer's Home Page) for a comprehensive look at gay network and cable TV (NJ: <http://www.jersey.net/~not2/gaytv-a.htm>).

38. Fred Fejes and Kevin Petrich, "Invisibility, Homophobia, and Heterosexism: Lesbians, Gays, and the Media," *Critical Studies in Mass Communication* 10 (4), 1993.

39. David Galligan, "Berlesques: Uncle Miltie's Unmatched Moxie," *The Advocate*, August 7, 1980, pp. 27, 29.

40. Vito Russo, *The Celluloid Closet* (New York: Harper & Row), 1981.

41. John A. Lee, "Going Public: A Study in the Sociology of Homosexual Liberation," *Journal of Homosexuality* 3 (Fall 1977), pp. 49–78.

42. Harry Waters, "Bringing Up Parents," *Newsweek*, November 6, 1972, p. 74.

43. Russo, *Celluloid Closet.*

44. Waters, "Bringing Up Parents."

45. Russo, *Celluloid Closet.*

46. James Heller-Jackson, "This Week in Queer History," *Q'zine Queer Radio* (Philadelphia: WXPN, <http://xpn.org/qzine/history.html>), March 9, 1997.

47. "Andrew Schneider, Interview," *The Advocate*, April 19, 1994.

48. Wilke, "Advertisers Battle Dr. Laura."

49. Wilke, "Advertisers Battle Dr. Laura."

50. S. Carter and Larry G. Burkum, "Tongues Untied: Public TV Managers and Potentially Objectionable Programming," presented to the Media Management and Economics Division, Association for Education in Journalism and Communication, Kansas City, KS, August 1993.

51. Joshua Gamson, *Freaks Talk Back: Tabloid Talk Shows and Sexual Nonconformity* (Chicago: University of Chicago Press), 1998.

Notes to Chapter Six

1. Joseph L. Casadonte Jr., Gay Media Resources List <http://www.netaxs.com/~joc/gaymedia.html#List>, February 2, 1998.

2. See MVS Media (Amsterdam, Holland: <http://mvs.nl/mvsuk.htm>); Frequence Radio Gaie (Paris, France: <http://www.radiofg.com/playlist.html>).

3. Thaksina Khaikaew, "Thailand Restricts Transvestites, Transsexuals on TV," Associated Press <http://content.gay.com/channels/news/transgender/051999.html>, May 1999.

4. *"This Way Out: The International Lesbian and Gay Radio Magazine"* press release (Los Angeles: Overnight Productions, <www.qrd.org/qrd/www/media/radio/thiswayout/twohome.html>, June 2000.

5. Ibid.

6. Douglas Price, "Gay Radio Gives a Signal That It's OK to Be a Swan in a World of Ducks," *Detroit News*, February 26, 1993, p. 1F.

7. *This Way Out*, press release.

8. Ibid. <http://www.inthelifetv.org>.

9. "Queer As Folk." UK:

10. "Queer As Folk," (UK: <www.queerasfolk.org.uk>). Also see "The Boys of Manchester: On the Set of *Queer As Folk, In the Life*, <http://www.inthelifetv.org>.

11. Rob Owen, "1TV Notes: Showtime's 'Queer' to Be Set in Pittsburgh," *Post-Gazette* <http://www.post->

Notes to Chapter Seven

1. Michael Wilke, "Commercial Closet: C1TV Debuts," *Gay Financial Network* <http: //gfn.com), January 10, 2000.

2. Gay Cable Network (New York City: <http://www.gcntv.com>), 1997.

3. Ibid.

4. Wilke, "Commercial Closet: C1TV Debut."

5. Ibid.

Notes to Chapter Eight

1. Daily News Archive, *Feed Magazine* (New York: <http://www.feedmag.com>), June 15, 2000; Larry McShane, "New Springsteen Song References Diallo Case" (Associated Press: <http://www.nj.com/springsteen/stories/0608newsong.html>), June 8, 2000.

2. CNN, "Springsteen Brings '41 Shots' to New York," (New York: <http://www.cnn.com>), June 13, 2000. (Associated Press and Mark Scheerer contributed to this report.)

3. Henry Louis Gates Jr., "Blacklash? African Americans Object to Gay Rights-Civil Rights Analogy," *New Yorker*, May 17, 1993, p. 42.

4. Also see Surina Khan, "Calculated Compassion: How the Ex-Gay Movement Serves the Right Attack on Democracy," 1998 Report from Political Research Associates, the Policy Institute of the National Gay and Lesbian Task Force, and Equal Partners in Faith (Surina Khan and Political Research Associates), reprinted from *The Public Eye* (Somerville, MA: <http://publiceye.org/equality/x-gay/Calculated_Compassion_TOC.htm.>), Overview, p. 1.

5. Michael Wilke, "Commercial Closet: Gay Ads Promote MTV," *Gay Financial Network* (New York: <http://gfn.com>), November 9, 1999.

6. Delia M. Rios, "Gay Papers Spoof Falwell's Teletubby 'Outing,'" Religious News Service, February 13, 1999.

7. Ibid.

8. Dudley Clendinen, "Anita Bryant, b. 1940, Singer and Crusader," *St. Petersburg Times*, *http://www.sptimes.com/News/112899/Floridian/Anita_Bryant__b_1940_.shtml*>. November 28, 1999.

9. "Uncle Donald Presents Gay Freedom Day Parade and Celebration: Gay Parades of the Seventies," <http://www.backdoor.com/castro/parade/parade/parade.html>, May 21, 2000.

10. Paul Gibson, "Gay Male and Lesbian Youth Suicide," In *Report of the Secretary's Task Force on Youth Suicide*, Vol. 3, ed. Marcia R. Feinleib (Washington, DC: U.S. Department of Health and Human Services, 1991); Jaye B. Miller, "From Silence to Suicide: Measuring a Mothers Loss," in *Homophobia: How We All Pay the Price*, ed. Warren J. Blumenfeld (Boston: Beacon Press, 1992).

Further Reading

Allen, Donna, Romona R. Rush, and Susan J. Kaufman, eds. *Women Transforming Communications: Global Perspectives*. Thousand Oaks, CA: Sage, 1996.

Brandt, Eric, ed. *Dangerous Liaisons: Blacks, Gays, and the Struggle for Equality*. New York: New Press, 1999.

Capsuto, Steven. *Alternate Channels: The Uncensored Story of Gay and Lesbian Images on Radio and Television*. New York: Ballantine Books, 2000.

Cruikshank, Margaret. *The Gay and Lesbian Liberation Movement*. New York: Routledge, 1992.

Dawson, Jeff. *Gay and Lesbian Online*, 4th ed. Los Angeles: Alyson, 2000.

Duberman, Martin. *Stonewall*. New York: Penguin, 1993.

Hogan, Steve, and Lee Hudson. *Completely Queer: The Gay and Lesbian Encyclopedia*. New York: Owl Books, 1998.

Holmlund, Chris, and Cyntha Fuchs, eds. *Between the Sheets, In the Streets: Queer, Lesbian, Gay Documentary*. Minneapolis: University of Minnesota Press, 1997.

Howes, Keith. *Broadcasting It: An Encyclopaedia of Homosexuality in Film, Radio and TV in the UK, 1923–1993*. New York: Cassell, 1993.

Marcus, Eric. *Making History: The Struggle for Gay and Lesbian Equal Rights 1945–1990: An Oral History*. New York: Harper Collins, 1992.

Richards, David. *Identity and the Case for Gay Rights*. Chicago: University of Chicago Press, 1999.

Robertson, Pamela. *Guilty Pleasures: Feminist Camp From Mae West to Madonna*. Durham: Duke University Press, 1996.

Rutledge, Leigh W. *The Gay Decades, From Stonewall to the Present: The People and Events That Shaped Gay Lives*. New York: Penguin, 1992.

Smith, Patricia Juliana, ed. *The Queer Sixties*. New York: Routledge, 1999.

Streitmatter, Rodger. *Unspeakable: The Rise of the Gay and Lesbian Press in America*. Boston and London: Faber & Faber, 1996.

Thompson, Mark, ed. *Long Road to Freedom: The Advocate History of the Gay and Lesbian Movement*. New York: St. Martin's Press, 1994.

Waugh, Thomas. *The Fruit Machine: Twenty Years of Writings on Queer Cinema*. Durham, NC: Duke University Press, 2000.

Witt, Lynn, Sherry Thomas, and Eric Marcus, eds., *Out in All Directions: The Almanac of Gay and Lesbian America*. New York: Warner Books, 1995.

Witt, Stephanie L., and Suzanne McCorkle. *Anti-Gay Rights: Assessing Voter Initiatives*. Westport, CT: Praeger, 1997.

Contributors

Alan Amberg is the founder and president of *LesBiGay Radio*, the only daily prime-time program dedicated to the Lesbian, Gay, Bisexual, and Transgender (LGBT) community. It is simulcast on WSBC 1240 AM (Chicago) and WCFJ 1470 AM (Chicago Heights) and across the Internet from 5 P.M. to 7 P.M. (CST).

Jon Beaupre is a freelance producer for National Public Radio, the British Broadcasting Corporation, Pacifica Network News, Latino USA, and a number of nationally syndicated radio programs. He is also a part-time faculty member at California State University in Los Angeles in the Broadcast Communication Department.

Marle Becker is a host and producer of *OutFM* on WBAI-FM, New York. His participation in the AIDS Names Project led to his involvement in *The Gay Show*, a radio program that evolved into the present-day *OutFM*.

Karen Louise Boothe was president of the National Lesbian and Gay Journalists' Association (NLGJA) (1997–2000). She has worked as a broadcast radio journalist since 1982. Currently she is communications director of the Minnesota Democractic-Farmer-Labor Party.

John Catania is the director of communications and a contributing producer for *In the Life*. He was a production assistant, stage manager, and coproducer of the series. Prior to 1993, he was an actor and theater director for ten years.

Josy Catoggio is a long-time interviewer of LGBT authors and former member of the *IMRU* radio collective on KPFK-FM in Los Angeles. Her early work included conducting antihomophobic workshops and involvement with several feminist schools/retreats. She's currently a producer/host on KPFK's *Feminist Magazine* and occasional contributor to *This Way Out*.

Lucia Chappelle is the associate producer and cohost of *This Way Out*. She began volunteering at *IMRU* on KPFK-FM in Los Angeles in November 1973, and from 1987 to 1995 she was program director.

Debra Chasnoff is an Emmy award–winning documentary producer. Chasnoff was director and producer of *It's Elementary: Talking About Gay Issues in School* (1996), along with Helen S. Cohen, coproducer. Chasnoff is also the director and coproducer of *That's a Family!* released in June 2000.

Meg Christian was one of the founders of Olivia Records and a leading songwriter and performer during the early feminist movement.

Nicholas Cimorelli is host of *Health Action* and one of the early members of Gay and Lesbian Independent Broadcasters (GLIB), which produced *Out Looks* on WBAI-FM, New York, through the 1990s.

Chuck Colbert is a freelance syndicated columnist with an exclusively gay-beat angle. His work has been published in the *Boston Globe, Boston Herald, Washington Post, Philadelphia Inquirer, San Francisco Chronicle, Harvard Business Review*, and *National Catholic Reporter*, among others. He is a past member of the board of directors in the National Lesbian and Gay Journalists' Association (NLGJA). He was a Surface Warfare Officer in the Navy in the early 1980s. Currently, Colbert is a graduate student in divinity at the Weston Jesuit School of Theology, Cambridge, Massachusetts.

Brendon Constans is the producer/creator of *Pulp Non-Fiction* and producer of *Queer Youth TV* on Santa Cruz Community Television. He has edited numerous projects for Queer TV.

Debra D'Alessandro is the host of *Amazon Country* on WXPN-FM, Philadelphia. She has more than ten years of experience as an activist, educator, and performer in Philadelphia's feminist and gay communities.

Thomas Davis is president and general manager of WTTT-AM and WRNX-FM in Amherst, Massachusetts. The station is a member of the Gay and Lesbian Business Coalition.

Steve Walters-Dearmond is a former commercial broadcaster who became involved in community radio after moving to Dallas to work at a major telecommunications company. He is the coordinating producer of KNON-FM's *Lambda Weekly*.

Robert Drake is a print journalist, entrepreneur, and Peabody Award–winning broadcaster in Philadelphia. He has hosted and produced WXPN-FM's *Q'zine* since 1996. The program was originally known as *Gaydreams*.

John Vivian Frame is host and coordinator of *Queer Radio* in Brisbane, Australia, on subscriber-owned community broadcaster Four Triple Zed Radio, the first FM radio station in Queensland. He hosted the 1999 AIDS Candlelight Vigil. It was at the 1993 Vigil that he was encouraged to take part in the show.

Cindy Friedman is the news director and NewsWrap coanchor of *This Way Out*. She volunteered as a program producer for Los Angeles's KPFK-FM for many years and has worked extensively for women's and feminist causes for nearly twenty-five years.

Joshua Gamson is the author of *Freaks Talk Back: Tabloid Talk Shows and Sexual Nonconformity* and *Claims to Frame: Celebrity in Contemporary America*. He is a sociology professor at Yale University and is on the research advisory board of GLAAD.

Uwe F. Goetz was one of the founders of *Eldoradio*, which began as the first gay and lesbian radio station in Germany (1985–1986) and later evolved into a two-hour program (1987–1989) on Radio 100, Berlin's alternative radio station.

Greg Gordon is the coordinating producer, cohost, and founder of *This Way Out*. He also served as a former production coordinator of *IMRU*, the Pacifica-broadcast lesbian and gay radio program at KPFK-FM, Los Angeles.

Paul Graham is a radio and television broadcaster and columnist in Manchester, United Kingdom. He is also a programming consultant for the British Broadcasting Corporation. He is the host of the radio program *Gaytalk*.

Hilary Hamm is a computer technician for a Santa Cruz Internet company and a nonlinear video editor and producer for *Queer TV* in Santa Cruz, California. She was born in Northern California and has lived in Amsterdam.

Denise Hill became involved in KDHX-FM in St. Louis as the executive producer and host of *Coming Out of Hiding* (1989–1998). She continues her involvement with KDHX as a theater reviewer. Hill is currently the music editor of *Intermission Magazine* and the technical architect of a Web site that promotes jazz in St. Louis.

Chuck Hoy is an assistant professor in the Communications Department at Grambling State University in Grambling, Louisiana. He has conducted and published several studies on gay and lesbian media.

Charles Ignacio is the executive producer of *In the Life*, the nationally acclaimed PBS magazine series on gay and lesbian issues and lifestyle. He worked at PBS affiliate WNET-TV in New York before producing the pilot in 1992.

Lidell Jackson was one of the hosts of *The Gay Show* on WBAI-FM, New York, in the late 1980s. He is an activist and was one of the founders of *Color Life* magazine.

Charles Karel Bouley II and **Andrew Howard** are drive-time leaders on Los Angeles' KFI-AM. Karel is a singer, songwriter, journalist, and comedian. Howard is a writer for the screen and stage. Previously the radio duo worked as a team in Seattle, Tacoma, and San Francisco. They are the founders of *Equality through Pride*.

Mary Kennedy is cofounder and producer of *Pridetime*, and a publisher who has been involved in the gay press since 1976. *Pridetime* is a local LesBiGay public access program that has aired in the Boston area since 1985.

Heather Kitching has cohosted *Queer FM* since 1994 with former cohost Craig Maynard and currently with Jensen Didulo on CiTR 101.9 FM in Vancouver, Canada.

Michelle King was a producer, host, and programmer for KDHX-FM, St. Louis, and has worked in the music industry for about eleven years. She is an ex-stripper and served in the military.

Nancy Kirton recently returned to *OutFM* as an associate producer, doing mostly fifteen-minute segments. She covered the dyke march of 2000 and some of the boro pride events. She continues her work with Identity House, a counseling and psychotherapy referral organization of thirty years.

A.J. Lahosky is the segment producer and webmaster of *10%-Qtv*, a weekly TV magazine show that airs on Rogers Television in southern Ontario.

Tom Kwai Lam is the founder of *Queer TV* on Santa Cruz Community Television. He describes himself as a "radical ferrie, a queer hippie, and a

Gemini communicator and artist." He is also a Web designer, video producer, photographer, and writer.

Christian Left is a singer and songwriter in Santa Cruz, California. He appeared on *Queer Youth TV*, speaking and singing on behalf of gay fathers.

Joe Liberatore is the founder of the *Gay News Network* (GNN), a nationally distributed news magazine program based in Washington, D.C., that can be viewed on commercial and public access television.

Sande Mack is the director and editor of *Electric City* in San Francisco. Mack has been an activist, actor, comedian, and singer, and is one of the founding members of *ACT UP Media* and *Electric City*.

R. Paul Martin was involved in the coordination and production of several WBAI-FM radio shows since 1981, including the present-day *Back of the Book*, which began in 1986. He was one of the producers of *Gay Rap* in late 1981, the executive producer of its successor *Gay New York*, and the Gay Men's Collective coordinator (1982–1984).

Tom McCormack is a recording artist and cofounder of the Gay and Lesbian American Music Awards (GLAMA), the only national music awards program to celebrate and honor gay and lesbian musicians and songwriters.

John McMullen worked as a radio broadcaster and an Internet software developer before becoming president of GAYBC, a primarily Web-based company that streams audio news, talk, and entertainment programming across the Internet.

Cece Pinheiro is a member of the board of directors for Santa Cruz Community Television. She is a gay/lesbian rights activist, lesbian mom, youth advocate, school community coordinator, cochair for the Santa Cruz chapter of the Gay/Lesbian Straight Education, and president of the Council of Classified Employees.

Cathy Renna is the Director of Regional Media and Community Relations of the Gay and Lesbian Alliance Against Defamation (GLAAD). She reported on the Matthew Shepard murder and subsequent trial, and continues to cover significant events within the LGBT community.

Alan Ross started Gay Fathers in 1979 and was president until 1985, when he became host of *Gaydreams* (1985–1990) on WXPN-FM, Philadelphia. In

1989, the program won three Lambda Awards from the Gay and Lesbian Press Association.

John Scagliotti began his broadcast career in radio news and programming. He has produced two major PBS documentaries, *Before Stonewall* (1986) and *After Stonewall* (1999). He is the creator of the highly acclaimed PBS series *In the Life*.

Marvin Schwam founded Gay Entertainment Television (GET) in New York City in November 1992 and became its president. GET was the first serious attempt at creating a national gay cable television network.

Allan Smales is a computer consultant, software specialist, and host of *Pot Pourri*, which airs on Joy Melbourne FM in Australia. He was born in Melbourne and spent his childhood mainly in a small farming community in Victoria.

Pamela A. Smith is producer of *Amazon Radio*, a program with a black lesbian perspective that airs on WPKN-FM in Bridgeport, Connecticut, and is self-described as a "computer fanatic, who lives with her lifelong partner, Susan."

Doug Stevens is a country musician and performer who has entertained audiences internationally. His latest release is titled *From Christopher to Castro*, a collaborative effort with his band, *The Outband*.

Mark Weigle, a singer and songwriter, grew up in Minnesota and moved to California as an adult. He spent seven years as a teen counselor at a crisis center, gave up his day job in 1998 and since then has produced *The Truth Is* and *All That Matters*.

Frieda Werden cofounded WINGS: Women's International News Gathering Service in 1986. WINGS is an independently and internationally syndicated news and current affairs program by and about women. As an extension of her feminist activism (beginning in the mid 1970s), she has been involved in several radio initiatives throughout the world.

Wayman L. Widgins produced TV and film while studying at the University of Pennsylvania, Philadelphia, and cohosted a public access show in New York before becoming involved at WBAI-FM as producer and administrative coordinator of *OutFM*.

Chris Wilson is a native Californian. She created "Audiofile" in January 1997. She and her partner, Pam Marshall, along with Christopher David Trentham, coproduce the award-winning music series that can be heard internationally on *This Way Out.*

Lisa Winters is the founder of Bronx Lesbians United in Sisterhood (BLUES) and the Bronx Lesbian and Gay Health Resource Consortium, a health and resource organization for Bronx queers. She has also served on many boards of directors and advisory boards, including Community Planning Board #11, New York City Gay and Lesbian Anti-Violence Project, the Commission on the Status of Women, and Bronx Mental Health Commission. She is a social worker and attorney and continues to reside in the Bronx.

Arnel Valle is the producer of *Electric City*, the longest running queer television program in San Francisco. He is also a Web designer and worked a number of years as a crisis counselor. He is working full time as a production facilitator for San Francisco's public access channel.

Index

About the Authors

Phylis A. Johnson is an associate professor at Southern Illinois University at Carbondale. Her fields of interest are diversity and communications. She has published widely regarding the role of radio in society; conducted the first national gay and lesbian radio broadcast survey in the United States in 1994; and has conducted research on African American radio's impact on urban youth. She has more than twenty years of broadcast experience in Philadelphia, Houston, St. Louis, and other markets across the United States.

Michael C. Keith is a member of the Communications Department at Boston College. He is the author or coauthor of fifteen acclaimed books on the electronic media. Of special note are *Voices in the Purple Haze* (1997), *Signals in the Air* (1995), *Talking Radio* (2000), and *Sounds in the Dark* (forthcoming). Keith is the coauthor with Robert Hilliard of *Waves of Rancor* (1999) and *The Broadcast Century and Beyond* (2001), and also the author of the most widely adopted textbook on radio in America, *The Radio Station*, now in its fifth edition (2000). Prior to joining Boston College, Keith served as chair of education for the Museum of Broadcast Communications in Chicago, taught at George Washington University and Marquette University, and worked as a professional broadcaster for over a dozen years.